After Now

AfterNow:

When We Cannot
See the Future,
Where Do We Begin?

BOB STILGER, PhD

2 0 1 7

MILL CITY BOOKS

Mill City Books
2301 Lucien Way #415
Maitland, FL 32751
407.339.4217
www.millcitypress.net

Printed in South Korea

Book design and infographics:
Isabel Sandoval / Zulma Patarroyo
www.pataleta.net

Sumie and calligraphy brush work
Barbara Bash

Editor
Megan Scribner

Foreward
Margaret J. Wheatley

Afterword
Mary Catherine Bateson

ISBN-13: 9781545609743

Dedication

I dedicate this book to those who died

and to those who survived Japan's Triple Disasters

of March 11, 2011. I dedicate it to those whose

lives have ended or have been touched

by disasters all across this wild

and beautiful planet we call home.

I dedicate it to all of us who gather together

to hospice the old and midwife the new as we

create a future that affirms life.

I also dedicate this book to Naohito Nakatsugawa

and Kazuko Nakatsugawa, my Japanese

host-parents, who have supported me with their

love and kindness since we first met in 1970.

And I dedicate it to my spouse, Susan Virnig,

and my daughter, Anne Lucy Stilger Virnig

(otherwise known as Annie), who have given me

unconditional love throughout our lives together.

Acknowledgements

So many in Japan and here at home have stood with me to make this book possible; I cannot even begin to name them all. I am humbled and heartened by the extraordinary kindness of the thousands of people I have met in Japan since the Triple Disasters. I am deeply honored to have shared space with them as together we have tried to find our next steps and new stories. To all of them, I offer a deep bow of thanks.

I am especially indebted to Taka Nomura, Hide Enomoto and Hide and Yuki Inoue, who have become much more than close friends and colleagues — they are among the people I trust most in the world. Taka also provided the forward for the Japanese edition of this book, which was translated by Mizuho Toyoshima. Deepest thanks.

I could not have written this book without all I learned from the young leaders I met in Japan over the last seven years and those from around the world, who I met and worked with during my years at the Berkana Institute. They helped me discover so much about being alive. I always feel the presence of two people, in particular, from those years. One is Maaianne Knuth from Zimbabwe, the founder of the Kufunda Learning Village, and the other is Manish Jain from India, co-founder of the equally inspiring Shikshantar. I've known Maaianne and Manish since 2000 and their fire and clarity continue to inspire me as we grow older together.

This book was made possible because of Yuka Saionji Matsuura's constant support. Yuka has stood by my side with compassionate insight and guidance. Her wisdom and kindness and her consistent presence and counsel have served as a compass as I found my way.

Here at home, my deepest thanks to Lynnaea Lumbard, the other co-president of NewStories, and the members of the NewStories Board, who had my back every step of the way; to the people who read and responded to the sixty or so blogs I wrote from Japan and gave me a sense of not being alone; and to the people who donated funds to cover my expenses at different times in this journey.

My gratitude to my spouse, Susan Virnig, who was involved in significant portions of the work in Japan that eventually led to this book. She was both my editor and thinking partner as I brought this book forward.

This book has its wholeness because of my editor, Megan Scribner. Friends said I needed some professional help and I found Megan. Deepest gratitude to her for her editor's eye and artist's heart. The beauty of the book grows from the sumie brush work of my dear friend Barbara Bash and the illustrations of Zulma Patarroyo, the graphic facilitator I have worked with on many efforts across the US.

And finally, I must turn in thanks to those whose presence in my life has been profound.

The first is my host grandfather in Kyoto, Naokazu Nakatsugawa. From the time we met in 1970 until his death in 1989, he was my spiritual guide. The second is my dear friend and colleague, British socio-economist and futurist Robert Theobald. Robert and I traveled many roads together from the time we met in 1969 until his death 30 years later. We learned so much together. The third is Joanna Macy, who I regard as the elder of my heart. Joanna's fierce wisdom has helped me find my way. And, of course, thanks to my dear friend Margaret Wheatley, whose views of people and leadership continue to inform and inspire me and whose invitation into The Berkana Institute changed my life.

I am grateful to Meg for her poignant Foreword, *Turning to One Another* and to Mary Catherine Bateson for her wisdom and perspective in her Afterword, Toward a Common Future. And, of course, deep gratitude to voices from my larger community as they have stepped forward to offer their perspective on *AfterNow*.

To each of you, deep and everlasting thanks.

Contents

FOREWORD:
Turning to One Another
by Margaret Wheatley

NEARLY EVERY CULTURE has incorporated into their cosmology or theology a realization about change. Change is just the way life is. When a Buddhist teacher was asked to describe the essence of Buddhist philosophy, he replied: "Everything changes."

Yet Western philosophy, especially in this global era, has built upon a different belief: We do not partner with nature, we demand that nature yield up her secrets so that we can become Masters of the Universe. We seek to control and alter nature to suit our petty human needs. For the first time in history, humans have changed the environment rather than working in partnership with life's powerful forces for growth, change and destruction.

As ecologists are quick to point out, nature always has the last word. Natural disasters are intensifying: more Category Five cyclones, catastrophic fires on many continents, erratic weather patterns of intense cold then heat, drought then floods. These are nature's last words. And each of these events are made worse because of where we've built and what we've built: nuclear power plants on geologic faults; dense building on flood plains or sea fronts; housing near polluted industrial sites. We are not Masters of the Universe — we are simply arrogant children possessed by magical thinking, believing we can get away with our defiance.

The great tragedy of this arrogance is that it is everyday people who suffer the most from fires, floods, droughts, and earthquakes.

1

They have neither the choice nor the money to choose to live away from danger, nor to stop the arrogance from manifesting in new projects and building developments. However, it is people and their communities that are the greatest resource once disaster strikes. For many years, after witnessing and working in post-disaster scenes, I became confident that humans have the capacity to get through the very worst experiences as long as we stay together and support one another. These times of trauma and great loss also offer us, paradoxically, the experiences of joy and grace.

I was puzzled when I first heard people describing these experiences as times of joy. They always did, but it took me many experiences before I realized that when we are working together with the intensity and clarity that disaster work requires, we are in communion with one another. Rather than separate individuals each seeking ways to help, something greater than ourselves emerges as we all pitch in and do whatever we can, whatever the present situation requires. This is a transcendent spiritual experience that feels joyful — we are together, truly present, no longer separate selves. The Bible promises this: "Whenever two or more are gathered, there will I be also."

This is the blessed part of post-disaster recovery work and an important sign post of what's possible when we forego ego needs and work together in common cause. However, as days wind into months then years, we are challenged by overwhelm, fatigue, despair, and government bureaucracy. We can't accomplish as much as is needed; obstacles block the way forward; solutions don't work, new problems occur; we run out of money; people give up; government assures us that it has things under control but doesn't. This is the predictable pattern of long-term recovery efforts. It's extremely difficult to keep people focused and working well together when the time period expands from immediate response to years of rebuilding and creating out of the rubble of disaster.

Once again, the medicine that keeps us going, that prevents us from giving up, is each other. Our relationships become primary — we can continue in this very hard and challenging work because we are together, with people we can depend on. We comfort, console and cheer each other up. We take turns being exhausted and depressed. We keep going because we can draw on another's strength when our own falters. And when we feel energetic and excited, we can offer it to our colleagues who are taking their turn at being exhausted and upset. We humans can get through anything as long as we're together.

As recovery efforts grow into months, then years, we find energy and perseverance from focusing on more local work, specific projects and activities. With this narrowed focus, results become visible and our spirits are renewed. We feel useful. As projects succeed, we learn how to do the work of creation and rebuilding with more intelligence. As people's lives are stabilized and they become more hopeful about their future, we feel their gratitude and love.

The Chinese character for "perseverance" is a knife suspended over a human heart. While there are many interpretations available, I have come to appreciate two. The first is that as we engage in work we care about, our hearts will be opened and expanded. From our cut open hearts, we feel more compassion, generosity, altruism. We want to be there to serve others, we no longer feel so self-protective or guarded, we have less fear of opening to what is rather than what we want to be true. The second interpretation describes the knife as risk — at any moment, our dreams and plans can be cut asunder. Yet still we persevere, because this is the work of the heart.

It is necessary that we learn as much as we can from Japan's Triple Disasters which is why I so appreciate the details in the stories and practices Bob so carefully and lovingly relates. Here are a few of the rich learnings I gleaned from reading this:

- Japan's ancient culture of community, patience, acceptance and perseverance was a strong foundation to invoke and then build upon.

- More recent processes for bringing people together to console, support and then create a future worth struggling for really do work. We can trust them and need to both learn them well and champion them.

- Governments, and the dependency they breed, are not the answer. In fact, they are the source of far too many problems and have a dis-spiriting impact as recovery efforts continue. We can't stop them, but we need to recognize their both adversarial and negative impacts so that we can effectively counteract them with sound community-based processes.

- With our eyes and hearts wide open, those of us who want to serve in post-disaster recovery efforts (we usually don't have a choice) must develop an unshakable faith in the human spirit and people's capacity to engage together well in creating their own future.
- This work is very difficult but not to be avoided or put off learning how to do it. Our skills will be required as global culture reaps the whirlwinds of nature's response to our intolerable arrogance. We need to prepare now.

Thank you, Bob, for everything here. You have written both a parable and a handbook for our time as you followed the path with heart, encountered the knife many times over, and persevered with emerging clarity and dedication. I am grateful for the gift of this book and ask that we take this into our own hearts and minds so that we can bravely serve well in the catastrophes yet to come.

Meg Wheatley

Note to Readers

ON THE AFTERNOON OF MARCH 11, 2011, massive, overwhelming, incomprehensible disaster struck the northeast coast of Japan. Life for those in the region would never be the same.

This book is about the awakening that follows disaster. About the minutes and hours and months and years that come after now. It is about what happens when we're smacked on the side of the head and open our eyes, startled out of the trance in which we have been living our days. It is about the opportunities always present, often invisible, to create the lives we want, now.

As the waters from the tsunami flowed back into the ocean, as the last bricks fell from buildings almost destroyed, people began to turn to one another. They grieved, they laughed, they prayed. And they asked, what now?

This book is about my journey with the Japanese people over the last six years. I write about my own story of awakening after plunging into this disaster. I share stories from people who found where to take their first step, and the next. I offer the tools and processes and worldview I introduced as people came together to discover and create what comes after now.

This book is built around two big ideas. The first is that after disaster, we find our way forward, together. We come awake, together. Disaster obliterates the past, plunges the present into chaos and cocoons the future. We need each other to see and build the new. The second big idea is that we don't have to wait for the overwhelming tragedy of disaster to make the communities and lives we want. We can engage each other with respect, curiosity and generosity and begin to co-create what we want, now.

We live in a period of precipitous, unpredictable change. The book is for those who want to make this time of transformation more livable and less insane. It is for those engaging with others around questions that matter and who have something inside that keeps asking what else is possible now. We are the hospice workers and midwifes, honoring the old and letting that which is ready to die go. We welcome and co-create our new normal. I no longer think of us as "agents of change" — that implies that we have control of the outcome. We need to let go of the pretense that we can know what will result from our actions. We need to embrace radical uncertainty, showing up as fully as we can each moment, each breath.

In Japan and all over the world, we are living in the messy middle where many old forms are falling apart and new possibilities are in early stages of development. The ground is pulled out from under us on a regular basis. It is important to not get distracted and try to clean up the mess — trying to make everything perfect, removing the tensions, covering over important differences. Our work right now is to learn to coexist with the messiness. We need to keep trying things, to keep learning. We need to remain focused on our purpose and follow the braided strand of intention and surrender as we find our way forward — with each other.

Whether it is changing our lives or changing something in our communities, it is almost impossible to do it alone. None of us is equipped with all the knowledge, skills, intelligence and experience we need for the work on the long road of transformation. We need to pool our talents, our skills, our resources. We need to create new structures for learning, ones that make it possible for us to take the time to chew our own experiences, to learn from each other's insights, and to interact with those from outside our immediate systems who have other knowledge and wisdom we need. All of this requires community. Hopefully this book gives some clues about how to reach out, find and form that community, and get on with what needs to be done.

Through this book, I share what I have learned in Japan — before and after the Triple Disasters — and from working around the world with people building community and new futures. I tell stories of my experience and the stories of others who have worked hard and long in Japan. I share the ideas, methods and processes that have been helpful to me in this work. I invite you to use these in your work, creating community and finding the new future.

I hope this book is beneficial as you create your new story. I hope it helps you find the confidence to begin and to continue. Read it from cover to cover if you are so inclined. Pick it up from time to time and look at different sections. Treat it as a farmer's almanac of ideas and possibilities to ponder and explore.

NewStories, the nonprofit I established in 2000, supports people everywhere who are discovering what is AfterNow. In our Learning Lab, we find ways to support those who offer their leadership in these uncertain times. In our Action Lab, we provide space for promising initiatives in different parts of the world. In our Stories Lab, we work to understand and reveal the role stories play in this time. We also provide strategic convening services, working with communities and organizations who are ready to create a new normal. Come visit us at www.NewStories.org and www.AfterNow.Today

And please, connect with me on Facebook, LinkedIn and Twitter where I am, not surprisingly, bobstilger.

Blessings on our many journeys.
June 18, 2017

The arrow points near the epicenter of the earthquake, as well as the location of the Fukushima reactors. The entire northeast coastline was hit by the tsunami with greatest impact closest to epicenter

Introduction

IN THE PITCH BLACK, early-morning hours of March 11, 2011, my phone rang. Startled, I answered and heard my daughter Annie's frantic voice calling from New Zealand. "Are they okay? Have you heard from Obaachan and Ojiichan? Are they okay?"

I had no idea what she was talking about. The news hadn't reached my home in Spokane, Washington. My heart sank and my fears rose as I listened to Annie tell me what little she knew.

Hours before, at 2:46 in the afternoon Japan Time, a 9.0 magnitude earthquake struck in the Pacific Ocean just off of the northeast coast of Japan. Forty-five minutes later, a 50-foot high tsunami wave traveling at more than 50 miles an hour hit the shoreline, laying waste to all in its path. The next day, the Fukushima nuclear reactors began to explode.

Annie was worried about the Nakatsugawas, our host family and dear friends, who live in Kyoto, near Osaka in the southwest and 500 miles away from the Tohoku region where the disasters struck. News was sketchy and for hours it was impossible to get through to the Nakatsugawas. Eventually we discovered they were safe, but for the people in Tohoku, life would never be the same.

The morning before the disasters struck, most people in the area were leading full lives. Connected, interdependent and reasonably content, spending their days nestled in a familiar normalcy. That afternoon, everything changed. The Triple Disasters — earthquake, tsunami and nuclear explosions — would be the greatest environmental catastrophe to hit a country in living memory.

By the time the waters receded, nearly 20,000 people had lost their lives and another 500,000 lost their homes, jobs or both. Businesses, hospitals, schools and homes — destroyed. Gas lines ruptured, train tracks gone, roadways missing. Everywhere they looked, their world was in ruins.

In Fukushima, the disaster from the exploding reactors was largely imperceptible, yet harder to comprehend with a devastating impact that will last for lifetimes.

Strong, self-reliant people now found themselves sleeping on school floors with hundreds and sometimes thousands of strangers, depending on others to bring them rice-balls three times a day for meals. Days turned into weeks and months with almost all sense of purpose in life destroyed. For those in the disaster area, it was being in a nightmare that would not end.

Those outside the disaster zones felt a sense of helplessness. They did not know how to support the people of Tohoku but knew everything had changed.

Beyond the personal loss, the physical devastation and the disturbing uncertainties about the nuclear explosions, the disasters struck at a deep psychological level. Such tragedies not only obliterate the present, they also destroy any pretense of a knowable future.

Japan faced a tremendous challenge to not only clean up from the Triple Disasters — but to find a new future.

What was possible?
Where to begin?
How to make a new path forward?

These were the questions facing Japan. Over the coming years, as I worked with the people of Japan, they became my own.

Approaching Japan

I first arrived in Japan as a student at Waseda University in 1970.[1] Forty years later, in 2010, I was invited to Japan to introduce work on dialogue, leadership and building healthy and resilient com-

---

1   For more of my own story and background, visit the AfterNow.today website

munities. On March 11, 2011, the Triple Disasters struck and on April 5th I flew to Japan. I would devote much of the next six years of my life to service in Japan.

This book is about my journey in Japan before and after the disasters. This book is about what I have seen and experienced and wondered in a lifetime dedicated to building resilient communities. While this is my personal story, it is also the story of the people I know and worked with in Japan. It is a story of what is arising in Tohoku — the disaster region — as well as in the rest of Japan and in places throughout the world. It is a universal story of people everywhere who are gaining insight into their own lives in a world where the future is obscure. It is the story of people who are calling together others in their communities and organizations to find a new way forward — realizing that they first need to rediscover where forward may be. It is our story — yours and mine. The question, of course, is what story will we each tell? How will we stand up? What will help us find our way forward?

For 2011-2014, I spent 4-5 months a year in Japan. My time has decreased since then, but I still return regularly. During those first years, I worked with people up and down the coast, from Iwaki south of the reactors to Otsuchi, just south of Miyako, in the north.

I wrote MIRAI GA MIE NAKU NATTA TOKI, BOKU TACHI WA NANI O KATARE BA II NO DAROU (*When We Cannot See the Future, Where Do We Begin*) to share my story with the people of Japan. It was published by Eiji Press in Tokyo in June of 2015 and has been well received in Japan, serving as a mirror and as a spotlight as people remember what we've been learning from the disasters.

In early 2015, my Japanese publisher told me the title they had chosen for my book — *When We Cannot See the Future. Where Do We Begin?* The brilliance of the title is all theirs. In Japan, the publisher decides the title, not the author, and they do so by going into deep discernment about the essence of the book. At Eiji Press, they concluded that this book really wasn't about disaster, nor was it about building communities — it was about how we move forward when the future disappears. In Japanese, the title is subtle and brilliant and its question is the core of that book and this one as well.

From the moment I heard it, the title started to work on me. Through the writing and my work, I've lived into that question, and I've realized that in these moments of blinding uncertainty, we must bring our attention to the present moment. Right here. Right now. We bring our attention to the people we are with and the resources we already have and to what's really important.

I knew when I wrote the first book that there would be an English edition someday and that it would be different from the Japanese version. Though many readers might have experienced disasters, I would be writing to people who had not experienced and may not know a lot about the Japanese Triple Disasters. It has taken some stepping back to see what story this book has to tell. After many discussions with my friends and colleagues, I turned to this English edition on the morning of March 11, 2016, sitting in my host family's home in Kyoto on the fifth anniversary of the Triple Disasters, known in Japan, simply, as 3.11.

On a plane ride to Japan in the fall of 2015, I had been thinking about the title of the English edition. I knew it needed to incorporate this sense of NOW as a point of departure. AfterNOW popped into view and I got off the airplane in Tokyo and immediately did a domain search. AfterNOW.org, .net, and .com were all taken. But there was a new domain extension — ".today" — which I immediately grabbed. It was perfect. It said it all. What's important is what we do after now, after this present moment. And we need to begin TODAY.

Disasters Happen

Now as I finish writing this edition, in the early months of 2017, disasters in many forms are taking place around the world: cascading wars in the Middle East; millions of migrants desperately seeking safety; host countries being overwhelmed by the influx of people; economies collapsing in Greece, Zimbabwe and elsewhere around the world; random mass killings happening on our streets and in our schools and factories, and natural disasters destroying lives and property across the globe. Add to this list the systemic consequences of climate change, income inequality, brittle infrastructures, hate mongering and numerous other issues. Some might object if I called the election of Donald Trump a disaster, so I'll settle for calling it a precursor of unpredictable disruptive change, which, of course, is what disaster is. And let's not forget the more immediate personal disasters that come when a loved one dies, when a partner says "I want a divorce" or we arrive at work and are told to clean out our desk and go home.

We live in a time that signals unimaginable shifts in our lives. Scientists say these are moments of "punctuated equilibrium"[2], when systems shift suddenly and unpredictably. Popular language sometimes refers to this as the transition from old to new paradigms. In his book, *The Collapse of Complex Societies*, Joseph Tainter offers a compelling analysis of how the very complexity that societies generate as part of their growth contains the seeds of their collapse. Meg Wheatley's new book *Who Do We Choose To Be* offers vivid insight to patterns of social disintegration.

We have done enough damage to our global ecology that we can depend on more and more hurricanes, forest fires, floods, tsunamis, tornadoes, crippling snow and ice storms and the like. In addition, many of our structures and systems in areas ranging from health care to education, from transportation infrastructure to sanitation, are overloaded, overwhelmed, brittle and collapsing. We will continue to have disasters: natural and man-made, structural and physical, systemic and psychological, smaller and larger.

Whatever the cause, our lives and world are steeping in disaster.

---

2   Connie Gersick's 1991 essay on punctuated equilibrium is a brilliant analysis of this phenomena examined from a number of perspectives.

Disasters Shake Us Awake

Disasters end the lives of some and cause trauma and grief for many. They turn cities and countries upside down. They smack us on the side of the head, making us open our eyes and see the world and stories we are living in.

Disasters demolish our carefully constructed lives and dreams. They dissolve the ways in which we find meaning and make sense in our lives. They reveal how our lives are sometimes like a house of cards held together by stress and inertia. In disasters, the cards collapse, our present falls apart, and our future — the one we envisioned, the one we counted on — is gone.

Disasters wake us up. We live in times of both trauma and possibility. Even after great tragedy and pain, we have a deep human capacity to create something new. Disasters are also a huge wake-up call that release us from the trance of our old normal and the future that was laid out in front of us. Disasters can be the springboard to create the lives we actually want. In these times, we are invited to look closely at how we want to live our lives. Important questions become visible:

- What happens after now, today? What do we do when we can't see the future anymore?
- How do we proceed when our normal vanishes overnight? How do we open our eyes, see our world as it is, find those we need to be with and ask what is possible now?
- How do we live well in this breath-taking moment, between the old and the new, surrounded by what's dying and what's being born? How do we keep from closing down, turning from chaos to fear and control?
- How can we respond to these disasters so that we can discover and unleash our creativity? How can we see take advantage of these times to turn to each other to build something new?

When the future is unknowable, we bring our attention to now, to the present moment. We bring our attention to ourselves and to each other as we welcome in the unseen and create together that which brings us joy. And we join together to build a new future.

For me, this is the underlying lesson of the aftermath of the Triple Disasters. It is also what led me to first write Japanese version of this book and now this English version.

In Japan, the Triple Disasters created a space and a necessity for change. In Japan, a deeply collective culture, this space is both individual and widespread. The birth of the new is taking place everywhere. Especially in Fukushima and in the coastal areas hit hardest by the disasters, where the old normal is gone. There is no going back.

This book weaves together my experience of how disaster dissolves any knowledge of the future with the stories of how people in Japan found their way forward. The stories in this book offer insights about how they have begun to transform their lives.

On a personal level, I write about the journey I took as I fell into service in Japan. It also represents the chaotic, complex, confusing and uncertain journey each of us undertake when we follow life's calling and step into the unknown. I hope that reading about my journey will give you insights about your own.

I share stories from many people in Japan and from other places in the world, because I believe they are inspiring as well as informative. They give us a chance to take a step back and look in on the immensely rich journey of grief at the disappearance of the old combined with excitement about the emergence of the new.

I offer some of the approaches I used working in communities in Japan as they stepped together into new possibilities — tools, methodologies, approaches and views that sustained me as I worked with people across Japan to make sense out of what was happening. These were my starting points. I hope they will help you find yours.

There are many stories, voices and lessons in this book. You can read it from cover to cover or you can pick up the book at any point that speaks to you, read it and put it down. I suggest you follow the principle of start anywhere, follow it everywhere. You'll also find that I repeat certain core ideas throughout the book, sometimes using different phrasing to give a different access. Grab what works for you and build on it. Let go of the rest. There's a lot here. This book is not written around a single big idea. It is written around the big question of how to live when our past is obliterated, present chaotic and future cocooned.

Here's what you'll find in each chapter.

CHAPTER 1 — **Following the Thread** is the story of my arriving in Japan in 2010, more than a year <u>before</u> the disasters, as a teacher and dialogue host. My entry into Japan was made possible because of a deeply personal 40+ year relationship with Japan that has shaped who I am. In this chapter I share some of what I began to teach as I worked with people all over Japan. Beginning with Art of Hosting and its cousin, FutureCenters, I also started to offer my own research about *Enspirited Leadership* and about the values and principles of Life Affirming Leadership that guide us in our work to create healthy and resilient communities.

CHAPTER 2 — **Befriending Confusion** describes my arrival in Japan just weeks after the disasters. It offers both a glimpse of what it was like in Japan in the beginning days and, through my journals, what it was like for me to enter into this emotionally charged field. Those first few weeks set the stage for my work of the next five years. I hope my story helps you think about how you can step forward when everything falls apart and invites you to take a step back and look at our world today and the disasters we're living with.

CHAPTER 3 — **Finding AfterNow** illustrates the work of creating spaces for dialogue, discovery, innovation and co-created action that have been a core part of my work in Japan. These spaces and methods have many names. In my work in Japan we call them FutureSessions; they were one key to helping people in the disaster area build new lives and people throughout the country to shape a new Japan. This chapter is a discussion of the steps, stages, and features of creating systems for transformative change.

CHAPTER 4 — Reflecting and Changing Together turns back to the first years after disasters and shares the reflections, thoughts and stories of some of my closest friends and colleagues. We dialogued with each other about what has been shifting in Japan. For many, inside and outside of the disaster region, the Triple Disasters were a wake-up call, inviting people out of the trance of their lives and into questions about what's important.

CHAPTER 5 — New Futures Arising Everywhere broadens out and takes a look at the wider world. Everywhere people are in an inquiry about what it means to be truly human and the purpose of their lives. The stories from different regions are distinct and have their own unique flavor textures, but they are the stories of a time of shifting paradigms and of new possibilities being born.

CHAPTER 6 — Walking the Long Road Together describes many of the ideas and models and frameworks I've been introducing in Japan. We need tools and stories and ideas that help us walk the long road into lives that matter more. As I did my work in Japan, these were the ideas that I introduced frequently — different ways of thinking about our lives and our world that help us explore those new possibilities being born.

CHAPTER 7 — Discovering Right Action is similar to Chapter 6 in that it introduces some additional tools and ideas. In this chapter, my emphasis is more on how we discover where to stand, on how we find ourselves and each other and look with fresh eyes at the systems in which we live. I turned regularly to Theory U, Active Hope and the Cynefin framework to help people understand their journey.

CHAPTER 8 — Creating a Future Together chronicles some of the archetypal stories that have been shared with me after the disasters. These stories are like stepping stones into an unknowable future. They illustrate how we, as human beings, have an extraordinary capacity to create the new, NOW. For some, disaster is a catalyst for these journeys into the hidden wholeness of our lives. These stories may give you some clues about your own journey forward.

CHAPTER 9 — WhatNow gives an overview of what's happening in Japan now, in all its messiness. Disaster changes everything and it changes nothing. It's a blip in time when the old is cracked open and new light begins to shine. But working in that light takes a lifetime, not just a couple of years. This is very much a story in progress, one with many endings and many beginnings.

CHAPTER 10 — Living in the Messy Middle offers some concluding reflections on how we live in this time with obliterated past, chaotic present and cocooned future. It's my invitation to you, and to me, to continue to find the steps forward.

CHAPTER 11 — Voices From My Larger Community draws in voices from around the world who have reviewed AfterNow. I began to gather these as endorsements, and then realized they are a central part of the book itself. I am the author of this book, not the creator of the ideas presented. They have been co-created in community. These voices help to unpack the messages of AfterNow.

The book begins with a insightful Foreword and ends with a thoughtful Afterword written by dear friends and colleagues. Meg Wheatley's Foreword — *Turning to One Another* — examines what it means to live in a time of collapse. Mary Catherine Bateson's Afterword — *Toward a Common Future* — reminds us of the nature of these times in which we live. I am honored to be surrounded by these dear sisters.

A section of Additional Resources, including bibliography ends the book.

Following the Thread

CHAPTER

1

Following the Thread

PEOPLE OFTEN WONDER, "Why is this white-haired foreigner spending so much time in Japan?" The answer is simple. I love Japan. I believe in the strength and resilience people everywhere have. I know people can work together in community to create the future they want NOW.

> There's a thread you follow. It goes among
> things that change. But it doesn't change.
> People wonder about what you are pursuing.
> You have to explain about the thread.
> But it is hard for others to see.
> While you hold it you can't get lost.
> Tragedies happen; people get hurt
> or die; and you suffer and get old.
> Nothing you do can stop time's unfolding.
> You don't ever let go of the thread.
>
> — *William Stafford, The Way It Is*

My life has been a tapestry woven with several threads.

One thread of this story is Japan, and my nearly 50-year relationship with Japan. In 1970, I spent my senior year in college at the Waseda University in Tokyo and began a rich and rewarding personal journey with, in and through Japan. Susan Virnig and I met in Japan that same year and married in 1978. Our daughter, born in 1987, grew up within both Japanese and American culture, living many months of her life in Japan. For 40 years, my relationship with Japan was a deeply personal one. At the end of 2009, I was invited to bring my work from around the world into Japan — taking my relationship to another level.

Another thread is the strength and resilience people have. I discovered at an early age that kindness and wisdom — and their opposites — are pretty evenly distributed across gender, ethnicity, class and politics. I discovered that people have an incredible capacity to be creative and that most of us want to help each other. I found that when I greeted people with curiosity, respect and generosity, magic usually happened.

The other key thread is knowing that people can work together in community to create a future they believe in. I spent ten years in partnership with Margaret Wheatley and others at The Berkana Institute,[3] working with people all over the world to help them use what resources they had (natural, political, and relationship assets) to build the lives and communities they wanted, today. Our work at Berkana was to name, connect, nourish and illuminate new practices of leadership and healthy and resilient patterns of life on this small planet we call home.

Most of us do not create a future alone. And why would we even want to try? We need each other. We are a social species. We come alive in community. I bring people together for conversations that matter because as a species we have evolved together, in dialogue and in community. We evolved sitting around the fires, sharing and listening, dreaming and creating. We have learned and practiced trust and deep listening and speaking the truth. Some of us may have forgotten how, but we can remember.

Spirit works in mysterious ways. The three threads of this tapestry started to weave together with my entry into Japan more than a year before the Triple Disasters. In November 2009, I was presenting at the Pegasus Systems Thinking in Action conference in Seattle and was astounded to find more than 25 people from Japan. We started talking and I learned about a new climate of change in Japan — a country and culture that had been an important part of my life since to my year in 1970 at Waseda University. I shared ideas from my work with

3   The Berkana Institute was founded in 1992 by Margaret Wheatley and Myron Kellner Rogers after Meg wrote *Leadership and the New Sciences*, a critical introduction to what living systems to teach us about leadership. Berkana has pioneered use of dialogue, networks and self-organizing principles to create healthy and resilient communities and organizations.

leadership, dialogue and building healthy and resilient communities around the world and was soon invited to bring these insights to Japan in January 2010. I had no idea what the future would bring.

For many of us in Japan, 2010 was a year of forming new relationships. The Future Center movement started, the Presencing Institute of Japan opened with the Japanese translation of Otto Scharmer's Theory U, and the Transition Towns Japan movement started to grow. And the list goes on. Many of us doing this work to create a new future connected with each other for the first time. Looking back after the disasters, we said it was as if spirit had given us a head start.

Change was in the air in 2010. The political party that had ruled in Japan since World War II had been toppled from power. The economy was stalled at many levels. People of all ages, and especially younger people, were raising more and more questions about what kinds of lives they wanted to live. There was a sense of discontent — not that most people were about to make any abrupt changes, but they were complaining more about their lives.

In January, we tested the waters with a two-day pilot "Art of Hosting"[4] workshop. Yuya Nishimura, then organizer of a series of events called Dialogue Bar, brought together a group of 30 or so people and asked me to join them. The session was amazing. I remember writing in my journal that while this was the first time Art of Hosting had come to Japan, it was as if it had been born there. I started to understand in new ways the Japanese sensitivity to BA[5] (the relational space that holds us) which was interwoven with a deep comfort with silence and an ability to listen, listen and listen.

---

4   Since the beginning of this century, Art of Hosting has grown into a worldwide community of practice with several thousand members. All around the world people learn with each other about how to use conversation to find the knowledge and the leadership within any system.

5   BA is an important word and construct in Japanese. The least complicated translation is "space" but it means much more. It refers to the space in which we gather. Most of us know what space feels like when it is alive and connected as compared to a space that is oppressive. That energy — the feel of the space — is what is meant by BA. It is the relational space between us. There is a deep Japanese sensitivity to BA. It enables or blocks deep communication and understanding.

This pilot workshop led to two full Art of Hosting programs in May and then two more in November along with innumerable workshops and other sessions. All together I made four trips and spent almost 6 months in Japan in 2010. The ideas I introduced and the relationships I stepped into formed the foundation for my work after the Triple Disasters.

My work with Art of Hosting brought me into relationship with Taka Nomura, then with Knowledge Dynamics Initiatives (KDI) at Fuji-Xerox, just as he was beginning to introduce new approaches for creating innovation in business, based on the Future Center[6] model from Europe.

People in Japan were attracted to the ideas about leadership that I offered. My work on *Enspirited Leadership*[7] found immediate resonance and some of my writing was quickly translated into Japanese. People were attracted to the values and principles of Life Affirming Leadership we had been discovering over the last decade through the work of the members of the Berkana Exchange. My daughter, Annie Stilger Virnig, and I were invited to present at TEDxTokyo 2010.[8] The Berkana Institute's way of framing paradigm shifts — "The Two Loops" — became a powerful way to invite people to think about the changes happening in Japan.

---

6 FutureCenters now exist all over Japan; these are physical spaces designed to easily host FutureSessions. FutureSessions — designed and hosted dialogues, described in detail in Chapter 3 — can be offered in FutureCenters, as well as almost any other facility. The spearhead of this movement has been Future Sessions, Inc., a business founded by Taka Nomura after he left KDI in early 2012.

7 A summary of my work on Enspirited Leadership is available on the NewStories website. Developed as my doctoral thesis at CIIS in 2004, Enspirited Leadership is a framework that explores what happens when people step forward in response to a call to service. How do we find our way when called and what helps us take the first step and the next and the next? It's also described in the next section in this chapter.

8 You can see this video on YouTube.

These four frameworks: Art of Hosting/FutureSessions, *Enspirited Leadership*, Life Affirming Leadership, and Two Loops[9] would become the primary building blocks for all my work in Japan. They gave people a way to have a conversation with each other that helped them discover what was important in their lives. They helped to begin creating common language.

I've used them not only in Japan, but all around the world, when I've been engaging people to think about their lives and the changes they want to see. They're a starting point. In 2010, it was in the context of sharing these frameworks that I started building relationships with many people who would become close partners after the Triple Disasters.

Art of Hosting and FutureSessions

Back when this new century was just beginning, practitioners who were strong advocates of different social technologies like Circle, Open Space, World Café, and Appreciative Inquiry[10] started to talk with each other about how these different approaches complimented each other. Berkana was in the middle of these inquiries in part because of our launch of a leadership development initiative called *From the Four Directions*. We believed that the best way for people to uncover gifts and find enough clarity and courage to offer their leadership was to come together in sacred circles of conversations exploring their lives. People who met through From the Four Directions soon gave birth to the Art of Hosting movement.

Art of Hosting evolved as a self-organizing learning community where experienced practitioners offered their skills and insights through three-day training programs called, simply, *Art of Hosting Conversations That Matter*. The journey over the last fifteen years has been a pretty incredible one and there is no longer any single way to

---

9   I introduce the first three frameworks in this chapter. Later in Chapter 6, I introduce the Two Loops in detail and in its relation to the work people were called to do after the Triple Disasters.

10 These practices are described in the Additional Resources section of AfterNow.today

describe Art of Hosting. For me it is a growing set of practices and practitioners who support and learn with each other, some of whom offer different training and learning opportunities with the identity "Art of Hosting."

The underlying belief in Art of Hosting is that we're better together. We're smarter, more courageous, more humble and more alive, together. We discover our capacities, our yearnings and our gifts, when we enter spaces where we can respond to Angeles Arrien's invitation from many years ago:

Show Up, Be Present

Speak the Truth without Blame or Judgment

Listen for What Has Heart and Meaning

Be Open to Outcome, Not Controlling of Outcome

— *Angeles Arrien, The Four Fold Way*

Art of Hosting and FutureSessions in Japan

When the bubble of Japan's economy burst back in the early nineties, most everyone tried to get back on track — to be a global economic power where production and consumption were the path to happiness. But as the first decade of the new century was coming to an end, discontent and turmoil, as well as a sense of possibility, were just under the surface in Japan. People were looking for new ways to connect, create and discover together. Words like SHI-AWASE (happiness) and ARIKATA (ideal way of being) started coming into conversations.

In Japan, these new ideas were challenging; they were not in alignment with the all-consuming commitment to capitalism and material prosperity that overtook Japan after World War II. What happened in 2010 was that people in Japan started using Art of Hosting as a framework to listen more deeply to each other to speak their truth as they explored their lives.

Through the Art of Hosting, I met the wonderful mavericks leading the Knowledge Dynamics Initiative (KDI) of Fuji-Xerox. At that time, KDI was a leader in "knowledge management" work in Japan. Utilizing many of the principles of Kojiro Nonaka,[11] KDI worked with major companies throughout Japan to help them find and use the knowledge they already had. But one of the things KDI noticed was that while knowledge management was useful, it didn't really seem to lead to a lot of change. They started looking around to see where and how innovation was happening in companies and quickly discovered the European-based Future Center Alliance.[12] As the leaders of KDI and I talked, we saw an obvious synergy between the approaches of Art of Hosting and those of FutureCenters, and we immediately began to work together.

In Chapter 3 we'll take a closer look at FutureSessions, but let me lay in a bit of background here. In 2010, I worked with KDI to prototype Future Centers — a physical structure in which FutureSessions happen — as a dynamic space in business for innovation. Later, after 3.11, we started to explore how FutureSessions could be used as a vehicle for collaboration across all sectors of society as a way to co-create social innovation.

After the disasters, Taka Nomura from KDI and I kept talking with many others about how FutureSessions might help. We felt these could be the kind of spaces in which people in communities could come together to begin to create the future they wanted. We boldly declared there would be a FutureSession Week at the end of May 2011, just 2 ½ months after the disasters. It would be five days, with five sessions, beginning at the Takamatsu Castle on the southern island of Shikoku and concluding at the Catalyst Ba in Futagotamagawa, near Tokyo. We gathered people around different themes, such as energy, community planning, work-life balance, and asked them to dream about what could be. Organizing these five sessions took an extraordinary amount

---

11 Nonaka-sensei is a scholar and prolific writer who has spent a life time exploring the nature of knowledge and the relationships that make it visible. In his work of a lifetime, he explores how the tacit or hidden knowledge of organizations can be released when we create the spaces (BA) where people can generously share their truth, listen deeply to others and engage in dialogue to create something that's been invisible.

12 The Future Center Alliance is a network of places and practitioners in many parts of the world who are creating Future Centers as oases for innovation.

of time and energy; dozens of people stepped forward to help. The idea of needing special places to create a new future began to take hold.

We used this week to introduce participants to this new kind of space for dialogue, discernment and action. Through FutureSessions, sometimes in a single session, often through a series of sessions, participants pay attention to six different aspects of creating new possibilities together:

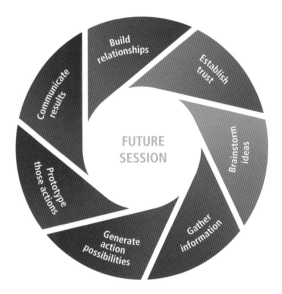

This is really the basic work of innovation and collaboration. Our first FutureSession Week generated substantial interest. In January of 2012, Taka and I decided it was time to bring together a community of people to take responsibility for this FutureSession work, so we called for a planning session. We thought maybe 30 or so people might come. We were amazed when more than 100 showed up!

An infectious energy was building. A self-organizing system emerged where people stepped forward to take responsibility for creating FutureSessions in their organizations and communities. Taka decided to leave KDI and start a new social business — FutureSessions, Inc. — that would provide support and an internet organizing space to connect these different local sessions and make them visible across Japan. Seeds were planted that grew into almost 100 FutureSessions all around Japan during the second annual FutureSession Week in May

2012. From five sessions in 2011 to more than 100 in 2012 — clearly there was something about FutureSessions that had strong attraction to people all across Japan. Every spring since 2011 there's been a FutureSession Week in Japan continuing to build this movement.

I began to say that going to a FutureSession was like going to an ONSEN (a Japanese hot springs bath). There are special rules for being in an ONSEN that frame the experience. People enter a room — one for men and one for women — and take off all their clothes. Then, they enter another room and thoroughly wash themselves, sitting in front of mirrors on little stools, side-by-side. I'm told that on the women's side they often wash each other's backs. We usually don't do that on the men's side. Once clean, we begin to soak in pools of water, indoors and out, very hot, except, perhaps, for an occasional dip into an icy cold pool. All these rules are well understood and add to the experience for all.

In the same way, special rules in a FutureSession help to create the setting for open and fruitful dialogue. The formal roles in the system's hierarchy (be it a community or organization) are left at the door. People encounter each other with a spirit of respect, curiosity, and generosity. There's a strong sense of wanting to invite newness in rather than just doing more of the same.

I had been drawn to FutureSessions because of their emphasis on innovation and taking action. I was quite intrigued with what felt like some very different attitudes about how the businesses in Japan saw themselves as part of these conversations. I was bowled over when people from Fujitsu, a multinational information technology company, asked *"What can Fujitsu do for people with dementia?"* and started to use the FutureCenter approach to explore and dream and create.[13]

I learned that there was a history of this kind of response in Japan. Roll the calendar back a couple of thousand years and business and community were exactly the same thing in Japan. Villages isolated by precipitous mountains relied on rice grown in irrigated paddies for sustenance. And it took a village, working together, to prosper. Business, economy, community — were all the same thing. In 2010 in Japan, more

---

13   A great deal has happened in this Fujitsu initiative over the last 7 years.
     Check out the website in Additional Resources.

businesses were starting to see that they wanted to go back to this earlier relationship, to reinvent themselves by coming back into community.

This exploration of how to create innovation in business turned to questions about how to use FutureCenters for community development. After the Triple Disasters, many of us saw that FutureCenters might be a key pathway for supporting people in Tohoku — and the whole country — in creating the future they wanted, rather than simply having government rebuild the past. We saw that these dialogical spaces where community people, businesses, nonprofit organizations, universities, government and others might mix could be places to develop insight and innovation.

My work in Tohoku and elsewhere in Japan has been to host the BA — that relational space that holds us — in which people come together to create a new future. We will explore this in detail in Chapter 3.

Enspirited Leadership

While I was starting to work in this intersection of Art of Hosting and FutureCenters in 2010, I met many Japanese — perhaps especially young people — who were asking: *"How do I discover what I'm supposed to do with my life? Where do I find my gifts? What is mine to lead? And once I start to see the beginning of an answer to that question, how the hell do I find my way forward?"*

I started introducing my framework for Enspirited Leadership as one way of entering those questions. It has been a foundation of my work in Japan now for many years, and my own understanding and ideas continue to evolve, especially through a series of workshops I started doing in 2016 in Kyoto, my home town in Japan. One of the participants at a recent workshop there nailed it by saying, "For me, this begins with an appreciation of our greater selves as enspirited beings who reach out to each other and begin to discover possibilities outside our imagination. We begin to trust emergence."

Turning back to the beginning of all this, back in 2001, I had been sitting with a group of people in their 20s and 30s at Castle Borl in Slovenia. Most were from Europe or Africa. They were grappling with big questions about their lives. They wanted to know how they could help the world and how they could live lives that had heart and meaning. I listened as they spoke with each other about their values and beliefs and the dreams that were growing inside of them.

From 2001-2003, I witnessed and supported a number of these younger leaders from different parts of the world as they found the confidence, clarity and courage to take their next steps. I listened and talked with them, trying to understand how they were living their lives and the challenges they faced. Their experience and questions seemed both similar to and different from how I remembered feeling when I was 25 years old and starting my first nonprofit corporation — but something different was present as well. This caught my attention; I wanted to understand this more.

While I was working with these vibrant leaders, I was also finishing my doctoral work at the California Institute of Integral Studies (CIIS). I changed my dissertation to focus on exploring whether or not there was a largely invisible movement for change being started by these leaders. I came to understand that the social movements I'd grown up with and actively engaged in during the sixties and seventies were ideological, strategic and tactical[14] As I listened to these young leaders' stories, I understood that the model of change and the leadership they were offering was enspirited, appreciative and emergent. This became the framework of my dissertation and my eventual book, *Enspirited Leadership*.

Fast forward from my dissertation research and writing, which culminated in 2003, to the Japan Art of Hosting workshop in May, 2010. We started talking about "participatory leadership." While some people got a sense of the idea, it was a bit of a stretch for others to figure out what this really was. I began to share the basic ideas of *Enspirited Leadership* with them. The young people, especially, felt a strong resonance — it helped them make sense of their lives, giving them a way of recognizing what they already know and are already doing. It also gave them some clues about how to step forward in the work that is theirs to do.

---

14 For a full explanation of this way of describing these movements, see *Comparative Perspectives on Social Movements: Political Opportunities, Mobilizing Structures, and Cultural Framings* in the bibliography.

Practices for Enspirited Leadership

These six practices are the foundation of Enspirited Leadership

LET YOUR CALLING
FIND YOU

Many of us want to be in service in these tumultuous times. It is easy for any of us to get overwhelmed. There is so much to do. Which opportunity or challenge do we respond to? I think part of the key is that we do not choose. We are chosen. You must **let your calling find you**. Calling doesn't always have to be big — and there doesn't need to be just one. When we stay open and listen with our whole being, we can hear the whisper of calling. It has to find us. Of course, we have to show up and be present — the other practices here help — but we are not in charge of how or when we are called. When you hear calling, follow it. Start now.

STOP AND BE STILL

To let our calling find us, we must **stop and be still** — a big challenge for most of us. For some it is meditation. For others, it is hiking the Pacific Crest Trail. Some find this space in a long, hot bath. The nature of the practice itself doesn't matter as much as the act of stopping. The act of stilling. It was after the disasters, when I was completely overwhelmed, that this practice help me find my way forward. My climb to the top of the Fushimi Inari mountain shrine, which I mention in Chapter 2, was the first time in my life I completely gave myself over to prayer and meditation, and since then it has become an integral part of my life.

STAY CONNECTED

Especially when we are working from calling, we must continue to **stay connected** with a close circle of people who accompany us on our journey. In Japan's collective culture, this is the easy part. People understand that they need each other, that they are stronger together. This isn't as true in other parts of the world where people often want to go off on their own and "prove themselves." We do our work, the work of our lives, best when we stay connected to others, sharing our stories and questions. We can cheer each other on when we feel confused and we can help each other not get lost in our egos. We are stronger, brighter, and better together.

When we do this work of calling — or any work of innovation for that matter, essential learning is available every step of the way. We're often in too much of a hurry to gather that learning. What's needed is to **chew your experience**. Stop, look back at what's been happening. Chew it. Savor the different flavors — the sweetness and the bitterness. Take in all the aromas. Mash it with your teeth and see what's essential. It is so easy to get busy and then busier still. But our minds and hearts can only take so much in before we have to stop and take stock — and chew.

CHEW YOUR
EXPERIENCE

When we are creating innovations, we often don't understand what's really going on. That's when it is time to reach out and **bring in more difference**. It is essential. Interacting with people whose experience and perspectives are different from ours helps us see more of an invisible whole. Holding the tension of differences usually allows something else to emerge. From the very beginning when I introduced this idea in Japan, people would tell me how tricky this was — how they wanted to be with like-minded people because it was just more comfortable. But as we talked, they also easily saw that they needed the questions, perspective and experience of people who saw things differently.

BRING IN MORE
DIFFERENCE

Finally, we must **embrace ambiguity and uncertainty**. I have spent most of my life thinking that I needed certainty. But I have discovered we need to stay with "what is," rather than insisting on some sort of false clarity. Studies in neurosciences these days tell us that the brain craves certainty. In our world these days we see countless examples of how people are willing to follow someone who says, "Trust me, I know what to do." But what's important is to stay with the ambiguity rather than jump to a dangerous "clarity." Our world invites us to act with our questions, to stay wide open as we work to create new lives and new communities. It is often not comfortable but it is necessary.

EMBRACE AMBIGUITY
AND UNCERTAINTY

Years after I started introducing *Enspirited Leadership* in Japan, I was hosting a retreat for people who were volunteering their time in the disaster area. One young man, who had graduated from college the previous year, spoke of his entry into the village where he was now living. With all of his earnestness, he would go to people in the village and say "I am Tetsu, and I'm here to help." They would offer him a big smile and welcome him and say "Please find what is yours to do." It drove Tetsu crazy. In school for 16 years and being told what to do every day and now "Please find what is yours to do?" Slowly he was able to quiet himself. He started asking questions rather than just saying he was there to help. He started connecting with others and be began to find a way forward. He was practicing Enspirited Leadership.

Whenever I start to feel a bit lost, I come back to these six practices — they help me remember how I need to be. At the same time, it's important to note that these practices are not meant to be an answer. They are an invitation to each of us to remember who we are, what we are doing and why. This is where we find the clarity and courage to take the next step. I've often explained this framework to groups and then invited them into a conversational exploration of the points as a way to become get clear about what comes next in their lives.

From the time I started my work in 2010, people in Japan have frequently commented on the rich atmosphere present in our various workshops. Using both my own presence and the social technologies of Art of Hosting and FutureSessions, I always invite people to remember what's important to them, connect them with each other, bring in silence and finally reflect on what we've been doing and learning. It opens the next steps of our leadership.

Practicing *Enspirited leadership* requires conversation. It thrives in community. It is not something we can do alone. We need each other. As people in Japan started to explore enspirited leadership, they started to stand up for what they really cared about. But they knew they couldn't stand alone. These six practices flourish in the BA we create with FutureSessions and Art of Hosting. The last three in particular require a gracious space in which we greet each other with respect, curiosity and generosity.

As I started introducing these ideas about enspirited leadership and how we change, together, and it became natural to introduce the values, principles and beliefs of what we called **life-affirming leadership**[15] at The Berkana Institute.

Life-Affirming Leadership

Our exploration of life-affirming leadership was center stage at the first Art of Hosting workshop in Japan. We began to talk about the attitudes and conditions that help any organization or system begin to fully realize its potentials.

I shared stories from The Berkana Institute where, over the last decade, we had worked with many networks, colleagues and friends to identify people, places and organizations that were creating healthy and resilient communities. At Berkana, we worked especially with people in the so-called "Global South" — the part of the planet often described in terms of its needs rather than in terms of its assets. We sought people who were learning how to build community with their own resources. And we found them. We connected with people from Pakistan, India, Zimbabwe, South Africa, Senegal, Mexico and Brazil — as well as people from Greece, Canada and the U.S. They helped us develop a new understanding of how to build community. This group became known as the Berkana Exchange. Over several years, as members of the Berkana Exchange gathered to learn from each other, we were "Alive in Community," which became the title of a publication that our key staff member, Aerin Dunford, and I wrote about this work. In the Exchange, we were all doing different things and sometimes had conflicting ideas about what was important, but beyond and through those differences, we felt a sense of camaraderie — we knew we "fit" together and we started looking for the texture and pattern of that fit. Together we surfaced and articulated the core values, principles and practices present in what we called "life-affirming leadership".

Through this work, I learned about the texture, aroma and color of resilient communities. In these communities, people are connected

---

15   At Berkana we looked for leadership that affirms life. "Life-affirming leadership" described our way of thinking and talking about leadership as power-with, rather than power-over, and our way of inviting people to look at the extraordinarily generative powers of life.

through relationships, churches, clubs and affinity groups. They have done stuff together and generated enough trust and knowledge about each other that they know who to turn to. They know each other's stories. People step forward when it is their turn to offer their leadership and step back when their turn is over. When times are rough, they find their first step, then the next and the next.

Many of us find ourselves called to work in what might be called unconventional ways. Rather than joining large corporations or universities or nonprofits, we choose to engage at local levels. But can any of this local work really make a difference or are we just playing around doing nice things while civilization as we've known it collapses?

For me change is local — if something new doesn't happen somewhere on the ground, nothing is really changed. Transformation is translocal. And transformation is the prize. How can local actions lead to transformation? We spent years inquiring into this question in the Berkana Exchange. Together we articulated the values, principles and beliefs that guided and connected our work.

It's easy to toss around words like self-organizing and emergence, but what can guide us in working with community in all its messiness? How do we work well with an amalgamation of decentralized, distributed, complex and sometimes chaotic people, patterns and possibilities?

The perspective I brought to Japan was informed by this decade of work with Berkana. I started sharing the principles of life-affirming leadership right away in Japan because it was clear that people needed a different paradigm — a new world view — that could help them make better sense of what to do with their lives.

The worldview we articulated together at Berkana had these principles:

Every community is filled with leaders.

What a radical thought! Our normal view of leadership is that only a few special people are leaders and they have a right to power, prestige and respect. But we posed a different point of view and set of questions:

- What if a leader is anyone who wants to help?

- How could we organize our communities to encourage each of us to step forward, offering our gifts?

When there's a crisis, if we instinctively work by the principle underlying these questions, we can create a fluid dance of leading and following that gets the needed work done. Egos, grudges, fears are set aside as people step forward to do what's needed.

I saw this in Tohoku right after the disasters and I still see it today. It happens naturally every time and in every place where there is a disaster. The stories in Chapter 8 are filled with this kind of leadership. We can — and must — create the conditions for each of us to step forward when we are called to do so.

Whatever the problem, the community has the answers.

I remember when my friend, Maaianne Knuth, told of visiting a rural village in Zimbabwe in 2001 as the country was entering a severe downward spiral. She had just started Kufunda Learning Village[16] to address "how people could recover their sense of pride, wisdom, and capacity in working with their own knowledge and deepening their resourcefulness."

When she arrived, she noticed that there were no gardens and she asked, "Why aren't you growing food? People looked uncomfortable, but no one responded. Maaianne asked again, "Why aren't you growing food?"

Finally, someone spoke up and said they had not received seeds and fertilizer from the World Bank in the spring. Maaianne asked, "Do you expect you will?" People reluctantly answered, "No." The next question was pretty obvious, "What did you do before the World Bank gave you seeds and fertilizer?" People said they didn't know. Maaianne said, "Let's go ask the elders." And they did. They started to learn and

---

16   Kufunda is a special place of learning in Zimbabwe. Started in the early years of this century, Kufunda helps people in Zimbabwe and around the world learn about participatory leadership and dialogue, permaculture, raising children, healing ourselves and other themes. Much of its current focus is on youth and women's leadership.

grow crops as the village did in the old days — perhaps, not surprisingly, like what we call permaculture today.

This is just one example; there are hundreds, thousands, like it. In any community, there's someone who knows something about the problem or opportunity at hand. You can depend on it! Working with communities to discover what they know creates a foundation of knowledge and a basis for action. When the limit of that local knowledge is reached, the community can seek knowledge beyond its boundaries.

Magic happens when we encounter each other with respect, curiosity and generosity.

I actually didn't use these three words in the days of the Berkana Exchange. They became visible to me only through my work in Japan. When I started doing my work with Art of Hosting in Japan in 2010, I started to understand the Japanese idea of BA — the space that hosts our relatedness. I now know that we can encounter each other with the totality of our being. We can arrive with a deep openness that is filled with curiosity and respect for each other. We can move with a generosity of spirit in which we know that the more we give freely, the more we have. This is the way in which a generative, appreciative future is created.

Self-reliance and interdependence work together.

The reality is that we have what we need to begin building the communities we want. Just as it takes many people with diverse perspectives, skills and strengths to make a community, community itself becomes stronger when it is consciously nested in a weave of reciprocal relationships creating a fabric of interdependence with other communities. We stand on our own *and* we stand taller when we hold hands with others. It is true of individuals and it is true of communities as well.

Sometimes we think about this as the two economies of community. One is the internal economy — the goods and services that can be exchanged internally within the community. Transition Towns in Japan have often started as local exchanges of goods and services — "I'll cut your hair if you will fix my plumbing." The other economy is the external one where what's produced in community is sold or exchanged elsewhere, bringing external resources into community, such as when one community produces fish and another produces saké. They're delicious together and so both communities benefit from the exchange.

Thriving resilient communities pay careful attention to both economies — to what they can do to be self-reliant and to the ways in which they are interdependent with outside communities.

We must live the world we want, today.

If not now, when? If not here, where? If not us, who? How long must we wait to give birth to the life that is growing inside us? The people I worked with in the Berkana Exchange, said, "Let's do it now." This is exactly what I hear from people in Tohoku.

In the last five years, I have heard many people in Tohoku, and then the rest of Japan, talk about happiness. They say that the disasters have made them think about what's important in their lives and to see that there is no reason to wait. Over and over, they speak of how they used to think and live before the disaster. One resident said, "We had a dream, but we said, I need more money or my children need to be older before I can do something else, and we go back to sleep in lives we don't really like. Six years later, we wake up with no more money and children who have lived with an unhappy parent for most of their lives."

Wake up to the world that is around you. Begin today.

We don't have to wait for external help. We have many resources with which to make things better now.

We have what we need to build the lives we want. The Triple Disasters were a big awakening for people everywhere in Japan. They realized that government or some other authority did not have the power or ability to come in and fix everything — they had to do it themselves. And they had to do it working with the resources at hand, looking around and finding a place to begin. There are many examples of this in towns in Japan, such as the residents of Kesennuma making canvas bags from ship's cloth or making dried flowers in Otsuchi.[17] It was our earlier work in the Berkana Exchange, where people were making beautiful purses from discarded rubber tires in India and discovering how to plant crops without the World Bank in Zimbabwe that helped me see these new patterns in Japan.

We turn to each other and we look around and see the resources and knowledge we already have.

We walk at the pace of the slowest,
listening even to the whispers.

We are on this journey together. When we are creating a new future together, it takes time. Frankly, this principle annoys me sometimes. I'm an activist. I want to get things done *now*. I see a problem and immediately jump to the solution I already see. But that means I'm skating across the top of Otto Scharmer's U.[18]

I need to slow down enough to actually see the world around me with new eyes — ones that are really open. We can and must learn how to slow down in order to go far, or as my friend Christina Baldwin puts it, "move at the pace of grace." We must learn how to listen to the quiet voices that see different possibilities. Some of us must learn to restrain our forcefulness and our sometimes conceit that we know what everyone should do.

We find a clear sense of direction AND we
take an elegant, minimum step forward.

Master plans work in situations that are relatively straightforward. We no longer spend much time in that world. Mostly we live in a world confounded with various levels of chaos and complexity. How then do we proceed?

When we sit together and listen deeply to and with each other, a future begins to appear. The quiet voice of that future calls us. When Maaianne began Kufunda Learning Village in Zimbabwe, she had no

---

17 See Chapter 8, "Use What We Have," for more detailed stories of how the residents of Kesennuma began making canvas bags from ship's cloth and the people of Otsuchi started making dried flowers.

18 The basic structure of Theory U is introduced in Chapter 7. See *Theory U: Leading from the Future as It Emerges*.

idea where it would be a decade later. She had a sense of where she wanted to go; she found where to place her first step. It was the same when Taka Nomura started FutureSessions in Japan; he had a sense of direction and he found where to take the first step. These first steps are close-in. They are most powerful when then are done with a measure of beauty and elegance. I remember when I first talked about elegance in Japan: we looked for a Japanese translation. Finally, I said it is how your mother looks when she steps into the room in her finest kimono. People got it immediately. We invite beauty in with a flower arrangement in the middle of the circle. We stand in a posture of pride and confidence as we begin. We step away from sloppiness.

We begin.

We proceed one step at a time, making the path by walking it.

We take a step, and then another step, and another and another. Along the way, we need to frequently pause to listen to ourselves and listen to each other. Occasionally we are amazed by overwhelming success in a step that we take. More frequently, what happens is not all that spectacular. Many of these steps don't quite take us where we wanted. Often something goes wrong. In all cases, we pause and learn.

I remember a story I heard years ago when I visited the village of Curvela in Minas, Brazil. A young educator had put an advertisement on the radio saying, "I think there must be a better way for our children to learn. If you think so too, please come sit under the mango tree on Thursday afternoon." I can't imagine a better setup for a good story — a new story. When I visited, his organization, the Center for Popularization of Culture and Development (CPCD),[19] it was 25 years

---

19 The teachers' invitation led to a pre-school program built around Paulo Freire's principles. As the children grew older, new offerings and dimensions were added. Now, the young women and men who complete the crafts school in metalworking, woodworking, fabric design, herbal medicine and business management are among the most sought after workers throughout Brazil. The Popular Center for Culture and Development uses the principles that guided the formation and evolution of this continuum of learning as the basis for supporting a network of community workers — called *caring mothers* throughout the province

into a practice of what I call "emergence with rigor." They were able to create a powerful enterprise because they had gained a sense of direction, they started, they experimented, they learned, and they found the next, next step.

Local work evolves to create transformative change
when connected to similar work around the world.

This final principle is crucial in moving from change to transformation. It is easy to get puffed up and enthralled by different theories and ideas. It happens to me all the time! But we need to remember that all change is local. These ideas don't mean much until they show up on the ground, in a place, and are owned by the people there. *And*, even that alone is insufficient.

How do we take what we've learned and created to shift entire systems? What do we do to create transformative change? What can we do to amplify the changes we find most desirable while damping down those we don't want?

We live in a time when everything is changing. Our future is no longer clear. But much of the time we continue to act as if we know what will happen, holding on to our plans and assumptions about what should happen next.

When disasters happen, our present is shattered and we must re-envision tomorrow. This re-envisioning is not theoretical. It must be based on new experiences that are almost always local and often isolated. When similar work is connected at wider and wider levels of systems, those who are doing the work are connected, inspired, and informed by each other and conditions are created for deeper innovation and change.

One of the big needs after the disasters in Japan, were these kinds of connections. Many of us worked to make them happen. They happen naturally over time, but we can nurture systems of connection and learning and speed things up by working with these life-affirming leadership principles to seed transformative change.

As I listened in to what people were saying and to the questions they were holding, I started bringing forth processes, practices and ideas that seemed to me might be useful. I kept returning to these four practices: conversation through Art of Hosting and FutureSessions, *Enspirited Leadership*, Berkana's principles of Life-Affirming Leadership, and Two Loops. They helped to create a framework for people to think together about what is important to them, what gifts they have, and how to bring them forward.

In many ways, my work in Japan in 2010 was to invite people into conversations they didn't know they wanted to have. A growing number of people started to see they were not alone in their hopes and fears. These weren't lists of things to be checked off. They were doorways of inquiry into what was really going on in our communities and our lives.

They started using these four frameworks as a way to keep in conversation with each other. We'd have deep explorations about what it means to "bring in more difference" in *Enspirited Leadership* or what it means to say "Every community is filled with leaders."

I left Japan in November 2010 with great appreciation for my many new relationships and for what seemed like a growing willingness on the part of people in Japan to ask new questions. I remember thinking that I wasn't sure if people were actually going to do anything more than talk about changes sometime in the way-off future. I couldn't really tell how strong the energy was to actually change anything. But it felt like a promising beginning. I planned to return in April of 2011 to nurture FutureSessions and to begin writing a book about the changes surfacing in Japan.

Forty years before I had done my undergraduate thesis work on the 1868 Meiji Restoration which ended Japan's 250 year feudal Tokugawa Era and ushered in the modern era of the Emperor Meiji. Many of us saw the current time as an echo of that era, of a new restoration brewing.

None of us anticipated the looming disasters of March 11, 2011, when the earth would shake, the oceans would rage and a nuclear power plant would explode.

Befriending Confusion

CHAPTER

2

Befriending Confusion

IN JAPAN, TIME STOPPED ON MARCH 11ᵀᴴ, 2011. Literally, clocks stopped at 2:46pm when the earthquake struck and have been preserved in memorials all over the region. The next minute and the next years would not be the same as those before.

The Triple Disasters of earthquake, tsunami, and nuclear explosions erased the old normal. The earthquake brought down buildings, mangled the roads, trains and utilities, and through subsidence, dropped the ground itself as much as three feet. The tsunami washed away everything in its path, devastating cities and towns and ending lives. The radiation explosions started the next day and cast a cloud of uncertainty over everything. At the same time, the disasters brought down barriers to discussions, swept away walls and toppled beliefs that what had been, must be.

Three weeks later, when I stepped off the plane at Narita, there was more than stillness in the air; there was an eerie silence. More than the dimmed lights or the stalled escalators, everything felt different. This sense became stronger as I traveled by bus to my hotel in the Roppongi district of downtown Tokyo known for its lively clubs and night life.

It was dark. The lights and electronic signs were turned off to save energy, few cars and even fewer people on the streets. Usually invisible through the pulsing urban energy, the stars were almost bright.

The devastation was limited to mostly the coastal areas in three northeast provinces of the Tohoku region (see maps in Introduction). But the impact was felt across Japan. Weeks after the disasters, a TV station executive in Shikoku, some 600 miles away from Tohoku, said to me: "I thought Japan was over. I thought our country would end." The sense of a tentative, uncertain future permeated the air.

I soon realized that this was a terrain I had never faced before. My work in helping others visualize the future had always been based in their present, their current situation. But here I was entering a time outside of time: the past obliterated, the present chaotic, the future cocooned. Discovering where to begin, and how to continue all the while getting lost time and time again — that was the new pattern of my years and my journey with the people of Japan.

As I talked with more and more people and saw a never-ending kaleidoscope of images, I was overwhelmed by the scope of the tragedy. It was impossible to take it all in. It was as if the ground was being pulled out from under my feet, time and time again. I didn't know where to begin. I could feel my own panic rising. This happens, I think, to each of us when our normal is destroyed. We feel lost and uncertain. How do we befriend this overwhelming sense of confusion?

Grasping for a way to make sense of it all, I turned to my friends and the people around me, started listening to their stories and sharing my own reality. I began to write. My personal journals, which then became blogs, were one of my main ways to make meaning out of my experiences in this new Japan. The following is a selection of journal entries from those first few days.

Journal Entry, Wednesday, April 7, 2011 — Tokyo

My colleague Yuya Nishimura, founder of Dialogue Bar, invited people to join us for an evening of dialogue. Almost 80 people came. It was the first time any of them had shared their own inner turmoil since the disasters hit four weeks earlier.

Our dialogue was quiet tonight. People are unsure how to give voice to their inner feelings. There is a subdued energy, people sensing that everything has changed. Normal is gone. Forever. And what exists now is a blind spot, waiting to be seen.

The change is an energetic one. I'm not just talking about the lights turned off everywhere and the rolling black-outs. People are saying things like: 'We have less energy and life is better now. I'm spending more time with my family. My sense of what is important to me is different now.' People are talking about wanting new indicators for success. One of the things brought up frequently was the Gross National Happiness[20] project of Bhutan as a possible measure — something almost unimaginable in Japan before the Triple Disasters.

Journal Entry, Thursday, April 8, 2011 — Tokyo

This afternoon we had a gathering of 35 business people at Fuji-Xerox's Knowledge Dynamics Initiative (KDI). I joined my friends and colleagues Taka Nomura and Yayoi Kubota to host what we had planned as a FutureCenter Pre-Program. Conceived at the end of 2010, it was to kick off 2011 FutureCenter activities. We almost cancelled. But in our planning meeting yesterday we said that Japan needs FutureCenters now more than ever.

People arrived quietly. Even those I knew from last year would not meet my eye. The space was still. Uncomfortable. People arrived not knowing if they were really ready to talk with anyone about anything. They didn't know if they wanted to be there, but they had come.

We invited them into pairs and then into groups of four to talk with each other about what was happening in their lives. We asked them: What is the same and what has changed? What is possible now that was not possible before? We kept inviting them to go deeper into their fear and their hopes. Three hours later, the space was alive with energy.

The change was incredible. I became quiet and sensed into what was happening. I heard a loud voice in my KOKORO *— (heartmind) saying:* **We have been released from a future we did not want.**

20　The fourth king of Bhutan, Jigme Singye Wangchuck first used the phrase "Gross National Happiness" in the1970s and in the early part of this century, Bhutan got serious about using GNH rather than GNP — Gross National Product — as a way to measure progress. They lit a fire around the world.

Journal Entry, Saturday, April 10, 2011 — Kiyosato

I've been in Japan four days. Listening, sensing, trying to understand what is present here, and what is possible now, that was not possible before. Last night, around a fire, some of us gathered to talk about the Art of Hosting journey in Japan. I left after one round of conversation, jet lag and too much listening filling my brain to the point of overflowing. But, ah, that first round...

We talked about how Art of Hosting is "simply" a way of being with one's self and with each other. When I starting doing this work in Japan last year, I said that this was the first-time Art of Hosting had come to Japan AND, it was born here. The deep, deep listening and respectful attention to relationships that is core to Japanese culture is at the very heart of Art of Hosting.

There is also something about the subtle and profound grounding of Shinto that permeates Japan. It shows up as this deep appreciation of the inter-connectedness of life. It shows up in Tea Ceremony, in IKEBANA (flower arranging), and yes, even in Sumo, the ritualized wrestling of Japan. It is a way of being. One friend asked me what was different between Art of Hosting in Japan and elsewhere in the world. In Japan, I think, it is this rapid remembering that we already know how to be with each other. In Japan, we know how to be in respectful, supportive relationship. Some of this has been forgotten or set aside over the last 50 or 100 years, but it is still deeply present. The challenge for the Art of Hosting in Japan is to learn how to use this deep quality of being-ness to act together in new ways — to create a new future, now.

Journal Entry, Sunday, April 11, 2011 — Kiyosato

I sit here a little broken hearted this morning when last night I was just beginning to see some new clarity. All I know is that so much help is needed. Help in finding and using a starting point. Help in seeing how to work with what is already available. Help in seeing how to help people regain authority over their own lives.

I need to write my way out of my grief. I am at the KEEP[21] in Kiyosato, a project for sustainable living started 65 years ago. The beautiful, loving people here know how to host hospitable space. Last night we began a conversation about Fukushima. A month ago, Makoto Yamamoto, long-time leader at the KEEP, drove the KEEP's bus 250 miles to Fukushima and found 43 people to bring back here to this beauty. He went because his heart was broken and he needed to do something. A new set of relationships began.

Makoto found his way to Koriyama, the largest city in Fukushima Province and the Big Palette, a sports complex, which provides emergency housing to 2000 people in some of the best conditions available. Makoto's idea was to bring people to the KEEP for respite — but when they leave, their space disappears and they have no place to which to return. So, it's a nice idea, but not enough. Every day the combined governments of the Fukushima region bring in ONIGIRI *(rice balls) to feed the 2000 people. They all have food, but for four weeks they have been eating only rice balls.*

Deep grief. Deep trauma.

The people of Yamanashi — the prefecture around the KEEP — will take their turn at helping to feed people. Yamanashi can only feed them seven times. Why seven times? It is not a limit of basic foodstuffs I'm told — it is the limited hands to make it into meals and serve. My grief shrieks: there are 4000 hands at the shelter. And of course, many, perhaps most, are in shock. But some are ready to begin to move. How do we work with and through the grief?

So much uncertainty and confusion. Two thousand people who weeks earlier had been fully present in their lives. Strong, competent,

---

21 The Kiyosato Educational Experiment Project or KEEP was started in 1938 by Dr. Paul Rush. Seisen Ryo, a hot springs inn and conference center at the KEEP, has been used for many transformative gatherings.

going about their independent daily lives, now crowded together and waiting for someone to bring them rice balls every day. Their past was gone. Their present was unimaginable. Their future, invisible.

It's all so confusing. Where do we find the places to begin? How do we get the insights and strength to continue?

There's a sense from our meetings this weekend that it is essential that the Tohoku region and all of Japan be recreated in a new paradigm, not rebuilt in the old. How do we all — all around the world — stand with and support this recreating so that we may learn and get courage to do it ourselves?

Journal Entry, Monday, April 12, 2011 — Kiyosato

I've returned from a nice long soak in the ONSEN *— snowflakes falling on the calm water. A quieter time, after another day of powerful conversations and deep listening. This is a beautiful place, with nourishing air and fantastic food. It calls forth a deep presence.*

I notice my proclivity towards action. I have been an activist for more than 40 years. Those waters run deep and I treasure them. But, of course, I cannot — even in my wildest dreams — be a problem solver here in Japan. But I can show up. I can be present. I can listen with my whole heartmind. I know my presence makes a difference. I will support where I can. In each conversation, tears are followed by laughter that is followed in turn by silence. There is such a collective sensing in here. A knowing that we are all in this together.

Journal Entry, Tuesday, April 13, 2011 — Kiyosato

Mt. Fuji revealed itself today in all of its grandeur. A subtle impression on the horizon, this silent sentinel is always on the rim, hosting Japan. Often hidden by many layers of clouds, it is always there. Sometimes just a glimmer.

I love it when Fuji-san shows itself. It helps me to quiet my spirit and simply be present:

Stay present.

Be where I am.

Notice what calls my attention.

Act with respect, compassion and dignity.

Stay clear while staying unattached.

Be prepared to be surprised.

Stay connected.

Yesterday we met for a day to sense what we could see about next steps forward. One of us, Kato, had just returned from Sendai, a region he has been to many times before. When he got off the train, he knew the difference. Not just the broken buildings and fields of rubble — but what was in the air. It felt different. Subdued, almost glazed over. He saw some young people and talked with them. Wandering aimlessly in the destruction they wanted to know: What can we do? Of course, he had no answers. Almost overwhelmed by his own sense of grief and loss, he could only stand with theirs. Devastation. Devastation. Overwhelming devastation made even more real by the proximity of spaces where life looks like normal. Stores destroyed. Stores shuttered. Stores open. Side-by-side.

By the end of our day together, there was still no clarity. A sense was present that some of what we might do is around youth and youth leading. There was a sense that this place, the KEEP, has a new purpose. A wondering if it might be one of the FutureCenters — places of innovation to discover the future — needed now in Japan.

This morning an idea began to crystalize. Makoto leaves tomorrow for Fukushima for three days. **He goes to discover what they have — not what they need.** *He goes to find some youth who have dealt with their grief enough to be ready to stand with each other to discover a next step.*

Contours of a possibility began to be visible. We will host a 3-day event at the KEEP in the middle of May. It will be for around 100 people. Most of them will be youth. The majority will come from Fukushima and they will come from three sources there — youth living inside the sports complex shelter who are starting to come back to life, youth serving in the shelter, and youth from the "normal area" around the shelter. They'll be joined by 25 or so youth from the Kiyosato area and 25 or so from Tokyo and other parts of Japan. We will come together to embrace grief while continuing to stand with it. Connect with each other. Regain some measure of authority over our own lives. Discover the elegant, minimum next steps that will support people all over Japan in organizing themselves.

Journal Entry, Wednesday, April 14, 2011 — Tokyo

The earth shook twice in Tokyo this morning as I sit here at my hotel desk. These quakes are now considered mild — just a little more than 5 magnitude and both around 100 miles away. This is part of the new normal here: the earth shakes from time to time. People notice immediately (sometimes aided by iPhone Apps that give an alarm).

I notice, I wait, a little surprised, but not really, and wonder how long this will last and whether I should be doing something other than sitting here, watching the shaking.

A little later, downstairs and outside into a lovely, sunny Tokyo morning, spring has popped completely into being here. The cherry blossoms have moved past prime, but on my street, gorgeous purple tulips now mark the path. Such a contrast.

the earth shakes
purple tulips bloom
life finds a way to be normal.

Last night my friend, So Yoshida, invited me to join a small gathering at his Dialogue House. Forty or so people came. Most were folks I had met and worked with last year — teachers, students, personal coaches, web designers, business people, government workers, facilitators. As I listened, it was clear that people were searching for the right way to stand with and behind people who live in Tohoku. Junya Sano, who has left his job teaching social innovation to graduate students at Rikkyo University, is starting a non-profit organization for this purpose. There's a boatload of people wanting to volunteer, people starting nonprofit organizations, corporations wanting to help.

The sense I picked up is that trying to think of ALL of Tohoku is paralyzing. Volunteers need to find an area where they can form more intimate human connections. Once they are in that place, they need to listen and listen and listen. They need to find the local people who are starting to step forward with some leadership and work with them. They need to know that there isn't a need to rush in to fix things.

I received a crucial e-mail from Meg Wheatley today:

> In times of turmoil, people from the outside tend to go in and ask: "What do you need?"
>
> For someone who is only just coming to grips with the fact that their old life is gone, this is an overwhelming question.
>
> Instead, the question to ask is: "What do you have?"

Asking what they have is something they can put their head and hands around. In addition, questions that start from the place of what "we have" will almost always lead to a conversation of what "we need." But the list of "needs" that arise out of a sense of "what we have" are very different from those that come when we just focus on needs.

We know that what's important now is continual hosting of the grief everyone feels. Some of the people who were there last night were also at the KEEP over the weekend. They spoke of how important it was that we spent the first day just being in the confusion together, before we started to move to develop some ideas that might be of help. Grief, confusion, listening. Each of these need space before action comes.

In this collectivist culture, grief and emotion travel subtly and rapidly through the cultural membrane. People outside Tohoku feel guilty for having grief when they have not personally experienced the devastation of Tohoku's people. But the grief is everywhere. People speak of how often, and how easily, tears come to the corners of their eyes. This grief will be present for a long time.

Grief and disorientation is present all over Japan. Another colleague talked about how she has found ways to switch the feeling off — to be able to act as if normal is still here. It gets easier to distance oneself from this emotional field when further away from Tohoku. But the emotional field is present everywhere.

Journal Entry, Friday, April 16, 2011 — Tokyo

I remember years ago watching Bonanza, an old western on TV. A gnarled old man picked up one stick and broke it and said: "Boys, if you stand alone, you're easy to break." He then put a bunch of sticks together and asked one of them to break the bunch — which, of course, he could not. And he said: "Stand together and you can't be broken." But how do we stand together, when the future we knew has disappeared?

As I started to talk with others about this question, a new image started to come into view. Together we will create a new garden. We will clear the earth and heal it, we will begin to see what to plant where, we will prepare the soil and plant new seeds and keep weeds away. We will nourish the new growth together and find a great harvest. Together we can grow healthy and resilient communities.

Journal Entry, Saturday, April 17, 2011
— Tokyo-Onagawa-Ishinomaki-Tokyo

Early morning in Roppongi. It's just after 5am on a Sunday and the streets are already lively. I rush, a little late, to join a Young Global Leaders group going to Miyagi Prefecture — the hardest hit coast in the tsunami zone. I am the only foreigner and the only one not young.

There is something almost surrealistic about getting on a bus in urban Tokyo on a spring morning and going north. Sakura (cherry blossoms) are giving way to leaves. As we travel through the countryside, it looks just like normal, green, glowing Japan in the spring. We stop at a roadside rest area filled with people and food. Lively conversation on the minibus is interspersed with naps. I'm with young men and women who have done things like starting Ashoka Japan and Tokyo Social Venture Partners — local "chapters" of worldwide communities of social entrepreneurs. All are active in various leadership roles in civil society.

Like me, this is their first time to travel to the disaster area. Hours after leaving Tokyo, we cross some invisible line and suddenly we enter an area where the tsunami struck. The lively conversations on the minibus quiet and we all look around. I see a rowboat in the middle of a rice field. Huge trees are scattered like toothpicks.

Then, mysteriously, we cross an invisible line again and are surrounded by fields being worked. No change in elevation. But the tsunami had not come. We go further and now, an elevated highway creates a barrier. Life as usual on one side. Destruction on the other.

When I got on the bus this morning I knew I would be unprepared for the sight of this massive destruction. What's more startling than the destruction is seeing life "as usual" so close alongside and intermixed with the destruction. It's like I am in a world that works for many, surrounding life that works for none: used car lots with sparkling cars a short walking distance from a wasteland; McDonalds and Sunday afternoon traffic jams just minutes from destroyed lives; young adults walking hand in hand towards their homes, only a song away from those who no longer have a home. We sit on the minibus, all talking about how striking this contrast is. **Grief, confusion, listening: each needed before action comes.**

People from a small non-profit that normally runs a school stepped forward to coordinate one volunteer center. The job needed to be done. They are stretched way beyond their capacity and invisible to international agencies like the Red Cross that will not acknowledge their work or support them. My organizing self says a network of these nonprofit organizations is needed: they could share learning and experience and approach international agencies with one voice that would be hard to ignore.

We arrive at the volunteer center with its makeshift campground on a school grounds. Roughly 500 people stay here now…. There are two warehouses, one for supplies and one for food that flows in from all over Japan. Donations from thousands of individual people who want to help. People everywhere are doing whatever they can to support. Of course, sometimes mistakes are made — like the cooked rice, which spoils quickly, donated who heard there was no water. We continue on and begin to encounter some of the worst destruction. It is almost mesmerizing as we drive along. Kilometer after kilometer of debris.

Cars in houses; houses on cars. Massive accumulation of trash that was important stuff in people's lives six weeks ago. I've seen it on TV. I've seen it on YouTube. I've seen pictures on the Internet. Nothing prepared me for the visual assault of this destruction. And I remember: just minutes away, people live seemingly normal lives. And this is just one neighborhood in one city.

We drive to a bluff above the harbor in Onagawa Town, some 55 feet above the sea. A hospital stands on this bluff. Its first floor was flooded when the tsunami struck.

The water today is a sparkling blue; this little harbor has a lovely entrance. It is an idyllic scene, until one looks ashore. On the ground at the foot of the bluff we stand on, the destruction is immense. One green, four-story apartment building near the sea was picked up whole and crashed on its side. A car rests atop the shell of another tall building. A family walks through the rubble of their former home.

The level of the land dropped almost 4 feet because of the earthquake. Then the tsunami came. The tsunami came at nearly 50 miles an hour, almost 60 feet high.

As our group stood in stunned silence overlooking the devastation, we noticed a woman standing to the side, staring at the destruction with a sad smile. One of our group approached her and asked for her story. "My house was down there in the rubble," she said, pointing at the remnants of a cement foundation. "When we heard the warning, some of us ran up the hill and into the hospital and up to the second floor. Some of my neighbors just climbed to the flat roof of that

3-story building next door. See the building skeleton left standing? That was the roof they climbed to before they were washed away."

I carefully asked her how she had chosen to live in such a dangerous place. "As you can see, it was so beautiful. On hot summer days, a breeze would blow through. We never imagined...."

A bike resting on top of a debris pile catches my attention. Someone rode it through these streets six weeks ago...

I stop taking pictures. This can never be captured in a picture, I know. Taking them is just a way to set aside the anguish, if only for a moment. To dwell in the horrific reality, while setting it aside.

We travel along the coast in our mini-bus, taking in the destruction. We eventually arrive in the downtown area of Ishinomaki City, where we have been assigned volunteer work by the center we visited earlier. It takes all 30 of us a little more than two hours to clear the remaining debris from this one sake shop. Mud shoveled from the floor. Bottles salvaged, cased and stacked. Meaningful possessions, now garbage, hauled away. We moved with what feels like startling speed and coordination for a team that had never worked together; our purpose clear.

Before we left Tokyo this morning, my friends Hide and Yuki Inoue had equipped me with over-pants, work gloves, a heavy-duty face-mask and goggles. They'd given my measurements to their neighbor in the village where they live. The neighbor coordinates the volunteer fire department and had said to them: "It is the least I can do," he said, "to thank and support you for going while I cannot."

All decked out and clumsier than usual, it is only when I feel my right ear's high-tech hearing aid dropping out of my ear that I realize somehow in the frenetic activity my left one disappeared. I carefully retrace my steps and search the muddy floor. Futile, of course. My hearing aid joins the debris of many people's lives. I still my irritation with myself: with so many lost lives, homes, businesses and livelihoods, how could I even think about complaining about this loss? I have so much, in so many ways.

I didn't even know the owner of the shop was among us. I had thought, "Ah, this is how it works." Volunteer crews go from building to building and clear away the debris. But then one man stepped forward and said: "Please, please each of you take a remaining bottle of my sake. It is the best in the region." How could he smile so much? I wondered. He literally beamed. He's not focused on what he lost, I knew. He is focused on what he has.

Minutes away from where we have toiled, we stop at a mega store for a bathroom break. It is filled with people and everything normally available in mega stores. Unbelievable in its own way. Darkness has settled now. We've begun the long trip back to Tokyo. No injuries. Hot showers and every food imaginable in Tokyo restaurants. Clean clothes. Comfortable beds. By the time we arrive, the volunteers back in Ishinomaki will be asleep in their cozy tents in the brisk winds, having spent another full day doing labor that tired me after two hours. I am grateful to have had the opportunity to go. Grateful to have worked alongside such purposeful friends. Grateful

for the real gratitude the sake shop owner expressed for returning his washed-out shell of a shop to him. Grateful for health and breath and spirit. I'm still just in the experience of this. Unable to make meaning. A bit overwhelmed. It has been almost 24 hours since I woke to begin this day's journey. Time for sleep.

In times of turmoil people from the outside tend to go in and ask: "What do you need?" For someone who is only just coming to grips with the fact that their old life is gone, this is an overwhelming question. Instead, the question to ask is: "What do you have?" This wisdom from Meg's earlier e-mail was such a life-saver for me. It helped me remember where to direct my attention and what I should invite others to see.

But what do we do when the things we never imagined happen? What do we do when our national economy collapses, as it did a decade ago in Zimbabwe, or on a personal level when we suddenly find ourselves unemployed with no income? What's next when a tsunami sweeps away not only our home, but also much of our town and the people we loved? Where do we turn when the hospital that has provided vital services suddenly announces it will close its doors?

We turn to one another. We talk and we listen. We grieve. We determine what we have and we begin to use those resources to build again. We find ourselves in a place of colossal loss and boundless possibility. We find a place to begin and we make a new path, step-by-step.

We walk on.

Looking back, I realize that five practices helped me find some semblance of peace and harmony in these difficult first days. They work together and are part of a larger whole. They can guide us to a place where are able to find the next minimum elegant steps. They assist us in finding the way to invite others on this journey of re-imagination and co-creation.

BE STILL.
SETTLE DOWN
Go for a long walk. Meditate. Do what you can to find equanimity and dispel the anxiety that paralyzes or leads to hasty action.

STAY CONFUSED
Be willing to stay in a state of confusion. Stay confused and stay together for long enough, and real clarity will emerge and right action will appear.

5
PRACTICES
Five practices to help find peace and harmony in difficult times.

GET CONNECTED
Alone, disasters are too much to handle. We need community. Find those who can hold you, host you and help you to not get lost in chaos and grief.

LISTEN
And then listen some more. Stay away from premature conclusions and actions. Listen to everything that is said. Listening without limits, we begin to see more of the whole.

EMPATHIZE
Let listening permeate to the very core of your being. Open your heart as wide as you dare. Stay present to grief, joy, hopelessness and possibility.

Cracking Open the Past

For the next three years, through the spring of 2014, my life was filled with these kinds of days. It was an intense time for all of us. We were witness to the wreckage of people's physical and emotional lives as well as to the resilient spirit of many we encountered. We discovered that disasters have many faces. Some were bowled over; their old lives destroyed and everything that helped them make meaning lost. Some pushed as hard as they could to resurrect the past that had just disappeared, diving into action. For these people, there was a pressure to close the cracks, to recover, rebuild, and reclaim the old normal.

For others, there was also, just below the surface, a sense of release. A sense of letting go of old ways of being, old ways of doing, and old ways of thinking. There was a sense of relief at no longer needing to pretend that everything was okay and do things the way they always had. Under all the chaos, there was a sense of new possibility.

Throughout it all, we tried to determine where to place our feet and learn how to walk together, creating a new future.

Let me go back, before the disasters and set a bit of further context here.

Most of us feel at least a begrudging contentment with our lives. We may complain but we have no real intention of changing anything. Even the things we don't particularly like are at least familiar to us. There is comfort in the familiar. On the other hand, stepping into the unknown is frightening. So, we hang in there, living our daily lives, with a routine that we don't particularly care for because leaving it behind is just too scary.

Such was the case for many in Japan prior to the disasters. While the country was still relatively prosperous, there had been a growing sense of discontentment since the 1990s, when the economic boom of the seventies and eighties came to a screeching halt. The relentless movement to a "knowable future" — one that was basically an extension of the past — had ceased to capture some people's imaginations or feel like a goal worth pursuing. Much as in other countries across the world, it was becoming increasingly difficult for people to have an unfaltering faith in maximum economic growth as the pathway to happiness.

In 2010, when I was working in different parts of Japan, I kept seeing signs of this discontent. If the space was safe, people would turn to each other and talk about their dissatisfaction. They didn't like many aspects of their lives: the hours at work were too long, what they did was boring. There was too little satisfaction and too much stress. But even then, in 2010, I don't recall many people talking about happiness. The word was rarely used.

It was also clear that most people were not prepared to do much more than talk. Yes, change would be nice — but it was not something they were willing to act upon. They were resigned to their lives. Sound familiar? When working in parts of North America and Europe I hear these same refrains. People are dissatisfied with their lives but unwilling to make changes. They would rather put up with the security of the familiar than risk reaching for happiness and fulfillment. What does it take to get us to act? Can we change without overwhelming disaster?

I often contrast Japan's response to the disasters in 2011 to those of 1995. The Great Hanshin Earthquake that struck Kobe in 1995 was the greatest disaster in Japan in many, many decades. In 1995, most people felt Japan was on the right course. Yes, the economic bubble had burst, but many thought that Japan could find the path to material prosperity again. It would take a little more effort to get back on track, but it was doable. Sure, a few adjustments might be needed, but generally speaking, things were okay. For most, the prescription for success, the direction forward, was the same as it had been for the last 50 years since World War II: We work hard. We achieve economic success. We prosper. Life is good and will get better and better. The old normal was something to which they could still return.

When the Triple Disasters hit — sixteen years after the Kobe earthquake — discontent was already in the air. Increasing numbers of people wanted something different. People wanted change, but what change they wanted wasn't clear.

It was an agonizing time. But along with the grief and loss, people were released from some of the restricting patterns and habits in their lives. They were shaken, sometimes to their very core, and began to ask fundamental questions about their lives. Suddenly, old ways of living were gone. New ways needed to be created — <u>now</u>.

People started asking questions about what kind of life they wanted. In almost every dialogue I have facilitated since the disasters, as well as in many informal conversations, I've heard people talking about happiness. In many ways, thinking about the "happiness" has become the way to ask: What is the life I want to lead and am I living it now?

This tentative exploration of happiness was part of a cracking open, part of the new light coming in. This new light illuminated a heretofore unseen landscape and invited questions about what's important, about how we want to live our lives.

In Training to Be a Sacred Outsider

2011 was a heart breaking and heart strengthening year in Japan. I believed that dialogue and FutureSessions could be an important key in helping people to come to grips with their grief and begin to envision the future. But how, when, with whom? Those were big unknowns.

By late November of 2011 I was back home in Kyoto, exhausted and very, very unclear. I felt embraced by autumn's beauty and yet also felt so lost. One morning, I hopped on a local train from the Tambabashi train station near my host family's home. I didn't know where I was going. I heard the conductor say Fushimi Inari and I hopped off. The Shinto Shrine of Fushimi Inari spreads out over a mountain and I spent the day climbing to the top. Stopping frequently to meditate and pray, I released everything. I bowed down and said I have no idea what to do. In my release, in my surrender, images and ideas started to flow in. By the end of the day, I knew my next step. It was later still that I realized

I had been following one of the practices of *Enspirited Leadership* by stopping and being still and letting spirit come in.

I also learned a critical lesson: Intention should always be braided with surrender. I was holding clear intentions for the unfolding of dialogue and FutureSessions in Tohoku. I wanted to do what I could to open spaces in which people in Tohoku and all over Japan could talk with each other about what kind of future they wanted. I intuitively knew that it was important. I held that intention and I had to surrender, time and time again, to how it would happen. I had to just keep showing up, listening, always listening, to discover where to place my next step. I had to keep coming back to the present moment — to who and what was in the space — and work from there. It was astonishing, frustrating, exhausting, energizing, filled with grief and with joy. I learned the difference between giving up and surrender. Giving up is walking away. Surrender is showing up to what actually is — not what we thought it might be or wanted it to be.

Working for many years with communities around the world had given me some expertise. I had some skill at designing and hosting dialogue and helping communities see into their future. I kept looking for the pathway forward — listening, being quiet, turning to my many friends and colleagues in Japan to help me find the way. Those years were filled with the kindness and patience of many people who helped me find the simplicity and directness to make this work understandable.

In Japan, I discovered that my expertise and skills needed to follow my listening, not precede it. Through this, I began to understand the difference between the stance of the "expert outsider" and the "sacred outsider." The expert outsider arrives with answers. The sacred outsider arrives with listening. I am in training to be a sacred outsider.

For several years now I've been sharing this idea of sacred outsider with others. It feels archetypal. Though most of us don't always act from this space, I believe that this is something we know how to do for each other; it is something down deep in our bones. We arrive quietly, working from our listening. From that listening we witness others. We hear their stories. In the process, they begin to see themselves in a different light. They are able, literally and figuratively, to re-member themselves, to discover more of who they are. From our listening, we sometimes find a question to ask. Perhaps we even notice a piece of insight or wisdom we feel called to share. But our deep posture is that of the witness. It is not for us to give answers. Rather it is to co-create a space for discovery of new answers and new possibilities, together.

Listening and Learning:

As my work continued to unfold in Japan, I was overwhelmed. When I stayed in Tokyo there was always another meeting, something new to attend to. I knew I needed quiet to do this work. I knew I needed to walk and be in nature and visit the temples and gardens I love. I knew I needed to be with my host parents, now in their late-eighties. I remember the first time I took a train from Sendai at 4:30 in the afternoon and arrived at my Kyoto home 500 miles away just before midnight. I wondered if I were crazy to do this kind of "commute," but as I spent the next afternoon walking in my beloved hills of Kyoto, I knew this was a wise decision.

As I kept listening, talking and reflecting, my work became clearer to me. My work was first to host the spaces for whatever conversations wanted to happen and to continue to introduce ideas about how we create the future together. I was to go where called. Planning meetings, dialogue sessions, FutureSessions, evening conversations.

For formal sessions, a translator always accompanied me. But I was also in many informal conversations on my own. People were so kind and tolerant of my limited Japanese. Through the limitations of my language skills, I began to learn something new. I realized that we have an over dependency on words and frequently make the mistake of thinking we understand what a person means, when we only hear the words they have spoken. I began to learn that listening was a "whole body sport." I had to listen with all of me — beyond the words. Listening, listening, listening — and the path forward appears.

And such chaos. Everything kept changing. I remember being really irritated at first when people I was depending on suddenly didn't show up. I started to realize this is just life. It is messy. I looked for tools and models to help me understand and stand with ease in what was happening around me. I tried to understand more about the various steps and stages of working with communities to create AfterNOW — today.

Finding
After now

CHAPTER

3

Finding AfterNow

You must give birth to your images.
They are the future waiting to be born...
Fear not the strangeness you feel.
The future must enter you
    long before it happens.
Just wait for the birth,
for the hour of new clarity.

— Rainer Maria Rilke

THE CHAOS AND CONFUSION I encountered when I returned to Japan after the Triple Disasters is more than most of us encounter in our lifetimes. But, we are often slapped by what seems like endless disruptions to our lives. We're frequently overloaded, distracted and stressed. The world around us is often hard to look at without just shaking our heads.

I'm neither a pessimist nor an optimist. I live my life with what Joanna Macy calls "active hope." This cartoon, published towards the end of 2016, gives a sense of what active hope actually is.

© JM Nieto.

Doing what we can — and what we know is important to do. Sometimes we act alone, doing some good, but perhaps not really changing much. What's often more powerful is when we do it together.

But with all the tensions and suspicion and exhaustion, how do we do it together? How do we talk with each other about what's really important, learning that our differences are assets not liabilities? How do we listen to each other, speak our truth, and figure out what to do AfterNow?

What I have learned from my work in Japan and from many years in other communities around the world is that we need spaces grounded in curiosity, respect and generosity to find our way together. In Japan and in this book, I refer to these kinds of spaces as FutureSessions. How do we create them — these kinds of spaces where we connect, dream and act, now?

This question shifted in some critical ways with the 2015 publication of my Japanese book, *When We Cannot See the Future, Where Do We Begin?* The title has invited me into questions and dialogues that have subtly and substantially altered most of my ideas about change and transformation. In the past, my focus had been on the future, moving towards a horizon. But when the future is invisible — as it seems to be these days — how do we focus? Where do we place our attention? We place it on NOW — right here, the people we are with, and the resources we have on hand. To focus our attention on what is really important. From that space, we can start to co-create and an AfterNow begins to emerge.

In this chapter, I'll explain what I am seeing about the systems, structures and processes that can help us co-create our AfterNow. Today.

I want to be clear, however, that this is not a "how to" manual. Creating these spaces is more art than procedure; more spirit than science. While there are certain things we can do, and watch for, this work is much more than a well-ordered and organized process. Looking into NOW is chaotic, messy, energizing, and frustrating! I want to share some of what has been helpful to me in understanding this work and point out the broad processes, stages and tools that I find helpful.

There are multiple and intertwining steps. First, we must settle our own anxieties, take deep breaths, and be open to what will happen. Next, we begin by inviting together a small group of people to help us deepen our understanding of what we really want. We come together with a few others as a design team to guide the work. And then finally, we convene people from diverse backgrounds in conversations that matter and which lead to action. These are not linear steps. As we move along, we often swirl back to re-engage with the questions and activities from earlier stages to go deeper. We keep engaging with each other — in face-to-face meetings, on video conferences, on phone calls, in Facebook or LinkedIn, using Google Docs, DropBox, Slack, text messages, e-mails and other forms.

There is an underlying flow that's important regardless of the form of engagement. I've discovered that seven steps help us relationship and co-creation with others.

1. Cultivate our own presence and equanimity

We each carry within us a divine spark of life. When we are able to engage with others from our place of calmness and center, we enter into discovery in the flow of life.

We create the future we want together. We create it from NOW, as ordinary people who listen to each other, tell each other the truth, trust each other enough to try new experiments, and reach out to invite others in. It grows from the very core of our being.

Sounds easy, right? We all know it is not. Our lives are too busy, filled with too much to do and far too many invitations to move towards fear. Sometimes we let our anxieties and fears completely overshadow that spark.

Whenever I am about to engage with a group of people I try to quiet myself. I am not always successful, but I know how important it is to let go of my anxieties, fears and worries. They are there, but I try to not let them "own" the rest of me. I glance at them, thank them for the information they provide and remind them that they are not in charge. When I can show up as a non-anxious presence, I can invite magic in.

It's easy to get pulled towards learning one more methodology, getting one more tool, studying one more aspect of design or mastering one more model. Don't get me wrong — these are important. If I didn't think so, I would not be introducing them in this book. But the foundation in work of discovering AfterNow is twofold: Be yourself and invite others in.

The frameworks I introduced earlier from *Enspirited Leadership* and the life-affirming principles from the Berkana Exchange are two pathways into discovering how to be ourselves. Whenever I find myself in a free fall of confusion, I start to regain my presence and equanimity by returning to these frames.

2. Pay attention to the air, to the space that surrounds us

Pay attention to the BA I love this word BA and all it represents. I've used it and defined it several times already in this book. It's important enough to keep emphasizing. BA is the air we breathe, together. It is the space we occupy. It is the sense of where we are and who we are with. The Japanese have named this sense BA. Even without the word, most of us know the sensation. We enter a room and feel the grief present. We walk on the street and feel a tension in the air. We step into a park and feel a playful energy.

In Japan, there's a simple expression for someone who is not aware of the BA — they KUUKI-YOMENAI (can't read the air). Learning to read the air — being still enough to sink in and notice the subtle energy of people individually and collectively — and then acting in ways that invite people to lean into conversation without anxiety — is essential. Paying attention to the BA helps us find our own harmony and allows us to invite others into theirs.

Part of BA has to do with the physical spaces we work in. Preferably those that are airy and light, close to nature, present to beauty. Many years ago, architect Christopher Alexander, without calling it BA, described some of the physical aspects of these kinds of spaces in his book, *Timeless Way of Building*[22]. In the beginning of his book, Alexander wrote *we know what the quality without a name — this aliveness — is like in our own lives. This quality can only come to life in us when it exists within the world that we are part of. We can come alive only to the extent the buildings and towns we live in are alive. This quality without a name is circular: it exists in us, when it exists in our*

---

22 Christopher Alexander's 1979 book set the stage for exploration of what's now called Pattern Language –looking for the patterns of relationships.

buildings; and it only exists in our buildings when we have it in ourselves. Alexander then went on to ask what is it that makes a space come alive?

In the 70s, just as I was really learning about facilitating and hosting, that question captivated my attention. Alexander described the basic patterns in a space that created aliveness — relative position of windows and doors, relationships of height to other dimensions, presence of light. While we usually don't have a chance to re-architect the spaces in which we work, there are always things we can do to bring out the aliveness and beauty-uncluttered, a simple circle of chairs, some flowers in the center, ample light.

And, as Alexander so wisely pointed out, a key part of BA is "what we have in ourselves." When we enter a room with respect, it helps to create a good BA. The choice is always ours. We can enter with suspicion, fear and judgment. These feelings make the air in the BA heavy. We can enter thinking no one will want our ideas, or we can enter thinking our ideas are the most important. Both of these attitudes weaken the BA. If we choose to enter with an attitude of respect and welcome for all others who arrive, then we begin to invite magic into the room. We begin by knowing that we need each other.

As human beings, we're naturally curious. We understand that we only know a little bit and that we need to find out more. We know we need the ideas, perspectives and experience of others. But we also get afraid. We think that we're supposed to have the answers and that asking questions shows a weakness. It's not true. Our questions — the things we don't know — open the possibility of creating something new. The Nuu-chah-nulth tribe of Vancouver Island reveal this deep spirit in a core aspect of their worldview: "It is unkind not to ask for help."[23]

When we arrive with generosity, we immediately invite in the generosity of others. I mean generosity at all levels — our spirit, our ideas, our knowledge, our questions and the many resources we have available to us. A BA that is filled with generosity is filled with possibilities; together we have enough to find a place to begin.

Whenever I am in a space with others — whether it is a planning meeting or a major community conference — my intent is to show up as a non-anxious presence and to really be interested in the ideas

---

23   See Tsawalk in Additional Resources: Bibliography

and opinions and hopes of others in the room. If I have that presence, I can invite others to do the same. By coming in with this intention, my presence itself extends this invitation.

As organizers of, and participants in, this work of creating a new now, the single most important work we can do is with our own spirits. The more we can be present to each other without being overwhelmed by our own fear and anxiety and the more we can embrace curiosity, respect and generosity, the more likely we will be able to do the work we need to do, together.

3. Find a few others who care

One thing that stands out for me in all the stories I've heard is that we do this work of creating what's next best when we work **together**. We're smarter together, we're better together, we get more done together. This way of being is a deep cultural competence in Japan. For thousands of years, people in Japan have depended on each other to grow rice, build community and prosper.

The Triple Disasters introduced something more into this cultural competence. Across the Tohoku region, and all across Japan, the disasters were an energetic push for people to stand up for what they want. People who before might have politely waited, stood up and said, "This is important; I need to do it. I'm not waiting anymore." What's unusual in my experience around the world is that people in Japan are both standing up <u>and</u> standing together.

This is so important. I come back to this as a foundation: standing up <u>and</u> standing together.

In the United States, people stand up, but often we don't stand together. Historically, people in Japan have been better at staying together than at standing up. When we can do both — stand up and stand together — extraordinary possibilities become available.

I've been sharing and nurturing this incredible energy of standing up and standing together with people all around the world. We need it everywhere. We find this energy when we enter authentic space — good BA — with other people who are exploring questions that matter.

How do you put this into action? Let's say that you have something you want to do. Something you want to stand up for; or as I suggested in Chapter 2, a calling has found you. Where do you begin? You begin by finding several other people who care about the same thing. Think of it as tossing a pebble in a pond. We want to generate larger and larger ripples. It begins with a few people who you call together for a dialogue. You begin by being brave enough to share the tender possibilities that are growing inside you and then invite those people to explore and bring life to what is emerging.

In the beginning, there are typically four steps.

- **Convening a Design Team:** We start to get to know each other. Who's here? What do we care about and what is important to us right now? What are the new and old stories we carry within us? How can we invite others to join us?

- **Naming the Challenges and Opportunities**. What is the particular challenge and opportunity that calls us together? It's like peeling an onion: We keep going deeper and deeper. What is the heart of the matter that concerns us right now? What do we care about and why?

- **Finding Focus.** Often what we care about is pretty big. What is our initial focus? What is the starting point? Where can we begin? What lies at the core of the invitation we might offer to others to join us?

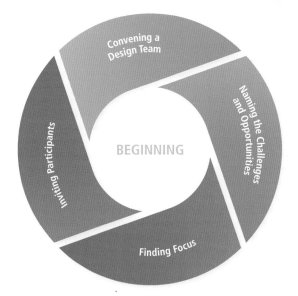

- **Inviting Participants.** Who should we invite? Who do we already know that cares about this challenge? Whose voice is needed? Most importantly: *Who can we invite who will come with respect, curiosity, and generosity?* Depending on the focus, we may issue a broad, open invitation; other times we may only invite specific people. Even with the broad invitation it is important to think carefully about whose voices will be particularly important and to find ways to invite them.

This process of convening, naming, finding and inviting is an iterative one, always reaching out further to invite in a broader range of people who want to co-create new possibilities.

4. Open a path for fresh action with questions

When we come together to learn with each other, to think with each other, to begin building a future together, questions open up new pathways. Our initial impulse for action often starts with on old and incomplete knowledge. If we actually want to create something new, we first need to be in inquiry with each other. Good inquiry always begins with good questions. Asking the right question opens up a conversation and keeps it engaging. A good question reminds us of what has meaning, triggers our curiosity and invites us to explore further.

The most powerful questions emerge when a design team sits with each other for hours on end trying to discover what the real questions are! We sit together, we talk and listen, we ask questions. We take our time, often with a fair amount of silence, discovering deeper and more important questions. As we do so, we strengthen our relations with each other and with the work we are undertaking. Patience is required, as are deep sensing and deep listening. When we approach the process with curiosity ourselves, really eager to discover what may reveal itself, our openness attracts the questions we need

One of the questions that we discover while sitting together will often become the "calling question" for a dialogue. Calling questions give off a particular aroma — one that attracts participation and arouses curiosity. Years ago, my Danish friend, Toke Moeller, worked with a group and discovered the question, "What else could a school be?" Simple. Crisp. Evocative. It became a calling question for many gatherings on learning and community.

FutureSessions grow out of powerful questions. The questions we choose to begin the process, and those questions that people discover through dialogue, are critical to the success of any session. Here's what I've found useful for choosing questions:[24]

- A well-crafted question attracts energy and focuses attention on what matters. Open-ended questions — ones that don't have a simple yes/no answer — are always best. They provoke the imagination.

- Good questions invite inquiry and curiosity. We're not trying to promote action or solve problems immediately. We're working to discover more of what is possible.

- Great questions are the ones that stimulate people to go further, uncovering more and more good ideas and possibilities.

- A powerful question
  - Is simple and clear
  - Is thought provoking
  - Generates energy
  - Focuses inquiry
  - Challenges assumptions
  - Opens new possibilities
  - Evokes more questions!

Powerful questions dance with clarity of purpose. Good questions help us understand our purpose. Purpose helps us find good questions. Look for examples of powerful questions that can open up conversations that matter in Additional Resources on AfterNow.Today.

---

24 The Art of Powerful Questions is a wonderful resource available through the World Café.

5. Gather with purpose

Let's face it. Most of us are tired. We're busy. We have more to do than there are hours in the day. We've all spent far too many hours in pointless meetings where nothing happens. They tend to be boring and frustrating. Too often, we organize gatherings without being really clear about why we want to call people together. When we're not clear, it is unlikely that the right people will show up and it is even less likely that those who do show up will have a productive dialogue.

After the disasters, I was part of many FutureSessions focused on purposes in the five different realms represented in the spiral below. In the beginning, in 2011, most of my work was around grief and possibilities.As the months and years passed, I engaged in more work is the other realms as well.

These realms flow into each other. Systems shift and transformation requires work with all five. It happens naturally and it can happen more powerfully with a bit of organization and insight.

Share Grief and Possibilities. Sometimes we just need to be with each other. We need to share our grief together. Unspoken grief becomes toxic. Held too closely, it causes us to die a little. We become lost and overwhelmed and uncertain. When we speak it out, it becomes fuel for change. It's the same with possibilities. We need to dream together. We need to be in a wild, open exploration of what is possible now that was not possible before. When we hide dreams away, they wither. Spoken out, they grow.

Both grief and possibilities can be fuel for fires of active hope. Good dialogue brings both out in the open.

Often, specific ideas begin to bubble up in this realm. But the main purpose is simply to help people get unstuck; to create a safe space in which people are able to speak from their grief; and to convene an energized space where the sparkle of new possibilities can become visible.

Take Local Action. We live in a time of agonizing needs and unparalleled opportunity. Many of us want to do something to improve our lives and our communities. Maybe it is starting a cooperative housing project. Perhaps it is beginning an aquaponics farm as a viable small business that gives 30% of its product to food banks. Or it might be founding a respite program where parents who are stressed to the point of breaking can leave their kids for several days. In these FutureSessions, people brainstorm ideas, develop plans and prototypes, determine their next steps and decide when they will come together again to share their results. People from diverse perspectives and backgrounds come together because they know what's important and they want to take action.

Sometimes local action takes the form of protest; other times it is the vital work of advising government or others about what they ought to do. My own emphasis and interest when it comes to action is what we can do now, together, with the resources we already have that we can mobilize to begin. In the years immediately following the Triple Disasters, people were coming together in communities and businesses to act together to build the new. Sometimes the work was haphazard.

Other times it was more organized. I believe that the actions and outcomes will always be more effective when they emerge from the kinds of dialogues hosted in FutureSessions.

Create Translocal Systems. "Translocal" means connecting people in different local areas who are doing similar work. All change is local. Change happens in a particular place; something new is created. It shows up in a local system. But most of us are concerned about more than a single change. We know that the challenges and opportunities in our world require systemic shifts. We're concerned about transforming the ways in which we live. What moves us from change to transformation?

One way transformation happens is that people who are working on the same themes in different local areas begin to connect with each other, share their learning, and think together about what happens next. This is what we mean by "translocal," connecting people in different local areas who are doing similar work. For example, in the Berkana Exchange, we identified six different themes ranging from "businesses we believe in" to "upcycling." Our work contributed to the growth of BALLE — the Business Alliance for Local Living Economies[25] just as it contributed to what's now a loosely connected movement of people around the world who are upcycling what would have been waste into useful products.[26]

If we want to transform the ways we live, we need to create and nurture translocal connections. We do this by inviting people working with similar issues and possibilities in different places together. This is the kind of work that was happening more and more in Japan's Tohoku region, three years after the disasters. Things were stabilized — it was time to look for the new.

---

25 See the bibliography in Additional Resources for details on this thriving movement to support growth of locally based, independent businesses.

26 See the bibliography in Additional Resources for one example of the planetary effort that recognizes waste as our most underutilized resource.

Envision Stories of Our Future. Many say that it will take 20-30 years to rebuild the Tohoku region or any other place shattered by major disasters. But what does it mean to "rebuild"? What will they "rebuild" to? Is it just more of the same? What will this future look like? Even before the Triple Disasters, things were difficult in the Tohoku. They were faced with an aging population, a declining economy, and the flight of young people to Tokyo. I often heard people in the rural areas say that they had a sense of not being as good as people in Tokyo. Returning to that past did not seem so inviting. But what would a different future look like? Could they imagine and create a future where people thrive in Tohoku and throughout all of Japan?

The Triple Disasters cracked open the assumptions and barriers of the past and made it more possible to move in new directions. All across the world, social, political and environmental upheavals are creating such openings. The challenge is how to take advantage of these openings for bold and imaginative thinking, engage with each other to imagine the kind of future we want, and then act together to create it.

Part of the challenge of envisioning a new future is finding new stories that capture our hopes and dreams. We are in a time when we need new stories everywhere in our world. But it can be difficult to imagine the new until we have a way to open ourselves to what's possible, to think beyond what we know. Processes such as Transformative Scenario Planning can help with this. In Chapter 6, I describe TSP and a few of these processes and how you can use them in your communities. Underlying each of these processes is the simple fact that we need new stories for the future that we can believe in and act upon.

This work of creating new stories is happening in many ways in Japan. The US based Pachamama Alliance's Awakening the Dreamer Symposium is prospering in Japan as one way to invite people to consider their dreams. The Goi Peace Foundation and Byakko Shinko Kai with their global Symphony of Peace Prayers are helping people find their "divine spark." The possibility that happiness could be the basis of new stories for our lives was being explored at the first annual Happiness 2.0 conference in Tokyo in early 2017. Joanna Macy's framework of Active Hope is helping people find their next story for how they will live their lives.

Deepen Learning. Everyone, everywhere is busy these days with hardly a moment to spare. This is particularly true in areas recovering from disasters. In 2013, I watched as colleague after colleague in Tohoku entered hospitals as they dropped from exhaustion. Everyone worked as hard and fast they could. While it would have been nice to pause and reflect — chew your experience — most simply did not have or make the time. When time might have been available for this, instead some expert would stand up in the front of the room and offer training. The immediate need for action was constantly overriding the need for rest and reflection. That's not how deep, generative learning happens.

Often when we're doing work that we think is important, we just keep trying to do more — and faster. We're usually learning a lot as we fly through our days, but until we stop and reflect on what we're doing, the chances are high that the learning will get lost. Often the best way to learn is to pause and talk with others who are engaged in similar work. Reflective learning environments help us share what we are seeing and what meaning we are making from our experiences. Doing so, we each get clearer about our own learning. When we combine our knowledge with others, we see even more. When we have a firm foundation in our own learning, we are then ready to ask real questions to experts from outside our immediate system. Suddenly, what they offer is no longer theoretical and abstract, but something that can be immediately grasped through the lens of our own experiences.

When we form different intentional structures — learning networks, social labs, communities of practice — where we can join together with others for the purpose of learning on a regular basis, we begin to create the conditions for true transformation.

The structure and methodologies of FutureCenters is one way to host and foster this learning. One example of this comes from Entrepreneurial Training for Innovative Communities (ETIC),[27] a Tokyo based-nonprofit created in the 1990s. After the Triple Disasters, it immediately organized to make it possible for people to make 3 to

_____

27 EETIC has been doing extraordinary work in Tohoku since immediately after the disasters. Learn more about their work all over Japan on their website.

9 month volunteer commitments. ETIC supported these volunteers with modest stipends as well as with learning opportunities. I worked with ETIC to offer FutureSessions which emphasized three levels of learning:

- Learning from self
- Learning together with peers
- Learning from teachers and wisdom keepers

Each of these levels is important. We begin with a STOP. Then draw a deep breath and ask: "What am I seeing? What am I doing? What am I becoming aware of?" Together, we reflect on our own experiences, engage in dialogues with colleagues doing similar work, and bring in perspectives and knowledge from beyond our systems.

This deepening of learning helps us become conscious of what we already know and acts as a compass as we find our next steps. The specific learning in each session with ETIC was unique — based on the questions and energy present — and ranged from a sense of solidarity in working with the unknown, to committing to keeping our own health and happiness as essential elements of anything we did in the wider world.

At the same time as this work with ETIC, I also became involved with the Co-Cre Project — the co-creation project — sponsored by Recruit Holdings, a major corporation in Japan. We started bringing in people working at the local level across Japan, not so much to form translocal networks for action, but to just pause and learn from each other. More recently, NewStories, working with other key sponsors in Japan, has created a Japan/US Learning Cohort of the leading facilitators of social innovation. In all of these examples, the purpose is to deepen learning and in each case the approaches used for FutureSessions are at the core of these dialogues.

6. Engage with others

FutureSessions are a way to engage in a group of people in conversations that matter which lead to action.

There are six overlapping stages in FutureSessions. They don't necessarily take place sequentially. Each is essential for success.

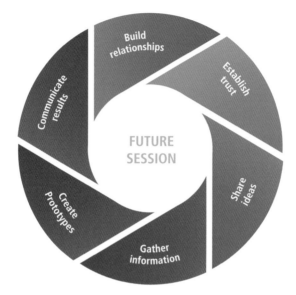

Build Relationships. Real change, deep change, requires people who are not normally in relationship with each other to come into relationship. It requires opening to the other.

We are often disconnected from one another. Just being aware of our relationship is itself a shift. Teams of doctors in the US have noticed that surgical procedures go better when the members of the team begin by introducing themselves to each other!

Building relationships happens in many ways. Sometimes it is in a dialogue — but that's not always the right starting place. I remember one of my colleagues talking about people in temporary housing after the disasters. "They don't want to be in relationship with each other. Their lives have been taken away. They don't want to be here. They hope they will leave soon, even though they know they won't." He said that rather than starting with dialogue, he was organizing different opportunities for people to play with each other. "If I do that first," he said, "then maybe they will start to get interested in each other."

Others have talked about how sometimes it is better to have some common project — building something, cleaning something up, organizing a festival — so that people work side-by-side and begin to be curious about each other. What's important is that people start to recognize each other as real human beings with their own personal stories.

Establish Trust. Our dreams are precious. Our grief is personal. Our fears can be overwhelming. It takes time for us to share our dreams, grief and fears. As we do so, we begin to create trust. One of those tricky paradoxes is at play here. Sharing who we really are invites trust — but it is hard to share who we are without trust already existing. We often have to take a leap of faith and be vulnerable with others to create trust.

To a large extent, trust has to be built over time and in place. In the beginning, perhaps, we "test" trusting one another. We know from FutureSessions work all over Japan that trust increases when people share their stories with each other — our personal history, grief and fears, hopes and dreams, or vision for what we want to do. When these stories is shared in a good BA, people begin to see more of who each other truly are. When this happens, trust naturally follows.

When we trust each other, dialogue flows more deeply. We are able to access more ideas, examine possibilities, create new models and organize ourselves for new collaborations. As we experience each other's integrity, generosity and good-heartedness, the trust deepens and we are able to create even more together.

Share Ideas. Every community is filled with people with good ideas about how to make things better. When we create a BA where people feel comfortable sharing those ideas, collectively we begin to make visible the range of possibilities needed to move ahead. In many ways, this is the easiest of all the stages, IF we have done the work to build relationships and establish trust.

People are usually eager — and sometimes a little shy — about sharing their ideas. Often working at first in twos or threes or fours is a good way to get ideas flowing. Appreciative Inquiry[28] can lead to sharing and talking in small groups that then leads to unrestrained brainstorming that begins to create an abundant list of possibilities. People then see that their idea is one part of a bigger picture that we create collectively. Simple techniques of "dotting" — giving each person in the room five big dots with adhesive backs to place next to their preferences in the room, or using some of the other methodologies offered in the Additional Resources section of AfterNow.Today, helps to bring forward those ideas most interesting for future consideration.

Gather Information. Once a community has started to surface the ideas it wants to seriously consider, it's time for more work. One of the things a community needs to know is what it doesn't know! When a community starts to get motivated because its own ideas are beginning to take on form, it is time for the research to begin.

This research can take many forms: learning journeys to other communities to see what they have done, engaging student teams from local universities to do research, identifying and interviewing people, businesses and other organizations who have some expertise in the area being discussed. FutureSessions are a good place to begin to organize information and its various methodologies are useful in talking about the information gathered and continuing to develop new ideas.

Create Prototypes. Eventually we're ready to try something. *Prototype* means we don't have to get it right. We're trying something to see what we can learn. It begins by coming up with a model or a plan. Prototypes range from preliminary to testable models. A prototype might be a detailed model using play-doh or drawings or words or other forms, or it might be a demonstration event. An idea for town planning might be

---

28 Appreciative Inquiry, developed by David Cooperrider from Case Western Reserve University in the 90s, is a powerful process used around the world to focus and amplify what we appreciate as a starting point for deep change. Additional Resources: Methodologies on the AfterNow.Today website.

prototyped with a three-dimensional model of an area being considered. A new program to match elderly in the community with young people as reading buddies might be prototyped as an intergenerational reading evening. A possibility of a new local business drying and preserving flowers might be prototyped by preparing an initial batch of flowers for a local farmer's market.

In other words, creating a prototype means going ahead and learning more about a possible idea by doing what you can with the resources at hand. We don't wait for anyone. Just start. When we build a model, or develop a demonstration, we see how our ideas work. We also see how the images held by different people may have sounded the same, but as we move ahead we discover differences that can make our work stronger. In the world of innovation, some people say, "Fail early and fail often." This is really just a reminder that we usually learn more from our mistakes than from our successes. Remember:

- We know how to do this.
- We know how to turn to each other.
- We know how to reach inside ourselves for inner strength.
- We know how to go alone when we must and how to stay together when we can.

Prototyping opens up a space of creating in the real world.

Communicate Results. Prototyping gives us something real and tangible to talk about with others. We've gone from ideas to seeing what we can make work. We try something, keep track of what happens, and then come back to another FutureSession to discuss next steps. Our work grows and deepens as we make what we've done visible to those we need to partner with as we go to the next stage. That next stage might involve:

- **Connecting with other possible participants:** Sometimes we try to grow the field of people involved in co-creating new possibilities and developing new collaborative partnerships. In other words, we want to make our work visible so we can connect with other people and invite them to join us.
- **Presenting to those who might support the work:** Sometimes we have taken a piece of work as far as we can with the resources

we have immediately available. Now it is time to take it to the next level. In a business, this may mean that we need to present our work to those in positions of authority in order to get decisions and budgets for proceeding further. In a community, this might mean it is time to reach out to government with ideas and proposals that have been tested. For a nonprofit organization, it might mean it is time to sit down and develop a next stage plan and seek funding. In each of these cases, we are communicating with those whose support is necessary to go to the next level.

- **Sharing with the community:** Other times we want to tell the community what we've been up to. We want to share our original concerns, the ideas we've developed, our research, and the prototypes we've produced as a report back to the community. By doing so, we open up our work in ways that can lead to unexpected synergies and may also surface those who are opposed to our ideas so we can dialogue with them as well.

These six steps — building relationships, establishing trust, sharing ideas, gathering information, creating prototypes, and communicating results — are what we do in FutureSessions. Sometimes several of these steps happen in a single session; often a series of sessions over an arc of time is required. As we work over that arc of time, we keep coming back together in FutureSessions, encountering each other in the ways described in this chapter. We use these steps to mobilize our communities to create the futures we all want. It is long-term work; it takes decades of being in the now to create a new future. It takes time. We have to keep connecting with each other, listening deeply, sharing our insights and hopes and dreams.

7. Move from Dialogue to Action to Community Transformation

This is another pattern I want to be explicit about. The "communicating results" step above begins to show this pattern. It is important that we keep a focused eye on the work immediately in front of us — the action we are taking. These days, we are often encouraged to "focus like a laser beam" on a specific aspect of our work or life. Yet, I find that we also need a soft gaze that takes in the larger system we want to influence and transform. I experience this soft gaze as a spiral with six stages:

These six basic stages can grow movements for community transformation. What's important is that we see this as a continuous cycle, a spiral, of deepening engagement as we search together for AfterNow. We move, with exquisite attention to each single stage of the journey, knowing that doing each well opens further possibilities.

Imagine. It all begins with imagination. For many years in my work I thought we needed to begin with clarity of purpose. I've realized that clarity of purpose is too narrow and constricting. When we focus too soon, we exclude many things that may be useful. We actually need to start with imagination. With curiosity.

We need to continually challenge ourselves to see more possibilities. Sometimes we do this through dialogue — asking questions such as, *What is possible now that was not possible before*? Sometimes it happens through brainstorming — quickly listing our different ideas and different approaches. Learning journeys, where a group goes out to closely observe what is going on in different systems, can also act as a stimulus for imagination. Slowing down, getting out of the old traps in our heads, and inviting in people with different ideas and perspectives are all ways to stimulate our imaginations.

When a design team meets for the first time, the first thing we need to do is look at what has happened so far and open ourselves to reflect on what else is possible. Through these actions, we imagine our way into the future and set the stage for a deeper inquiry.

Invite. From that place of imagination, the design team asks itself: Who do we need to invite in order to explore these questions? Who has a stake in this area? Who has different ideas and experience than we do? Who will it be important to involve if we are going to be successful in creating something new?

We want to stretch — but not so far that we break. We want to involve people with many backgrounds: women and men, old and young, people engaged in many different kinds of daily work. We want people with diverse knowledge and perspectives and we want them from different sectors of the community — business, government, nonprofit organizations, citizens, academia, and professionals.

We don't want to try to convince anyone about anything. This is not about selling or promoting. It is about attracting and inviting. Our work is to find the people with diverse experience and perspectives who want to be with each other — the people who can come together with curiosity, respect and generosity. We don't want to leave anyone out — but we don't need to try to bring everyone in.

Each time we convene a FutureSession, we need to remember that it is just the next step in a process and that there will be other sessions as well. The essential question to ask is,

Who needs to come now, to our next session?

Engage. Then, of course, we engage with each other. We come together in powerful ways that help us see our common concerns from a deeper perspective and as an invitation into new collaborative action. I've written about FutureSession engagement in the preceding section. I just want to situate it in this spiral. As we engage, we harvest.

Harvest. In any dialogue session, there are always many things going on. Many different levels of interaction. Sometimes we work in a circle of the whole; other times we work in a variety of small groups addressing the same questions or exploring different areas. At regular intervals, it is important to pause and invite participants to look back on what's been said by harvesting the fruits of their conversation.

Many things contribute to a good harvest. Sometimes it is as simple as bringing the essence of what has been happening at smaller levels of the system — pairs, trios, groups — into the middle of the room. Sometimes just a sample is needed, sometimes a more complete report. Using "post-its" to make maps on the wall of ideas and possibilities; having a graphic illustrator who is listening deeply to everything being said and bringing it forward in colorful illustrations; having sections of walls dedicated for sharing poems or quotes or resources — all of these can be part of this harvesting.

Sometimes we get more energetic and use a process like "Social Presencing Theatre" from Theory U, where a group of people listen and inquire deeply into the field and create a simple and powerful performance to make the invisible within the room more visible. Working with other non-verbal media — group body sculpture, play-doh clay models, drawing pictures — can give important new insights about what's happening. Graphic Harvesting — a skilled listener and artist making wall murals of what's being said — adds a powerful dimension to any gathering[29].

Make Visible. Often our intent is to grow our inquiry and broaden the community of people involved. That's the next step beyond harvesting. Often harvesting is of most use to the people who were part of a dialogue. It helps them remember the collective energy, the "air" in the room and what it felt like to be there. It captures and shares some of the ideas and context as well. That's great — but there is a next step in this dance. If we want to grow this inquiry and to nurture an overall cycle of change, we need to make what is harvested visible to the broader

---

29 Drawn Together through Visual Practice illustrates this wide field of harvesting.

community. This means we look for opportunities to go from the specific information of harvest to creating knowledge that can be shared more broadly.

It's exciting when a group sits with what's been gathered in the harvest and asks, *What does this really mean? What does it point us towards? Who needs to know about this?* These questions open the door to create different artifacts — blogs, articles, edited videos, photo collections, and specific tweets — that begin to share the deeper meaning present.

Connect. The next step in this spiral is when we use what we have made visible to connect our work and dreams and questions to more people. Earlier I spoke of this work as dropping stones in a pond. When we make our work visible, we send the ripples further in ways that enable us to connect with more people. We continue to use the spirit of invitation to welcome more people in, to share our explorations, our questions and what we are beginning to see as possible. We use both our hearts and minds to continually ask, "Who else can we invite in?" We use our knowledge as a basis for inclusion rather than as a means to exclude.

Imagine. The spiral keeps turning as we step again into a time of imagining and going through the six steps again, going deeper and deeper.

For three and a half years — from April of 2011 through the end of 2014 — I kept introducing these ways of thinking about dialogue. Sometimes I was invited to design and host different kinds of FutureSessions. Sometimes I was invited to talk about the structure and form of this work. My modest ability to speak Japanese was something I danced with continually. Another part of that dance was discovering both the power and the limitations of doing this work as a foreigner, an outsider. I could make almost no contribution to the rescue and emergency work required in the disaster region in 2011, so most of my convening was in other parts of Japan — often bringing people from Tohoku together with others in Japan. In 2012 and 2013, I showed up wherever I was called in the region. By 2014, my focus was shifting to helping people deepen their learning in the disaster area and across all of Japan.

By 2014 it was also time to pause, raise our heads and look around at how Japan was changing.

Reflecting
& Changing
Together

_____

CHAPTER

4

Reflecting and Changing Together

THOSE FIRST YEARS after the Triple Disasters were incredibly full and busy. Everyone working in the disaster area was running as fast as they could. Some ended up exhausted and hospitalized. The work was never, never ending.

My work deepened my relationship with many who were also called to serve. By the end of 2014, when the Japanese version of this book was almost finished, I realized I wanted to reach out to them to see what they were noticing. What surprised me (and now I am surprised that I was surprised) is that they all talked about profound *and* subtle shifts. Insights that would not be noticed in a rush: they needed time and reflection to emerge. They talked about the changes inside themselves and a new weave in the fabric of the culture.

Many days and nights had passed since the Triple Disasters took so much away. What did they leave behind? As people began to create a new future together, what were the fundamentals? What were the foundations? What was different and what was the same?

I asked friends who had worked in the disaster area to share their stories. Sometimes in the train or in a car, or across a table at a coffee shop, or even on Skype, I'd pull out my iPad and we'd begin. I asked a simple question: "What's shifted for you in these past three years?" And then we would follow the story that emerged.

This wasn't a data collection or a random survey or sample of anything — it was just a series of conversations with friends. Their comments help make visible what's shifting under the surface of daily life in Japan. There's a growing shift in consciousness, in the very way we make meaning. A shift in terms of what is important.

While my story collecting took place over several months and was almost always with only one person at a time, writing this chapter, I imagine all of us sitting around in a beautiful circle, speaking from our hearts. I suspect that each of us might have spoken any of these words because they come, I think, from a collective unconscious which is being revealed. But while our words flow together, I want to share them in the separate voices I heard.

You'll find the people I spoke with listed at the end of this chapter. The following are the important themes that arose from our conversations:

It Was All Here Before:

What if nothing is different? What if "it" was all here before? Obviously, I'm talking about something other than the catastrophic loss of life and property. A disaster of immense proportions did occur. The sense I got as I listened to people's stories was that 3.11 was like being doused with a bucket of cold water — being woken from a deep sleep. Startled, we looked around. Cracks and holes and faded colors were revealed. Beauty previously hidden was also suddenly visible. A veil of illusion had been ripped from the landscape of our lives.

Hide and Yuki Inoue felt that the foundations of society crumbled in the disasters. "A big hole opened and we saw things that we couldn't see before. Social, political and economic patterns all became more visible." Gunso said: "Unfortunately, it took these disasters to open that door. It allowed us to start."

"Many fundamental issues were already present, but 3.11 let us see the current reality in new ways" according to Riichiro. "We each make conscious and unconscious choices every day about what we will see. Most of us ignore a lot. We screen out our own feelings. We avert our eyes when we see a homeless person on the street. We shake our heads when something feels wrong and we don't know what to do. 3.11 broke many free from the trance of daily life."

For Hide Enomoto: "What shifted was a clearer or stronger reason for doing this work. In some ways, my work before was hypothetical. After 3.11, it became much more real. For example, in the past I was operating from a hypothesis that we have to make a transition or the economy will crash, or we will run out of oil, or some other disaster will happen. After 3.11, it was not a hypothesis anymore."

We Exist in Relationship:

We humans are a social species. We exist in relationship to each other. This is particularly true in a collective culture like Japan. Japan's origins are as a wet-rice agrarian society where everyone had to work together to survive. But Japan has been in a different "experiment" for the last 150 or so years since Admiral Perry arrived in Tokyo Bay with his black ships and demanded that Japan open to the West. Suddenly, Japan was thrust into modernity with the West's ways of measuring progress and making meaning in life.

Yuka reminded me, "Up until 3.11 more and more people were acting as if security in life came from having money and buying things. The disasters showed how vulnerable and fragile this system of material living was. That whole world of certainty collapsed. Many of my friends saw that we needed to depend more on each other."

"Before 3.11 we had come to think of ourselves as separate selves," Mikako mused. "You need to worry about yourself. You need to compete. But that doesn't go anywhere. I am not a separate self; I am part of the whole. The disasters helped us see our connection with everything in a way that creates a totally different sense of self. We used to think we were separated from each other. It's just not so. In the past, it seemed we had to struggle hard to connect. The disasters helped many find a new sense of the self that made it easier to turn and connect with each other.

"I have learned that things are always changing," says Yoichiro. "For me, the shift is towards sharing the BA in the precious presence of others. That is what is most important. It is not expensive. The most precious thing I can do is to offer my time and space with others to share each other's BA. After all, this same space and time will never happen again."

Koji added, "The more I worked after the disasters, the stronger my awareness became that I am part of the ecosystem. It is not just *my* work; it is the work we do together." Chie nodded and added, "My ideal society is where everyone can be themselves. It seems easier since the disasters for many of my friends to understand that idea. You live only once, and it is time to be yourself."

Time and time again, I heard people talking about how they need to discover their own "color" — not as a means to separate from others. Rather, as a means to have more authentic connections. This is a world of paradoxes, where words get slippery. The more we are able to let go of our need to be separate and self-contained, the more we are able to be our unique selves. Our very uniqueness, itself, results from our connection with others.

We Yearn for Real Connections:

Hide and Yuki recalled how right after 3.11 train workers were smiling and trying to do their best. "People really wanted to do a good job." Hide said. "They were really in touch with their own humanity," Yuki said it was like what she remembered after the 1995 Kobe earthquake, when she was a middle school student: "Neighbors started talking with each other and they couldn't stop talking with each other. There were many problems requiring their attention. They knew they could take care of them, together."

Mikako noticed, "People I knew were trying to be more authentic to their life purpose — to what is happening inside of themselves." Yoichiro commented, "Some people are beginning to notice that sorrow and fear are caused when we can't share now and here in the BA. In the past, many people were unable to share their space, their selves and their present moment. We could not communicate deeply. We looked very busy every day and the chance we could share this moment and this BA were rare. These phenomena cause loneliness and stressfulness. More people are noticing this, I believe, and starting to open more."

Finding these places to share authentically has sometimes been difficult in Japan. Ai, in her work with many rural communities, noticed that there were two kinds of gatherings. There were formal meetings and then there was the nomikai (after meeting party). "There was no middle space where people could really talk with each other without getting drunk. And then there was almost a purposeful forgetting of what was said in the nomikai, a separation from those real feelings and experiences." Yuka spoke of how she was a different person inside and outside of Japan. Outside she felt more able to share her beliefs and experiences; inside Japan she often felt that she needed to keep these hidden from view. The result was that sometimes she felt like an outsider in her own country because of her spiritual beliefs. "I thought people would think I was weird, and I was often trying to find ways of speaking about spirituality in a way that would be accepted."

Gunso spoke of how he often felt like his life served no particular purpose. Then he "met" the Mayor of Minamisoma on YouTube. "The Mayor said 'We're dying here and we need help.' I couldn't just keep saying that there was nothing for me to do. Quickly, I went there and the people of Minamisoma warmly accepted me. They offered me relationship and we had work to do together. It wasn't just donating money, but an immediate feeling of close connections." Gunso worked hard during those crazy days of 2011 and 2012. By the time 2013 began, he was exhausted, used up. And on January 1st, he was paralyzed by a major stroke and hospitalized. "Even though it took more than five hours to reach my hospital from Minamisoma, people kept coming to be with me. I realized I didn't have time to be depressed. The process of recovery from my stroke is the same as recovering from 3.11. I discovered where I could show up and found the people I could connect with. I hadn't paid attention to how much I was loved before," he said. "I never experienced anything like that before. The people from Minamisoma worried about me so much. Their love became my power. The existence of the people worried about me made it more possible for me to go on. When I was in the hospital, I had a lot of time to think. Many people came and shared their personal stories with me. I realized I was needed and loved and I saw what people loved in me."

This sense of isolation began to shift for many people after 3.11. There's something subtle here — I can almost describe the taste of it. Here's the sense I get. Before 3.11 a lot of people were unhappy. But they ignored those feelings, pushed them aside, and hid from them. But the disasters were overwhelming! Their spirits said, "I can't do this alone," and they started reaching out to others.

There was both a yearning for connection and the openings in which to connect. Rich pointed out that, "Many leaders were lonely in their work and in their community. They, too, came into circle with other people who had real struggles and they started to speak about themselves and to share their stories and to respect each other's presence." Rich felt this in his own life where he had only a few close colleagues before 3.11. "Now I have ten times more."

We became visible to each other.

A Hidden Wholeness:

This increasing sense of connection and relationship began to reveal something more as well: a wholeness that was present but had been hidden underneath busy and disconnected lives. As I listened to these friends, we found there was a growing movement towards this wholeness, towards a new sense of happiness, towards a new future.

One day, as we were driving along, talking about these questions, Norio mentioned how he was coming to understand that women were the key to the success of their efforts. "If men learn how to support women's ideas, things will go more smoothly. Within a small village, women and men can share different roles, and with equal levels. Within a small team, we can make a small prototype and then bring others into our idea. The power of people is getting stronger as men and women work together. Part of what's critical," Norio said, "is that compared to men, women can quickly change their mindset. Perhaps it is because women also come with children in their way of thinking — and something to protect."

Yoichiro noticed that "young people, especially, have a different culture that is not so materialistic. In the 20th century in Japan, we built a materialistic civilization where we worked very hard and bought a lot of stuff. Young people now are putting importance on quality of experience. Their consumption is very ecological; they use things for a very long time. Many young people are not buying cars or houses — they ride trains and rent. Why are these changes happening now?" he wondered

Koji sees this as a time when he and others started to invite more of who they are forward in all parts of his life. "Rather than thinking out of our heads, it became natural for us to feel our way ahead." Yuki and Hide began to be more aware of the whole system: "We can't just buy rice; we need farmers to grow rice. Of course, we knew this before, but in some ways we didn't see it. We saw," they said, "that we needed to start knowing our own personal feelings about our lives. We moved to Karuizawa in order to begin changing ourselves from a deep place. Now we have moved to the U.S. for a time to continue this process — to bring out our whole selves."

Yochiro sees that "young people are trying to build a new lifestyle. They seem to put importance on their time and their lifetime, community and quality of relationships. Things have changed for people in their 50s and 60s as well, especially those who took time away from their companies to go to Tohoku: they came back different."

Ai sees "a baton being passed; we are in the middle of a generational shift; people are standing up all over Japan. Before younger people could not stand up because they were afraid of their elders. Now maybe their elders are standing with them." For Norio, it is simple: "Teams work best when people with different values and experience join together. But to do this, I need to stay in balance, know my own role, and do my work."

We prosper together. We find our way as we lean toward wholeness with curiosity and openness rather than fear. For Hide Enomoto, his life has shifted in subtle ways. "I am satisfied with how I am approaching life. I'm not Pollyannaish; I know we all live in a story. This is a powerful realization by itself. I like this story that I am living in now. We can change."

For Chiki, this shift towards wholeness comes in similar ways: "I was able to see the issues as my own issues and I can be connected to so many people. The past and future — they are all connected. All issues and challenges are interconnected with each other. Chie sees that she "used to think that things were in categories — left and right and so on. Now it feels like there are more initiatives to work towards a common goal rather than seeing each other as divided entities."

This shift is pervasive. Hide Enomoto notices important changes in the Transition Town[30] movement in Japan. "Receptivity around Transition Towns has shifted; there are 50 Transition Towns now — twice as many as before 3.11. Even those not in Transition Towns

---

30 The Transition Town Movement started in Tontes in the south of England in 2006. In 2008 Fujino became the 100th Transition Town in the world and the first in Japan. The movement continues to grow in scope as a transition initiative with nearly 500 registered initiatives around the world.

are showing more interest in local programs. For example, in Fujino we are receiving lots of media attention. Fujino Electric Company is a pioneer in Japan — more famous than the Fujino Transition Town itself. Before 3.11 people asked: Why do I need to think about transition?" After 3.11 the question changed to 'how'. People said, of course, we must make a transition."

Koji spoke quietly about "needing to not deceive one's self." He saw this most clearly in a recent visit to Okinawa, on a morning walk with the women shaman of the island. "We've had this kind of sensibility before — these ideas about how to be and live in the world, but being on the island made it clearer to me. It was like climbing up a mountain and being able to see below. The disaster made things that existed before more visible. I had seen it many times looking at data. It was all there before. But it became more real."

Once we begin to see this wholeness that lies below everything, it is hard to forget. We may be lulled to sleep again, but upon waking we will have this memory of wholeness.

Work from Happiness and Joy:

As people have started to work with and towards this hidden wholeness, a new internal compass seems to come into existence — with north pointing toward happiness and joy. I heard this expressed in many ways since the disasters. Almost immediately after 3.11, people in Japan started talking about Bhutan's Gross National Happiness standard. I began to wonder, *What if happiness is a guide for our work? What would we do differently? How might our lives and our communities be different if our focus was on doing that which truly makes us happy?*

Yoichiro used to think: "Happiness is sometime in the future, when I complete my target or mission. I can be happy then in the future, but for now, I have to run. I have to run with pressure to reach that target. But I've learned that happiness has to be now and here. We can taste it now. Before 3.11 I thought the inside of me was empty, and I needed to get something from outside to fill me. Now I know it is all here."

Gunso's words were similar. "I've developed a relationship with what is simply fun and enjoyable. This feels important. Some people said we can sit in the aftermath of the Triple Disasters and we can still feel good. If we deny our own happiness because of our own hurt, it is not enough. We can be a power to change the existing system. After noticing this, the next step is how we can enjoy this process — how we can do it very enjoyably. In this process self-sacrifice is not needed and training is not so important either; rather, we work together and find joy and fulfillment."

Business As Usual Is Over:

It is not surprising that this shift towards wholeness, towards happiness and joy leads to a fundamental shift in how business is undertaken. Perhaps this is particularly true in Japan where business and community have been so closely intertwined.

"People are trying to operate in the harmony of the universe," says Mikako, "rather than the human systems that people have created to control the fear and make us safer. It doesn't make us happier. We have become saturated in terms of material prosperity — beyond sufficiency. Now, people are spending money in different ways. A sense of "local money" is emerging. Sometimes things are more expensive, but they bring more happiness. People live, talk and listen differently now. Perhaps this is the greatest part: people are changing how they listen."

For Koji, he sees: "In the past, the direction of the whole society was a stream that couldn't be resisted, and we kept trying to adapt to it. It's still that way, but after 3.11 the ways in which companies interact with society are changing. Companies must now demonstrate what they are for — their purpose. Then their ideas get sympathy and move forward. This is what we call entrepreneurship — the things they are trying to express in their being — entrepreneurship is not about starting companies; it is about learning to be yourself. Especially for young people it is not about money, but about meaning. Not just for society, but for their own uniqueness and happiness."

"In 2011, it felt as if our time had come," according to Chie. "There was more room for our imagination. This has started to close up again as some things stabilized. But people remember that the doors were once opened. Everything is intertwined with what happened after the disasters. I feel part of our ecosystem. It is something I can't do anything about. It is something bigger, something we can't control."

Hide Enomoto suggested, "Fewer and fewer businesses are in the old 'business as usual' mode. In Joanna Macy's language, they are moving into the great unraveling and the great turning."

Before the disasters, in many ways, people had grown distant from their own selves, from each other and from the places of home. Now people have learned to "be local" again. They are bringing business back to community. "No one liked the old situation," Rich said. "But many were counting on someone else to create the future for them. When 3.11 happened, people suddenly started to care for many reasons, including the fact that they were chosen to be alive while so many others died. People at the local level are the ones who know what is needed and genuinely want to change the course at the local level."

"Before 3.11," Mame observed, "I could not find where to start anything in my life. I had lost confidence. I see now that my mind was wrong. I didn't know how to listen to community. That's changed now."

2014, Three Years Later:

Three years after the Triple Disasters, so much had changed. Many people found new ways to step forward, making new pathways into an uncertain and invisible future.[31] The words my friends shared with me suggest that where people are going has changed as well. Their direction is different now.

And so much is still the same. Of course, some of the old reasserted itself. People are sometimes more comfortable with old certainties and ways of being — even if they didn't like them — than they are with stepping into the new. Yet even as some of the openings that appeared after 3.11 are pushed closed, there is a lingering sense of difference…

People are still applying to be "right arms" in the ETIC program that places, stipends and supports volunteers in Tohoku, but now, Koji says, "People remember what happened and they are applying to the program not just to contribute, but for themselves and for their being. They can't resist applying, even when they have many excuses

---

31   These new ways to step forward are described in Chapter 8.

— small children, their jobs, their comfortable lives. These hurdles are less of an obstacle; they are unable to resist the stream of change."

"Certainly, it is different now," Chiki says, remembering many different encounters. "Many people here are trying to live their own life from before — their old normal. Lots of people who wanted to change are giving up because they feel our situation is not going to change. There are people who are able to change themselves. But there are some people who can't or won't. The community of people able to change is getting smaller. I have to remember that each of us has different timing to be changed. I remember how, two and a half years ago, we organized a music festival. People talked about not being able to speak their own honest feelings because they were afraid of hurting others' feelings. I speak my own feelings every day, and frankly, I am a little tired of doing it. But there are still some girls who have not been able to share their own feelings yet. But each person has different timing. We must be patient."

Koji agrees, "The energy is different now, but still the flow of the society in terms of what is important has changed." Mikako feels "much more confident in terms of what we can create as human beings in spite of how helpless things feel. We can co-create a reality together. Something was broken free. Before 3.11, people read the books, but it never got down to their own context. The disasters shifted from the concept to the reality. It makes a total difference. Where people are doing their actions from — the source — has shifted. Even if we say the same things, where we speak from is different now. Of course, this is not true for everyone in Japan, but my world and the world of many of my friends is different now."

"We are becoming more attuned to the local," Rich suggests. "In the past, people in many parts of Japan thought they were raising their children to live in Tokyo, if they could. But people in Tokyo forgot their roots. As the tide reverses and people started going out to Tohoku, they began to see things they could not see before."

Yuka has noticed, "The younger generation in Tohoku who have lost friends and family feel they have to make a difference on behalf of those who have died. Those deaths have allowed them to speak of spiritual things."

Mame was looking for a way out of Japan before the disasters. "But I really want to live in Japan and make a difference here, now. I'm confident that the challenges and opportunities are here. It is my calling now. In the past I didn't believe Japan was that important in terms of change. I believe it is now, and I cannot escape. Things are happening again in government that worry me very much. Japan is getting worse and worse. We need to step forward, together."

For Norio, he says that his way of "thinking about the world isn't different than it was before the disasters — but it has been reinforced." Mikako senses an evolution of consciousness in many people "who are trying to live more authentically, beyond the stimuli of fear. It involves a lot of risk. We are here to serve the wholeness of the universe — not just survive. I talked about things like this before the disasters, but people looked at me like I was crazy — now I am accepted."

Chiki admitted that she "never thought that much about Fukushima before 3.11, but I realize now that it was that invisible context for my whole life. Now I have started to think about Fukushima and the rest of Japan and the rest of the world and the past and the future. They are all connected. Sure, I was concerned about Fukushima and other issues before. But now in front of my eyes I saw that we were going to lose things I hold dear. The people who are awake are the ones who feel like they must stay awake. They can blame others, or would like to blame others — but they know it is their responsibility. When we gather, we remember to stay awake."

In early 2011, Mame recalls "feeling sorry and miserable and incapable. But now, I have a continuous commitment. I am not giving up. My attitude is completely changed. I have something I can offer! I don't really know if I have been able to do things for people in disaster, put I have grown so much myself."

Yuka's story of the Karma Kitchen provides an example of this shift of attitude. Karma Kitchen is a restaurant where diners receive the meal they eat for free — and then they "pay it forward" with a contribution for the meals of those who come next. Yuka started "speaking about it to friends in 2009 — creating tighter bonds, wanting to do something to pay it forward. My friends said 'Interesting idea, Yuka. Good luck.' But they didn't step forward with me. The way I spoke about Karma Kitchen was exactly the same after the disasters — but people suddenly got it. We started in six months. People are remembering the ancient Japanese consciousness of ON OKURI (Pay It Forward) and it is spreading."

For Hide Enomoto, we are now moving beyond the "HA" part of SHU-HA-RI[32]. "Enough of introducing forms; it is time to share ourselves and what we see and hope more freely and more broadly. Time to create a new future together."

I keep returning to these stories to help remember the essence of my work in Japan and in the rest of the world. The story is far from complete and in Chapter 9, I'll give at least a glimpse of what's happening in Japan and what is not.

My companions in this circle of respect and relationship included:

- AI SANDA is a researcher with Recruit who is building a network of people from rural areas who are learning together about how to make strong, vibrant communities through an exciting project called Co-Cre (Co-creation). Her insights about how people can work together combine with a fierce determination to discover new ways forward.

- CHIE AIKAWA and I met in January 2010, when I first came to Japan to help others learn about the Art of Hosting. In the beginning, she translated my words into Japanese and helped me understand what people were saying. Soon, she was helping me see things that were invisible to me and helping me understand what was really going on. Chie translated me into Japan and Japan into me and became a person whose insights I cherished.

- CHIEMI KAMADA, otherwise known as Chiki, is a kind and strong young woman who, with others, founded Peach Heart — a support organization for young women in Fukushima who are facing many hard questions about how they will live their lives.

- HIDE ENOMOTO and I were introduced originally because we went to the same graduate program — California Institute of Integral Studies. Hide introduced professional coaching to

---

32 SHUHARI is a term that refers to the way of learning from a master, whether it be learning ink brush drawing or aikido. SHU is learn the form. HA is practice the form. RI is break the form. We learn, we practice, we develop our own mastery and go beyond.

Japan and also is the founder of the Transition Town movement in Japan.

- HIDE INOUE was a professor at Keio University and founder of Social Venture Partners Tokyo. YUKI INOUE does research and writes about social innovation. After 3.11 they moved to Karuizawa because they needed more quiet in their lives. And then they moved even further in 2012, going to the U.S. for a two-year sabbatical to discover more about who they truly are.

- KOJI TODA, otherwise known as GUNSO, was a truck driver from Chiba who felt completely confused after 3.11. After watching the Mayor of Minamisoma on YouTube, he felt called to go to Minamisoma where he became the director of the Minami Mirai Center — the South Future Center.

- KOJI YAMAUCHI is one of the founding members of ETIC (Entrepreneurial Training for Innovation Communities) and was the person who saw, immediately after 3.11, that ETIC should make it possible for young people to volunteer for extended periods of time in Tohoku as "right arms" to business and community leaders.

- MIKAKO YUSA is the founder of the Presencing Institute of Japan and translator of Otto Scharmer's Theory "U." A year and a half after the disasters, she and I had a chance to take 14 people in their twenties — seven from Japan and seven from seven other countries — on a learning journey to Tohoku.

- NORIO HONDA was born in Minamisoma and was an advertising executive before the Triple Disasters. He felt called into deep service to the people and lands of Fukushima. He works with many others to convene workshops and dialogues for the future across the region and has created a nonprofit supporting people returning to the communities closest to the reactors, from which they were evacuated in March, 2011.

- RIICHIRO (RICH) ODA is the founder of Change Agents and a key strategist for Japan for Sustainability. Rich, as he is known to his American friends, worked in business for many years before turning his attention to work in the social sector.

- YOICHIRO YAGI was a professor at Kagawa University in Takamatsu when the disasters struck. His own path took him to spend a year studying Appreciative Inquiry in the U.S. and then back to Tokyo to become president of his family's building maintenance and security company.

- YUKA SAIONJI MATSUURA is a leader of the Goi Peace Foundation and works with young social activists around the world. She's been a dear sister to me in all the work I have done in Japan since 3.11. Her clarity has often helped me find my own.

- YUKO ENDO, known also as MAME, is a woman who made her way to Tohoku because she had to help. She's helped me a lot! First as a translator and then as a partner listening deeply to what others were saying.

As I reflected on these many conversations, as well as the many other stories people shared with me in Japan, I found a variety of images to hold in heart, moving forward into our AfterNow.

IT'S CONFUSING.
No better word for it. I found I became more and more agitated if I tried to ignore the confusion and push it away. I had to learn to be comfortable with the confusion, not try to resolve it away. Eventually, I would find harmony in the confusion.

EMBRACE GRIEF.
It is real and it is overwhelming. Let it come, breathe it through. Befriend it. It connects you with more of who you truly are.

CULTIVATE ACCEPTANCE.
Learn to accept the "is-ness" of right now. Whatever is going on is just what is happening right now. It will be different in 10 minutes and different still tomorrow. Once we have accepted what is, then we have a place to stand – and a point of departure as we look for the next step forward.

COLLECTIVE CULTURE MATTERS.
The presence of collective culture is a game changer. I'm reminded of the African proverb: If you want to go fast, go alone. If you want to go far, go together. This is indigenous wisdom and indigenous cultures were collective. Unlike most industrialized cultures, Japan still retains its indigenous roots. Some things will seem painfully slow, but we will find our way forward together.

NO VICTIMS.
Sometimes bad things happen in life — horrific and unimaginable. But there is a powerlessness that comes when we think of ourselves as "victims." When we become victims, we get lost in that past, mentally bound to the images of our loss and unable to see into our own future.

WORK WITH WHAT WE HAVE.
We don't need to wait for anyone. We have enough to begin. We start by discovering what we have and by imagining how it might be used. It may be hard, even agonizing, but it is a solid and trustworthy place to begin.

PARALLEL REALITIES.
We each find our way forward the best we can. We each live in different worlds, yet our individual realities exist side-by-side. We must deepen our own capacity to live in our own reality while being aware of that of others. We must develop our capacity to hold the tension of these differences, knowing that newness arises from that tension.

EVERY PLACE IS DIFFERENT.
No two communities are the same. What works in one place will not necessarily work in another, but people in one community can learn from another. Forget about replication. Resist any impulse to go to scale. Cultivate a rich field of relationships in which each person and each community is the author of their own future.

New Futures
Arising
Everywhere

CHAPTER

5

New Futures Arising Everywhere

ALL AROUND OUR PLANET PEOPLE are making conscious choices about how they want to live their lives. Some make these in response to environmental, social, and political disasters. Others have had enough of dominant culture and decide they want to create something new. Still others discover what it is like to step into life rather than separating from it.

But how do we know what change is needed? When do we stay resolute and focused on a particular outcome and when do we stay in more of a flow state, learning our way forward step-by-step?

These are questions being asked in the many communities and networks I am part of in Japan and all around the world. Japan, six years after the disasters, is a very mixed bag. Good things are happening. Bad things are happening. About the only thing that seems crystal clear is that the future is, indeed, invisible. In Chapter 10, I give a glimpse of what's emerging now in Japan. Right now I want to zoom out and take in some stories from other parts of the world.

All around the planet we are learning — slowly, painfully, joyously. Together we are authoring stories of new possibilities for how we live on this planet. These stories are happening everywhere and I want share just a few from friends in Ukraine, Zimbabwe, South Africa, Greece and the U.S.

We all know that much is changing around our world, quickly. What does it look like when either the old normal suddenly vanishes or when we choose to turn away from the old and step into a new story? What does it look like when:

- A new era began in South Africa in 1994 with the end of apartheid, but the challenges of deep poverty and social and economic inequities are still staggering.

- An underclass is being created in the US where, since the 1996 welfare reforms, extreme poverty has grown sharply, moving from 636,000 to 1.46 million — a 130% increase. Alongside of this, incarceration rates doubled from a half million in 1980 to a million in 1990 and doubled again to 2 million in 2000; the curve leveled a bit with "only" a half million increase by 2010.

- In the early 2000s, Zimbabwe's economy started to unravel, with political violence peaking in 2008. Since then each year is different with new conditions and new challenges.

- In 2004, the Orange Revolution started in Ukraine and in 2014 people took to the streets again. Violence, turmoil and unrest thrive alongside a spirit of new possibilities.

- In 2005, Hurricane Katrina devastated New Orleans. The slow, painstaking process of reaching towards a new future continues 11 years later with leaps and sputters.

- In 2010, the Greek economy came unhinged and in 2011 the Arab Spring erupted. Each of these has been a catalyst for people to step forward and do things differently while much of what held things together in the past has dissolved.

- In 2016 in the US, the popularity of both Bernie Sanders and Donald Trump as presidential candidates revealed the deep the dissatisfaction with the status quo. Trump's election promises an era of unpredictable change.

Add to all of these social/economic/political shifts, the growing number of natural disasters are up from 100 a year in 1980 to more than 300 a year since the early part of the century. It is easy to see a world that is shaking. These are just a few of the many places where extraordinary changes are taking place. What does it all mean? There are convenient labels we can put on all of this: *We're in a time of shift from the old paradigm to the new. An era is dying and a new one is being born. This world is over.* I often resort to language like this because it holds truth — yet I know it is also very incomplete.

This began to be clear to me in 2001 as I walked alongside friends in Zimbabwe as that country started to unravel. I discovered that collapse didn't look like my old images of how things fall apart. The old, the dying and the new stand side-by-side. It's confusing and messy. *And* daily life still goes on. Some structures, and unfortunately some people, die. The old and the new learn to dance together. Sometimes they don't.

Obviously, Japan is not the only place where there is a break between the past and now. The changes I've witnessed there in the past six years have many cousins around the world. Let me offer some of the stories and insights others have shared with me.

It Starts with Me

This is the lesson everywhere. People are standing up for what is important. Those who keep standing for long and resist the temptation to martyr themselves know they can't do it alone and must stand together with others — lone rangers are a dying breed. They know that even when the work is hard, they must not lose track of their own health and happiness. This is, in fact, a spiritual practice.

The people I am listening to aren't trying to change the world or save it. They're paying attention to their little patch on the planet and trusting that others are doing the same. The questions become simple: *What's important? What can I do? Who can I turn to? What resources do we already have? Where do we begin?* People are working with the now, right here, today.

For Yuliya Filippovska, a young leader in turbulent Ukraine, this means "facing the conflict in my inner and outer world and going through it — sitting in the fire and bringing all emotions forward. I make the conflicts that rage below the surface visible — inside myself, the family, the team, friends and loved ones — so they don't take me by surprise. It's tough, but this is my responsibility as a Ukrainian citizen and a world worker!"

At Kufunda Learning Village in Zimbabwe, Jackie Cahi says much the same thing. "We try to be present and to bring intention and flow into our daily work. It's not always easy, but the regular coming together, the way we have learned to host each other and visitors has helped us all grow, listen, learn. There are still times when tempers get heated, when we fail to hold our ground, when our emotions and our old wounds overcome us, but we are learning always to come back to the whole, back to the centre, to trust the circle and each other."

People begin to see their lives as a blessing rather than a burden. Cornelia Emmert, a volunteer at Kufunda put it nicely: "It doesn't require anything special to be happy here. People have fun with their daily duties and occupations — laughing and singing whilst fetching firewood or working in the field or dancing while cooking. At any time, you will find people being in a good mood starting from the early morning. One day I wasn't sure if I should help collect bricks for building — it's a very exhausting job. But then somebody said: 'Come! It's going to be a lot of fun!'. This is the mentality I'm talking about. It doesn't depend on what you are doing. People will have fun out of any occupation. When people are waiting for something they will just start clapping a rhythm and begin to dance. Especially if the work is boring or exhausting, there will be new energy out of the dancing, singing and laughing because it makes everyone happy."

Dorah Lebelo Marema, a longtime activist in South Africa, sums it up: "People are realizing that we have to take care of ourselves — our health and well-being come first. We just have to take care of our bodies and do what we are called to. We look around and find the people who are passionate about what they want to get done and then we work together in an organic and passionate way. We don't need any taskmaster to push us — we can do our work, come together and connect with each other and enjoy each other and life."

Relationships and Community Are Essential

It's so easy to get lost when we try to do this work alone. We need each other. We need a fluidity in our relationships that allow each of us to step forward to act and lead when needed and then to step back and support the efforts of others. This sense of relationship and community is easy to see in the collective culture of Japan, but it also exists around the world.

Maria Scordialos, co-founder of the Axladitsa-Avatakia Learning Center in Northern Greece and the Living Wholeness Institute suggests "that at a deeper level the lesson we are learning daily in Greece is how to face fear with love through strong relationships of friendship and family based at a local level within a neighborhood or village. Most of the current mainstream system is based on fear — especially the fear of not having money. Insurance companies, pension schemes, earning large salaries are all coping mechanism that we have created to deal with this fear. There is an assumption in our Western world that becoming comfortable financially — buying our own houses, having a vast choice of what we can buy, choice of going wherever we want — is progress and leads to fulfillment. Yet we know that instead this creates an empty hunger. We consume and obtain, yet we still do not gain meaning."

In South Africa, community is what makes it possible for women to reclaim dignity and financial independence. Early this century, Sahra Luyt, a daughter and sister and wife of fishermen said that if she could bring women together in community, they could step out of repressive relationships. Through many struggles, she created the Southern Africa Fisherwoman's Association which has now enabled hundreds of women to step into a new life.

Likewise, Dorah Marema knew that the demands of climate change could open space for rural women to connect with each other and become self-sufficient. Her work at GenderCCA has "enhanced and increased women's productivity and diversified their sources of income. Together, women are the champions in the process of establishing cooperatives to run the various initiatives and save money from selling garden produce and other products. A participatory approach and ongoing capacity building have been important both for ensuring that the beneficiaries have 'buy in' in all aspects of the project cycle and for conflict resolution. Working together in these ways, women also have extra time to do other activities including beading, exchanging information about how best to package and sell their produce, counseling each other, giving each other tips on economic empowerment and strategizing on other income generating projects such as herb processing."

And, of course, at Kufunda in Zimbabwe, community and connection are key at many levels. The Kufunda Village itself is a community and each person in Kufunda belongs to their own rural community. Visitors find an instant welcome and become part of the growing community that spreads across the world. This community is connected by a common spirit, shared practices, continuing co-creation and exploration. Marta, a volunteer from Denmark speaks about how "this sense of community fascinates me and still now, from the other hemisphere, I feel this connection. I find myself living this journey of life; learning, being, laughing, witnessing and also failing, letting go, giving life and dying at the same time".

Individuals, professionals, organizations and governments keep turning towards each other: talking and listening, remaining adamant and compromising as they find a collective way forward. Almost no one wants to do it alone. Different people step forward with vision and leadership, but without a community going on the journey, nothing happens.

New Images of the Good Life

Doing what's important and turning to one another is part of a process of letting go of what's not working and being able to see the sprouts of new possibilities.

A few years ago, Jackie Cahi was at a Zimbabwe city bank in Harare waiting to meet some fellow Kufundees for protocol signatures. The bank is a hushed and formal space, lined with soft navy carpets and furnished in light wood. Staff wear a corporate uniform and clients queue quietly for their transactions. The Kufundees arrived like a flurry of fresh air into the air-conditioned atmosphere and everyone turned to look at them. It wasn't only the long dramatic dreadlocks, the casual, comfortable clothes and proud confidence that made them stand out. They carried the palpable energy of a different way of living — the energy of open spaces, clean air, ancient rocks and companion trees. The energy of freedom. They seemed like visitors from a brave new world where life is whole and healthy with unlimited potential.

At Kufunda Village people live the future today. Working with available resources, people build on the wisdom and resources they have for a more resilient tomorrow. "Living that future," says Jackie, "living a life of dignity, vibrancy, soul and spirit, living in harmony with each other and nature, living in wholeness, is an emergent process. Not always visible until suddenly we see how far we have come. Over the last decade, Kufundees come to accept responsibility, to step into their agency. We have concentrated on accessing our own resources, inner and outer — on journeying deeper into ourselves, our history, our healing, as individuals and as a village. We can acknowledge the old stories and start to let them go as we usher in the new. We help communities focus on what they have rather than what they don't. This is key to our work and helps build the individual as well as building the community."

Stepping back in time a bit, in 1955 the *Journal of Retailing* published an important article with the unassuming title "Price, Competition in 1955." Its core message was straight forward: "Our enormously productive economy demands that we make consumption our way of life, that we convert the buying and use of goods into rituals, that we seek our spiritual satisfactions, our ego satisfactions, in consumption. The measure of social status, of social acceptance, of prestige, is now to be found in our consumptive patterns. The very meaning and significance of our lives today is expressed in consumptive terms. The greater the pressures upon the individual to conform to safe and accepted social standards, the more does he tend to express his aspirations and his individuality in terms of what he wears, drives, eats — his home, his car, his pattern of food serving, his hobbies."

Co-creating a very different "way of life" from one based on consuming stands at the heart of Kufunda as it does in Maria Scordialos's analysis of the deeper meaning of current shifts in Greece. She writes "that this is not an economic crisis, nor is it about political instability of one nation. It is about the current Western civilization and the assumptions on which it is based falling down, collapsing and dying. The main assumption that's changed is that continuous economic growth is possible. The crash of 2008 created the crack in this assumption and the events in Greece are part of trying to keep this on a life support system. A recent study suggests that 95% of the bail-out funds do not go into the Greek system, but directly into the banks as a way of trying to rebuild the damage caused by irresponsible lending and hedge funds that in the end could not be insured. All the bailout and spiraling debts are based on the assumption of growth — that we can continue to live in a growth paradigm and that the economy is something that can grow infinitely. The IMF and other prominent economists are already beginning to admit that this might not be possible."

From South Africa, Dorah Lebelo Marema sees that "people are realizing that we have to take care of ourselves — our health and wellbeing come first. First, take care of our bodies and then do what you are called to. Create relationships with the people who are excited about what they want to get done. Working in an organic and passionate way, we don't need a driver to push us. We do our work, together — connecting, listening, eating, just being together."

Our egregious consumption of this planet's resources has shattering consequences and that arc of Western civilization is crumbling. Of course, many continue to find what satisfaction they can while conforming to well-established social norms and within the bounds of conventional culture. Some of these people hope that solutions will come from the outside, new technologies which will fix just about everything. Certainly, as our understandings of the workings of our universe continue to expand there are likely to be some remarkable advances. Others hope that an alien invasion from space or an apocalypse or the election of a new heroic leader will save the day.

I'll stand with my friend Dorah, who has been working with rural woman on climate change in South Africa for the last ten years. She sees how new technologies are always touted over the lifestyle changes that ordinary people can implement in their daily lives. Her organization continues to lobby and advocate for people-centered solutions that are context-specific, participatory and use local knowledge. Her organization, GenderCCA helps 1200 women in four provinces mobilize to claim their rights to food security and climate justice. It is continuous, demanding work that requires clear focus and great patience.

Less visible, perhaps, are the incremental changes people are making in their lives and even more invisible are the many who have stepped away and into something new. But many people are looking for new ways to live. Some just start to lead the way. They don't make sweeping promises. They turn to the people they are with and ask "What's important?" They keep their heads down and invite people to co-create the next minimum elegant step. These stories of creating the new, together, are everywhere.

What Are We Willing to Step Towards?

Collectively and individually, we are stepping towards what matters to us — right here, right now, in the communities where we live and with the people we love. We are stepping towards each other, towards health and happiness, and towards the land and nature. We are stepping towards making a difference, solving our problems, addressing our common cause. These steps are reminding us of who we truly are and, with that nudge, opening us to see and welcome in diversity and difference.

In New Orleans Bobbie Hill wrote me about her business partner, Steven Bingler, in the weeks after hurricane Katrina. "He began to convene planners, city officials, architects and other leaders to discuss ways in which we might build a model and framework for a recovery plan. Many people were suspicious of Steven's intentions. He did not let that consume him. We kept our heads down and plowed ahead until we had convinced people that we could all make it happen."

In the US, NewStories had an opportunity to engage with people in communities in West Virginia, New Mexico, Northern California and the Cherokee Nation as part of a listening tour for the Robert Wood Johnson Foundation on creating a "Culture of Health."[33]

---

33 The NewStories Listening Tour in 2016 was amazing. Find out about our Communities Report in the Bibliography

In community after community, we found people stepping towards health. They knew that if obesity, drug abuse, diabetes, unemployment and incarceration were to be changed, they had to do something. It was up to them.

The same kind of clear focus and great patience exhibited by Dorah in South Africa shows up here. Sometimes the results are more immediate — like people who shed 45 pounds in a year, or the area in North Tulsa where every year the 11-year gap in life expectancy compared to other parts of Tulsa is being narrowed down.

These small steps towards something new are mostly invisible. Yuliya Filippovska points out that "in these times it is so easy to fall into the rhetoric that there are no changes. In Ukraine, a new regime takes over the old one, and history repeats itself — nothing changes. However, a lot is happening that is hard to see (and where the changes are actually more sustainable). It is important to bring these stories from the parallel reality forward and to frame what is happening. This empowers people to keep moving!"

We just keep moving. People reach out to each other and start to do what's important. It happens both when circumstances force us to step from our old reality and when we look around and voluntarily step towards a new and largely invisible future.

And Then the Politics

One more thing that becomes clear is that *politics* and *government* can no longer be looked at as dirty words. Sometimes those of us who want to create the new act as if we can do it outside all existing structures of power and authority. That sense of freedom and separation may be important in the beginning when we're just trying stuff, but as we begin to see what works and are ready to amplify it, then we need to turn to policies and politics and governance structures — and change them as needed.

In Chapter 10 I share a little bit about the new story emerging in the fishing village of Onagawa that was 85% destroyed in the tsunami. It was the words of their young mayor that helped me begin to see this theme differently. In early 2016, he spoke to me of how he has three roles. First, he is an individual citizen who loves his community and has his own hopes and dreams. Secondly, he is a politician where the heart of his work is convening people and groups — listening to them and helping them listen to each other. Finally, he is the Mayor with the legal and administrative powers and budget of City Hall to align with what needs to be done. We need the presence of all three roles to create and maintain significant changes.

"What we are witnessing in Greece," Maria Scordialos points out, "is the need for systemic change in governance creating new ways for people to participate more directly with the decisions that influence their lives and generations to come. A new citizen agency emerging where local people on a small scale begin to fill the gaps that the government and the public services have not been able to. In the past five years we have seen local community clinics being established, community pharmacies, complementary currencies, time banks, exchange shops, community kitchens, food drives, homeless centers and care, neighbors helping one another again — a wellspring of solidarity emerging that protects both individuals and the commons. This includes squatting and takeovers of landmark sites under threat, workers continuing to run factories so that they will not shut down, local villagers taking on a huge Canadian gold mining company threatening their pristine environment. Citizen participation is creating a new direct democracy that brings meaning and self-organizing, where community begins to replace institutions, technocrats and bureaucracy. The neo-liberalism paradigm that has spread since the 1980s with the strong belief that a free market will heal everything and that any impediment to this happening — whether the human rights of people, the protection of the environment, the safety of the earth for generations to come — needs to be overcome. These beliefs have resulted in the increased trafficking of people, sweat shops, child labor, climate change, and indigenous lands and people threatened, and must be addressed through politics and policy change."

In New Orleans, Bobbie Hill describes how, early on as rebuilding started after Katrina, "We determined that we needed a public hearing type system that supported the work on the ground. We called this the Community Support Organization. The mayor's office, city council, city planning commission, the community foundation and each of the council districts had a representative that met in city council chambers every two weeks. We offered a planning presentation dealing with a specific component of neighborhood and city-wide issues then gave citizens a chance to ask questions. The sessions were broadcast on public access television live and in between meetings. At the end of all of these meetings both Planning District and Neighborhood Plans and the City-Wide Recovery Plan had to be approved first by the citizens, followed by the City Planning Commission, City Council, the Mayor, then the Governor. At the last Community Support Organization meeting prior to approval, community members stood up and announced that New Orleans and the diaspora were now a community of citizen planners. They understood the vocabulary, the necessity for smart planning, and that these plans belonged to them. Their final request was that the recovery plan that would eventually roll into the City's Master Plan have the force of law. They demanded there be a referendum to amend the City Charter to make this so. This, indeed, happened and is proof that authentic engagement is powerful and the right thing to do."

Dorah writes about how her work has shifted in South Africa. She's no longer out front leading the charge for a new society. Instead, her time is spent behind the scenes, writing proposals, building networks. She's always with a team, supporting others. "People are looking inside of themselves for solutions and then reaching out to other people, organizations and government to collaborate. Coming out of apartheid there was lots of money, but not anymore. We have kind of arrived, with 20 years of democracy, and donors are taking money elsewhere. People are being called to be more innovative, sharing spaces and resources, finding more synergies, creating enabling structures of policies and practices which can be changed, and providing a reference point."

My world is made of stories and when I contemplated the English edition of this book I reached out to some of my friends around the world to help me bring in their wisdom and experience. Those I turned to included:

- BOBBIE HILL from Concordia, Community Based Architecture and Planning in New Orleans. Bobbie's work focuses on helping people whose lives were ravaged by Katrina and other disasters across the country find their way forward. Our mutual friend Meg Wheatley connected us years ago.

- DORAH LEBELO MAREMA from Gender CC — Women for Climate Justice is someone I have referred to often as my fierce Zulu Warrior. We met nearly 15 years ago when Dorah was Executive Director of the GreenHouse Project in Johannesburg, a member of the BerkanaExchange. She has the fire of the present and the wisdom of ages as she stands up for people in South Africa and all over the world.

- MAAIANNE KNUTH from Zimbabwe and the world who was the first woman president of AIESEC, then the co-founder of Pioneers of Change and then the founder of Kufunda. We met back of the beginning of the century when Berkana, NewStories and PeerSpirit were launching From the Four Directions, a global leadership initiative which led to the BerkanaExchange and indirectly to Art of Hosting, both of which I refer to in this book. Maaianne was my first sister of the heart.

- MARIA SCORDIALOS from Greece where she co-founded both Axladitsa-Avatakia and the Living Wholeness Institute which does action research on systemic change, particularly in places where deconstruction of the present system is taking place. We came to know each other in the Berkana Exchange

- JACKIE CAHI, an elder with Kufunda Learning Village who has breathed the air of Zimbabwe her entire life. We met years ago after Kufunda was first founded and have been learning together ever since.

- YULIYA FILIPPOVSKA and I met 15 years ago when she was in her early 20s and a member of Pioneers of Change, a global network of young people committed to learning together about living lives consistent with her values. She's a treasure and a leader in Ukraine.

These stories are just a small sample of what's going on around our planet. Some continue to work in policy frameworks based on what ought to be and with measures and metrics for how we get there. I appreciate their work.

My own attention is more drawn to what is bubbling up at the grassroots. I believe we need to make that work visible and connect it to other work going on. In 2015, my daughter, Annie Stilger Virnig, started working for the Equator Initiative at the United Nations Development Program, available in the bibliography. She works with indigenous peoples and local communities around the equator who are coming up with their own solutions for climate change. It is another example of people stepping forward to reclaim their lives and in so doing, reclaim our world.

We do this reclaiming step-by-step, inch-by-inch. It is our individual, daily choices that matter. In the coming months and years, we will continue to find each other. We will connect with each other. We will share our failures and our successes and we will continue to create the lives and communities we want. Occasionally we will see each other; other times we will not. Sometimes we will be alone and sometimes we will be together. But we are a tribe reclaiming our right to be self-actualizing, interdependent, strong and compassionate human beings. We do this by the choices we make about how we live our lives.

Right now, we are surrounded by a cascading series of climate disasters, fractured economic structures and decaying systems in health, education, governance and more. Things are falling apart. Alongside this collapse the new is rising. People are finding ways to feed themselves and their neighbors, live in healthier ways, engage in work that has meaning, and create beauty.

When I look to Japan and Zimbabwe and Greece and South Africa and Ukraine and the United States, these two worlds of collapse and creativity exist side-by-side. I frequently find myself in the messy middle with one foot in the old and one foot in the new. My own clarity about who I am and the gifts I have to offer often disappears and then, after some agony and uncertainty, reappears. The good news is that these days I notice that I am more able to find my way forward, even when lost! I've been lost more times than I can remember in my work these past five years in Japan.

Gradually I've become more relaxed with uncertainty, comfortable with a future that is only occasionally visible, and content with focusing my attention on right here, right now, on what we have and who I am with.

Not long ago I was part of a small gathering of people from around the United States who are leading various thriving resilient community movements. NewStories has helped to convene the Thriving Resilient Communities Collaboratory (TRCC) as a space for collaboration and learning for people working in many related, but separate enterprises. Some come from national efforts like Bioneers, Post Carbon Institute and Movement Generation. Others come from local efforts like BayLocalize, Thriving Salish Sea and Transition Towns. Different words are used — sustainability, thriving, resilience. But even with all these different labels, they are reaching into the same sea of possibilities.

As I listened to many different people share their work, I was struck by how much we have actually learned about creating healthy, resilient communities. People have been out there working for decades, constructing alternatives to the existing dominant culture. Those alternatives are becoming solid. Sure, we have a long way to go — but we have, in fact, started to move beyond the prototype stages.

I hear the same story in many different places. In, Zimbabwe, at one level, the same old politics continues. At another level, people are getting on with their lives. They are figuring out how to get up in the morning and have a life that works again. They are doing their work — growing food, taking care of children, creating businesses they believe in. And they are doing so by connecting with each other, building relationships, sharing learning, and continuing to walk together into an uncertain future.

Greece? The same thing. With the financial collapse of 2011, many lost almost everything. Rural people and others living at the economic margins saw their scant savings disappear. They are now creating new local economies based on exchanges and many different forms of local currencies. They are discovering what they have, rather than simply being overwhelmed by what they don't.

The story is the same in Japan. In late 2013, I had a chance to spend an evening with people from Fujino, the first Transition Town in Japan. As soon as I walked into the room, I had a sense of a connected community. These were people who knew each other, joked with each other, worked with each other, and supported each other in practices to make a thriving community. It is early still. Most live in both the old world and the world that is emerging. But a new world is indeed emerging. As I wrote earlier, before the Triple Disasters, many times when people in Japan heard about Transition Towns they asked, *Why*? Now they say, *How soon can we begin*?

In 2014 and 2015 I had a chance to visit areas in the US and Canada that have been ravaged by climate disasters. I met with the people there who were rebuilding their communities. Walking through the downtowns of Cedar Rapids, Iowa, and High River, Alberta, both of which were devastated by major floods in 2008 and 2013, respectively, I had a sense of being in one of Japan's coastal towns decimated by the tsunami. Even though it had been 2-6 years since the floods in Cedar, visible wounds are healed both slowly and rapidly. Some first-floor businesses were still closed. Street and sidewalk repairs were fresh. After a disaster, there's a rush to cover the wounds, make it look like everything is fine. But sometimes this just covers the cracks through which something important and new might emerge. There's no simple solution. It is not a linear process. It is an invitation to learn how to stand in the fierceness of uncertainty.

As I have been in and observed many disasters around the world. While there is no linear process to the healing, it's become clear that there are different stages. I've noticed four.

The Great Unraveling. Sometimes everything changes in a long out-breath when all becomes quiet as the ocean recedes and then the full strength of the tsunami rolls forth. Other times it is gradual or sporadic as groceries disappear from shelves and banks close their doors. Sometimes we are shaken awake in time and we realize we are in a time of crises: danger and opportunity. Still other times are like the stories of a frog in boiling water — things happening all around us that we fail to notice — until it is too late to jump out and we "are cooked." (This frequently used story is actually untrue of frogs — they are smarter than that. Are we?)

In our hyper-connected world, there can often be a surreal quality to the unraveling. The old world and the broken exist side-by-side. Some have champagne and caviar in the President's Mansion while others queue for hours for a loaf of bread. A television broadcasts the frenzy of a World Cup as rescue workers pause for a bowl of soup in their search for bodies from a collapsed apartment building.

Emergency and Rescue. Everything is torn apart. People's lives are in danger. Shelter, water, food, sanitation, clothing, health care, and basic infrastructure are needed immediately. Help arrives. Everyone is running as fast as they can. Schools and stadiums are converted into emergency housing. Volunteers come, as do truck after truck with what's needed right now.

The response happens at different speeds in different places in the world. After a catastrophic disaster occurs, the devastation is immediately broadcast on television and through internet reports across the world. There is a world-wide call for relief, for support and action. But when the foundations of people's lives are slowly eroded away as they were in Zimbabwe and Greece, there are no pictures, there is no 24/7 coverage, no call for solidarity with the victims. Often, if mentioned at all, the judgment of "they brought in on themselves" is offered.

In the weeks after the Triple Disasters in Japan, people began to clear away debris, while also continuing the heartbreaking search for the bodies of people who did not survive. At first time passed slowly and then more quickly as the debris was cleared, roads repaired, new convenience stores constructed — and things begin to stabilize.

One of the many miracles in Japan was that by the fall of 2011 temporary housing had been built or found for some 300,000 people. By September, just six months after the disasters, it was possible to take a breath and look out to the future.

Resilience. Then the next stage of work begins. People start to come together, drawing on their own knowledge and resources to make a difference. Everyone's involved — individual citizens, community groups, governmental bodies, businesses, nonprofit organizations. Coordination is scarce — everyone is still running as fast as they can. Separations develop as people feel more obligation to and relationship with particular constituencies and certain funding sources. Yet cooperation also develops as people see someone else whose work can make a difference to their own. New ideas are developed and tested. Not surprisingly, initial attempts often fail. And people keep working.

There is so much to be done. There is an overwhelming sense that there is so much to do. People find themselves doing things they never imagined. Those most committed and involved start to get sick and sometimes are hospitalized.

New relationships are built. People have ideas they never considered before. Sometimes they feel a little guilty because the work is exciting and rewarding — shouldn't they just be sad? New businesses and services start to emerge. Things get better. There is a chance to take a deeper breath, to lift one's gaze from the immediate challenges, and to wonder what is next. This is what was happening in Tohoku by the end of 2013 and early 2014.

The Long Road. For some, it seems like the old normal is back. Things are okay, but not great. All the same issues that were there before the Triple Disasters are still present — but at least it looks normal. Some people simply want to rest in that old normal.

For others, there is a different call. Part of this stems from how everything on the inside has changed. Many of the stories I've shared so far in this book speak of that difference on the inside. Internally everything has shifted. Material prosperity is less important. Relationships and happiness are more important. There is a sense of another world becoming possible. This shift of consciousness is fuel for the long-term work.

In Fukushima and in the coastal areas, there really isn't an old normal to return to. It is gone. In other parts of Japan there is an awakened sense of the old normal not being good enough. Something else is possible. The questions for both situations revolve around the same fundamental question, *What future will we build?*

We also need to understand what we need to do this work. To answer the larger question, we need to answer the "smaller" questions: *What will sustain us as we step into this long-term work? How do we find the confidence we need? What skills and capacities are important? How can we see and think differently than we have in the past? How do we get up each morning and live fully as we step into an unknown future?*

Walking
the
LongRoad
Together

CHAPTER

6

Walking the Long Road Together

WE WILL FIND WHAT'S AFTERNOW TOGETHER. People across all of Japan — not just Tohoku — yearn for lives with more health and happiness. The same is true around the world. It is present everywhere. Often it is still a whisper, but everywhere people are learning how to stand up while continuing to stand together.

Some of us will step into this strangeness. We will find each other there. Doing so means developing the skills and capacities to move with a measure of grace through the first two stages — emergency and rescue and resilience described above. It also means developing the confidence, skills and capacities to walk the long road, together.

We will have more disasters and collapsing systems. We need to respond to them when they happen, bring with us the wisdom and learnings from other disasters, work with the insights and energy which arise, and continue to return to the work of the long road — building a future we want, together.

Tools for the Road

By the late summer of 2012, the long road was beginning to open in the disaster area. For more than a year, my work had been hosting and inviting and supporting people in other parts of Japan. My limited physical strength combined with my insufficient Japanese meant that I was not able to offer much in the emergency and rescue phase, or in the phase of recovering resilience.

An important opening came when I was invited to host others — and host myself — into being sacred outsiders in Tohoku. I was asked to co-host a learning program in Tohoku in August 2012, with Mikako Yusa, one of the members of the "dialogue circle" in Chapter 4.

Organized by Japan for Sustainability, this learning program was for seven youth from Japan and seven youth from the rest of the world, all in their twenties.[34] We went to Tohoku and visited with wonderful people in Ishinomaki, Ogatsu and Kesennuma. There was so much learning for the youth, and for me. I started to understand more about people's experience in communities affected by the disasters and what support they wanted.

This learning journey happened just after I received a grant from Give2Asia that would support my work in Japan. The journey itself was my first deepest step into Tohoku and opened the door for the intense, demanding, rewarding and confounding rest of 2012. After the Japan for Sustainability Learning Journey, I reached out to find the people I could partner with and who would invite me to do the work in cities in the Tohoku region: Otsuchi, Yamada Town, Kesennuma, Sendai, Fukushima City, Minamisoma, and Koriyama. We held many, many gatherings over the rest of the year. In both small groups and large groups. Sometimes it was simply to introduce FutureSession dialogue and approaches; sometimes it was in service of a particular purpose. It was an intense time of helping to open the spaces where people could talk with each other about their grief, about their hopes, and about what they were doing and wanted to do next.

Whenever someone in Tohoku invited me for dialogue or collaboration or FutureSessions, I joined them. The call of my heart and soul said "Just show up. Be there. Stand with the people of Tohoku." And I did. I was a listener as much as I was a dialogue host. I was a witness to people's stories. For people in many communities, those last months of 2012 were the first time they were able to raise their heads,

---

34 People in the US are sometimes surprised when they learn that in Japan as well as in Europe the term "youth" refers not just to teenagers, but to people in their twenties and sometimes into their thirties.

shake themselves off, see who else was standing, and begin to discover how to talk about this heart-wrenching time.

I returned home to the US in mid-December, 2012 and was back in Japan eight weeks later. Almost two years had passed since the disasters. Things had stabilized. The rescue and emergency phase was officially complete; organizations, people and money were being withdrawn from Tohoku. Japan's attention and that of the world were moving on. And yet there was still so much work to do. For the most part, the work of building a future had not yet begun. In some ways, we were just getting to the starting line for the long work ahead.

But everyone was tired — including me. Friends and colleagues were entering hospitals all over Japan — exhausted, sick, and confused. For two years, people had been working ridiculously long hours, with no breaks, giving everything they had. We had scrambled to find money to pay our bills while doing our work to help people and communities. Now there was a sense that we needed to get organized for the long haul. We each asked ourselves, *How could we sustain our efforts, the work, and ourselves?*

In 2012, my work shifted back to NewStories, the nonprofit corporation I had founded in 2000[35]. Lynnaea Lumbard, President of NewStories, invited me to step fully back into NewStories and by 2013, Lynnaea and I had become Co-Presidents. It turned out that there was a rightness to my circling back to NewStories. It was the right base for my work on the long road. This shift moved my gaze from Berkana's emphasis on leadership to our meme of stories at NewStories and helped me see how much a new story was needed — and emerging — in Japan. For those in the coastal areas decimated by the tsunami and those in Fukushima facing exposure from the nuclear explosions, there was no returning to an old normal, to their old story of who they were.

---

35 Berkana's 2009 experiment with self-organization led to terminal exhaustion. By the end of 2011, Berkana entered a period of hibernation. The shift from Berkana was awkward, annoying and a little heartbreaking. It was a challenge to explain to people in Japan's disaster area that the people at Berkana were exhausted and needed to rest. Among other things, I had to confront my own anger and judgments until I gradually came to understand that exhaustion comes in many forms.

And in other parts of Japan, the disasters had cracked open questions of what do they really want, now. What might their new story be?

We made a major push in 2012 and 2013 to keep introducing dialogue methodologies and FutureSessions throughout Tohoku. More and more people were thinking about what's next and how to begin. We planned for more FutureSessions wherever possible and ongoing assessments of what was needed to support a future that was still largely invisible and unknowable.

These early FutureSessions were important. They helped people grieve and reconnect with each other. They created space for people to share ideas and to begin to develop new actions. People across the region used FutureSessions and other approaches to begin to connect with each other around similar themes — food supply, elderly and children services, energy, and community planning. But it didn't feel sufficient. Something was — and still is — missing. Often what was lacking was any sense of an overall context.

Creating a new future is not just recreating the past. It takes another level of dialogue; it takes looking at the larger picture. Asking bigger, deeper questions:

- What do children in Fukushima need to learn to create a new future? Is it the same as for children in other parts of Japan? Probably not.
- How might the layout of neighborhoods and commercial areas and shopping districts in our communities shift from what they were before? See Chapter 10 for how this question was approached in Onagawa.
- We need our elderly in new ways now. How can we reintegrate them and their wisdom rather than moving them to the margins?

Many good things were happening — new ideas, new businesses, and new support structures. But for the most part, they were small, isolated *and* going in many different directions. Given enough time — like the 40-year arc of the local foods movement in the US that I describe later in this chapter — they would become more substantial. But we needed to do something now, not in 40 years. We asked ourselves, *What can accelerate and focus this change?*

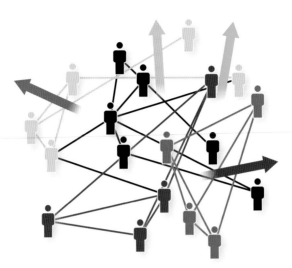

How could we proceed to do something that was bigger than each of us? I think this is the kind of question planners and policy makers ask all the time. But their work is usually done in times of stability, when the way ahead is relatively clear. Plans and policies are a guidance system when we know where we are going.

But what if we are stretching towards an unknowable future? What can give an overall sense of direction towards the new things we want to create? In Japan, these days some people speak of finding their "polar star," something that gives them a sense of a new normal.

How do we begin to find the new stories that would help us create a new normal? What would this new normal look like? How would we find our AfterNow, today?

Many of us working in the region were asking these kinds of questions. At the same time, there was a never-ending boatload of problems and issues needing attention, so the challenge of looking for a new normal was often pushed to the side. This is a common struggle that those recovering from disaster face. How to address people's immediate needs and keep a sense of a bigger picture?

It became clear to me that in addition to witnessing people and their stories and hosting spaces in which they could have dialogues, something else was needed. Different forms and models and tools were required to keep cracking open the present in search of a new normal and an emerging future. I started introducing a number of different ways of looking at the long road. There are, of course, a plethora of models out there. But these were the ones I found myself introducing out of my own experiences and in response to the stories and needs of the people I was working with.

In this chapter and the next, I'll share some of what I found most useful.

Berkana's Two Loops

Around the world many agree that we are in a period of change. Whether we speak in terms of climate change, looming global water shortages, overconsumption of natural resources, or stress in our lives — most people who stop to think about it know we are in a shifting time. It became clear that a framework was needed to ask people to consider important questions in their lives like, *What time is it in the world and in my life? Where are we? Where am I?*

Starting as early as 2010 in Japan, and continuing ever since, I have found that Berkana's Two Loops is a helpful way to start a conversation in which people begin to think with each other about all the different kinds of work needed in our world right now and to get more clarity about what it is they have to offer.

This simple model really isn't a theory of change, as some people sometimes refer to it. It's a map for thinking about what is important to each of us now and where our work lands in a larger system. It was co-discovered and co-created by a number of us from Berkana who helped organize a global learning village at Castle Borl in Slovenia in the summer of 2002.

The Two Loops has proved to be an effective way to help people think about what's going on and where they stand.

And I mean "where they stand" literally! I remember the first time I used Two Loops in Japan. It was a sunny day in May 2010; we went out into a courtyard area next to the meeting room we were using at Tokyo University. With everyone in a big circle, I laid the two loops out on the ground with rope, introducing and explaining as I went along:

There's a curve that life generally follows. Things get better and better, there are some bumps along the way, things peak, they fall apart. Sometimes it's a long curve, sometimes a short one. Nothing lasts forever. Conditions change. This is a simple picture of our reality.

Back in the latter half of the 20th century most people thought we were on an upswing — things were getting better and better. But such curves don't go on forever. They peak, and then they decline (as in the green arrow below). When that happens, some people push to reverse the decline (the red arrow) in order to get back to the "better and better" stage.

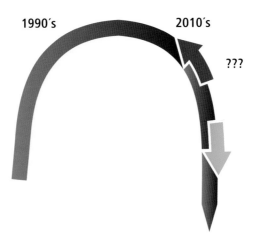

Let me tell a bit of the story from Japan in the context of these two loops. I mentioned the Japan of the 1990s back in Chapter 2, but want to expand on it here and look at it through the Two Loops lens.

When the bubble of a super growth economy burst in Japan in the mid-90s, many thought it was just a temporary setback. Many thought they just needed to keep on doing what they were doing and everything would get better again. "Surely we will get back on track." In the devastating Kobe earthquake of 1995, most people felt that Japan just needed to pursue economic prosperity with more vigor and commitment. For most, Japan was still on the upward swing of the first loop above. Keep going forward. Get back on track.

As the new century was born, some people were wondering if economic prosperity really was the key to happiness. Those who had been successful in the post-war economy were retiring and going hiking in the mountains. The younger people, those born in the final decades of the last century, weren't stepping into the economic machine in the same way their parents had. The people in their 40s and 50s were left "holding the bag" with little support from those older or younger than them.

By 2010, there was a sense that things were not working, that they were falling apart: a growing aging population, many of whom no longer lived with extended families; cracks showing in the public school system; economic stagnation; more and more pressures on the health care system; a general sense of malaise. Things just weren't as smooth and clear as they had seemed. Most people still thought they should push to get back to the old normal — to follow the red arrow back up the slope. Not everyone agreed with that, but many people did. Still, in many circles, people began to speak in terms of old and new paradigms.

Later, after the Triple Disasters in Japan, the green arrow — the decline — became much more visible.

What if what's needed is stabilizing existing systems and letting the parts that no longer serve us fall away? What if we're not trying to return to the old normal, but trying to create a new one? What if we are beginning to let go of the old paradigm of domination and control as we work to create more life affirming ways of living with each other and our small planet?

In Tohoku, especially in Fukushima and in the coastal communities, the old normal was gone. It was a time of great loss and fear. But there were also openings, even excitement, about what was now possible. People were often a bit reluctant to talk about the excitement part — they seemed to feel they were being almost frivolous and disrespectful when they admitted they were having more fun than they ever had in their lives. But both existed side-by-side — the grief and the delight.

In the fall of 2012, Hakozaki-san from Itatemura took me through a PowerPoint he had created. The PowerPoint compared Tokyo and Fukushima in terms of the traditional measure of progress — GNP. In the years before 3.11, Fukushima kept falling further and further behind Tokyo and when the disasters were brought into the picture, the gap between Tokyo and Fukushima looked insurmountable. Hakozaki-san suggested it was clear that Fukushima needed to find a new measure of progress. Perhaps happiness, not money, could be used to create a map for the future. Let go of the old. Create the new.

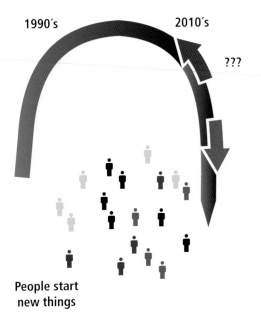

**People start
new things**

In the first decade of this century, more people had begun to step off the line of the old paradigm.

They started new things in many different arenas. Some left Tokyo to live in rural areas. Others began private schools that operated with different principles and values than public schools. Some experimented with renewable energy. Others set up small businesses that didn't require living in major urban areas.

This shift intensified after the Triple Disasters.

In the disaster area itself, people realized they couldn't wait for the government to make everything okay. They had to step forward themselves. I remember the first volunteer center I visited in April of 2011. I mentioned it back in Chapter 2. It was in Ishinomaki and the people there said, "We don't know how to do this. We're teachers. We work in a school. But someone had to step forward and begin to organize centers for the many volunteers and the donations from all over Japan."

And it wasn't just the volunteer centers. As rescue and recovery efforts created a base of stability, so much more work was needed. Support for the people in emergency shelters, support for children, support for the elderly, new businesses, new housing, and on and on and on. The list was endless and people stepped forward.

Most of what they were stepping into was chaotic and complex. There were no rules or guidebooks. But they had to start. They had to address what they saw in front of them. They had to learn as fast as they could. Initially most people worked in small teams in their local area, quickly working on the issues at hand. But as 2011 turned into 2012, people began to reach out to each other across the region. They began to form networks.

These initial networks were important. They enabled people to share information and experiences with each other. They talked about what they were doing — their successes, their failures — and about the changes happening inside of themselves. They began to learn from each other and see where they overlapped. This kind of initial connection was essential. It helped them remember that they were not alone.

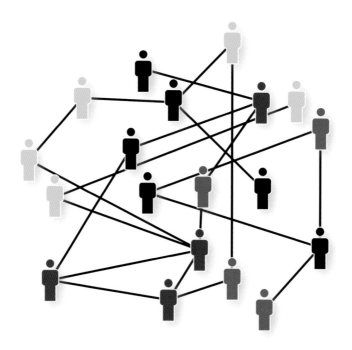

Creating the New

Soon, people who were working on the same themes started to reach out to each other, connecting within communities and between communities to share their experiences and generate new learnings. They began to form networks and to create groups and associations of people tackling similar issues, spread over different communities, businesses and organizations. Forming what is often referred to as "communities of practice," "social labs," or "co-creation labs." The network pictured above began to shift into something more like this:

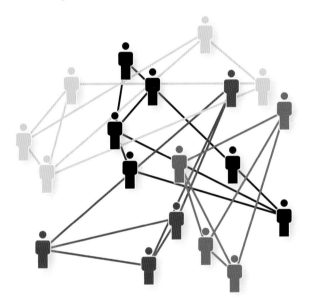

Social Labs and Communities of Practice

At this point, the connections became more refined. People started to seek out those working in the same areas (represented by the colors above), engaged in similar work. The learning started to deepen. Local change began to open the way for broader social transformation.

In Tohoku, some of the themes were very specific: radiation decontamination, growing healthy foods, and support for elderly residents. Other times they were broader: community reconstruction, finding new vision, creating indictors of success. In every case the purpose was the same — bringing people together to learn from each other's experience in order to create something new that makes the communities better. Together, they began to create a new paradigm — they were discovering a new normal for AfterNow. They were building on the long road.

Can this actually happen? Yes, it can. It takes time. It is messy and chaotic, but even still, AfterNow starts to emerge. It isn't — and I suspect can't be — carefully organized. Change is not an orderly process. Often it is only in looking back that we can see progress. Using the Two Loops to map the territory can be helpful in finding our way.

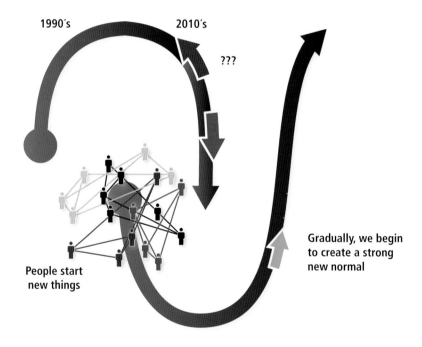

1990's   2010's   ???

People start new things

Gradually, we begin to create a strong new normal

Let me give an example of this phenomenon in a US context. Back in the 70s, some people started "going back to the land." They bought farms and began to grow their own food and, like most innovators and entrepreneurs, at first most of them failed. Some got discouraged and quit. Others kept at it, and kept learning. In 1974,

I invited poet and farmer Wendell Berry to speak at the EXPO '74 Environmental Symposium Series in Spokane. He said it was not only possible, but necessary to find more ways of producing food locally. His remarks led to the formation of Tilth, an early community of practitioners committed to local food production in Washington State. They started talking about what else was needed now. Eventually, among other things, they started working with other people living in urban areas to create Farmers Markets. When I co-founded the Spokane Farmers in the early 90s, it was a new and exciting addition to the community.

Now, almost 40 years after the local foods movement began, "buying local" is a common practice. Costco has a reputation for selling local foods whenever possible. Most supermarkets have local foods sections. All these changes made it possible for people to easily buy local food. Many didn't go through any sort of systemic analysis of the benefits of eating local food — it just made sense. New choices for local food became visible — and people began to cross over to the new.

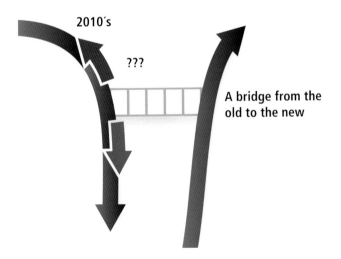

2010's

???

A bridge from the old to the new

The diagram on the next page can help us see what's going on and can be a useful way for us to figure out where our own work resides. Though as with all maps, it can't show all the variables.

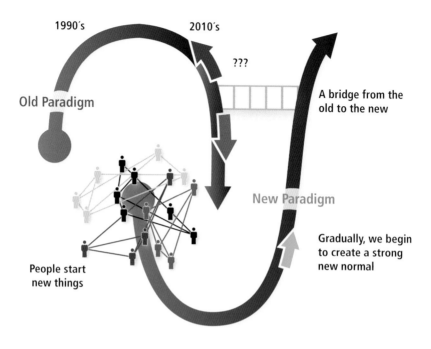

Here are some other things to keep in mind:

1. Much of what we do doesn't work! Things fall apart. We have to persevere, take one step at a time.

2. The social labs and communities of practice pictured in the diagram for creating the new are needed at all stages of the process.

3. People in the old paradigm also need to be learning with each other, as do the people building bridges.

4. Likewise, bridge building — inviting others to try something new — is going on throughout.

5. Finally, it is helpful to keep the whole model, the whole system in heart/mind. Many different people are doing the work they are called to do; offering their gifts and insights is what sets the stage for transformation.

I will often lay the two loops and the bridge out on the floor and ask people to go stand where they are now working. I then invite them into conversation with those nearby with the following questions:

- What is your work?
- How does your work help the overall system?
- What can you offer and what do you need from other parts of the system?

I have found that people see this as a helpful way to think about their own work — right now. I know it helps me release the tension that builds up in my body when I try, unsuccessfully, to figure everything out in my head. It helps me relax a bit into the chaos swirling around me.

Like the other frameworks introduced briefly in this chapter, Two Loops helps people see their work and their life as part of a larger pattern. Transformation happens both with agonizing slowness and in the blink of an eye. The work of transformation takes perseverance, persistence and patience. Two Loops helps to make the larger system visible. It also makes it easier to see the importance of the many different kinds of work required in a period of transformation. There are several other frameworks I want to mention as well. I use them less frequently than Two Loops, but each of them offers a way to see the larger system.

Berkana's Name-Connect-Nourish-Illuminate

As colleagues and I continued to work throughout the disaster area and across Japan, we became aware of the "spottiness" of our efforts. We were all doing good work in many different places, but how could it lead to a shift at the systems level. I was reminded of our work at Berkana when we started thinking about the progression from networks to communities of practice to systems of influence. We built a model on top of the Two Loops framework:

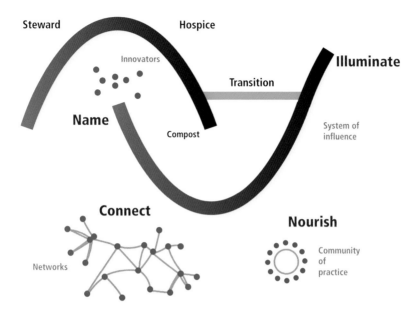

People who have stepped off the "business as usual" track of the first loop are early innovators who are trying new things. Often those things don't even have a common name in the beginning. Eventually a **name** begins to emerge. Because of that name, because of some common vocabulary, people begin to **connect** with each other, forming loose networks. Sometimes they begin to deepen their interactions and develop some disciplined ways of learning together. They become social labs and communities of practice that **nourish** each other's work. As this continues, they come to a point where they are ready to share, and they begin to **illuminate** their work to others, and begin to create systems of influence.

At Berkana we believed that these parallel and overlapping progressions — name, connect, nourish and illuminate — and the forms they take — networks, communities of practice, systems of influence — were important ways of thinking about transformation. As I've continue to use these frameworks, I've realized that what's most important in creating these systems of influence is where we start to find transformation — through a spreading influence things begin to happen, well, naturally.

There are many ways in which these systems of influence are created. Some of those I find most useful follow.

Reos Transformative Scenario Planning

Working across Japan, it became clear that a new story was needed — something that might help bring the good work occurring in many communities into a new coherence. Some of us began to wonder if Transformative Scenario Planning might help.

Developed by Adam Kahane and popularized by Reos Partners, Transformative Scenario Planning (TSP) is a way to engage a diverse group of people in imagining what might be. Traditional scenario planning work is *adaptive*. It works from a mindset that the future is somewhat fixed and we must adapt our actions to match the future that is coming towards us. Transformative Scenario Planning is different in outlook; rather than adapting to a future coming towards us, it invites us to be authors of our own destiny.

Adam began discovering this approach in 1992 when he was one of the facilitators for the Mont Fleur dialogues, which brought together a broad mix of South Africa's political, business and civil society leaders. They came from the left and right, the opposition and the government and shaped how apartheid ended and the future of South Africa actually unfolded.

More recently, TSP has been helpful for envisioning different pathways for South Africa's future. Using TSP, the Dinokeng Scenarios[36] brought together a diverse group of stakeholders, worked with them to generate enough trust so that they began to be willing to listen to each other and then to engage their imagination to think together about what was possible. Adam's book, *Transformative Scenario Planning*, published in English in 2012 and in Japanese in 2014, gives a detailed description of this process.

The basic idea here is that if we are going to shift a system, we need a new story of what else might be possible. Whatever the topic — prison reform, new food systems, peace in zones of conflict, building new communities — people with very different points of view must come together, build relationships and develop trust, and begin to

---

36   By 2010 conditions in South Africa were becoming tense. The promise of prosperity for all with the end of apartheid wasn't being realized. A culture of blaming was developing. The Dinokeng Scenarios helped to shift this.

envision new possibilities together. From a process point of view, almost all of the FutureSession stages and steps and principles described in the preceding chapter apply. Transformative Scenario Planning is organized around five key steps:

1. Convene a team from across the whole system.

2. Observe what is happening.

3. Construct stories about what could happen.

4. Discover what can and must be done.

5. Act to transform the system.

Independently organized and loosely connected local action creates meaningful change and can make things better for some people. TSP, like Berkana's Name-Connect-Nourish-Illuminate, is a way to situate work within a larger context with an eye towards creating a larger transformation.

Indicators of Success in Brazil

Any time we are committed to building new systems and making substantial changes, we must figure out how to measure and evaluate what we're doing. For the first two years in Japan, the emphasis was on getting the obvious things done. By 2013 there was enough space that people started to ask "How do we know if we are headed in the right directions?" In some ways, this is an easier question in times of stability, when there is a future ahead of us that we collectively see. We create plans and goals and have measurements and metrics to assess our progress. But what about those times — like the ones we live in — when so much is in a freefall?

Talking about this with colleagues in Japan, we started to realize that we needed new ways of measuring our progress. We needed new indicators of success, and I was reminded of some excellent work in Brazil.

In 2008, I had the opportunity to work with people in Sao Paulo, Brazil. They had organized a broad coalition of civic organizations — Nossa Sao Paulo — and had come up with an unusual way to create new stories for their future. The name translates as "Sao Paulo for All of Us" and they worked together to pass a new law that required the City of Sao Paulo to make their indicators of success visible. The law didn't say what the indictors should be; just that the city ought to be able to tell the public what it was planning to do. The law passed and local officials were left scratching their heads. They turned back to the civic organizations that had passed the law and said, "We need help!"

It took some time. Community meetings were held to help determine the themes for improvements and then task forces worked to identify a wide range of specific and broad goals. They ranged from a shelter for passengers waiting for the bus on a particular corner to a comprehensive health plan for older citizens. For the first time, all of these ideas and indicators were visible to the whole community. It was a grand mosaic. It was not organized in the methodical way of Transformative Scenario Planning — but it made new possibilities visible and started a public dialogue on what was important. It invited people to focus on what was important for them and to look beyond towards a larger system. Perhaps most importantly, it suggested to people that success was something that could be thought about and defined.

Nossa Sao Paulo continues to act as a catalyst for local action in one of the world's largest urban areas.

I told the story of Nossa Sao Paulo in many meetings in Japan in 2013. It became part of a conversation that sprang up about how new indicators for success were needed now. Just as the idea of scenarios was somewhat novel in Japan, the idea of consciously creating indicators of success was new. By bringing in these new approaches, it created another way of stimulating people's imaginations. It didn't lead to a "Japan For All of Us" initiative, but it has become part of the conversational fabric for people involved in social innovation. These days I hear people using the language of *indictors of success* as a way to focus dialogues about next steps.

US Community and Regional Futures Initiatives

In 2013, two years after the Triple Disasters, I continued to bring in other ways to help people think about what they wanted in their future and about what they could do right now to move towards those possibilities. I began telling more stories from my earlier years of work. Back in the 70s and the 80s many states as well as local communities in the US engaged in a variety of futures initiatives. I had the pleasure of working on a number of them. The Institute for Alternative Futures continues to do this work. When we started talking about new stories in Japan in 2013, my mind raced back to the early-eighties in Spokane, Washington — the community where I have lived since 1973. We created a community futures program — FutureSpokane — that is another example of how new stories for the future are created. At the time, I was the Executive Director of a nonprofit community development corporation, Northwest Regional Facilitators.

We found two unlikely partners who were connected to very different parts of the community — the regional public university — , Eastern Washington University, and Spokane's most elite women's civic organization, the Junior League. No one would ever have expected the three of us to be partners! After a lot of groundwork, we convened a "Committee of 100" — leaders with diverse expertise and interests and very different opinions — and brought them together for three full days to imagine what Spokane's future might be.

During those three days, the participants identified ten areas for community improvement and specific projects they were willing to invest their time, energy and social capital in creating. These ideas were publicized widely, and we invited anyone from the community to join task forces to further develop the ideas and to begin creating actual projects. It was an energizing process.

Twenty-five years later some of us who had led this community initiative came together to look at what had been proposed and what had happened. We were amazed and delighted to find that almost every single idea raised at that three-day Committee of 100 session had come to be a reality. Not because of a strategic plan or a single coordinated effort — but because the dreams and aspirations of the community had been made visible in a way that allowed people to work for the common good.

This experience turned out to be a good example of how to design a structured convening process that stretches over months and years as a way of engaging the community. This is long term work and we often don't see results until many years later.

Creating Reality on TV: South Africa

You've probably noticed a certain commonality in each of
the approaches I've named so far: they each make possibilities visible. I started looking for more examples of these kinds of approaches. I didn't expect that people in Japan would simply "adopt" any of
them whole — but I wanted to illustrate — , through my stories, that
there were many ways of creating more coherence creating the conditions for transformation or systems shift, and creating systems of influence. One example I started sharing was how this had been done on
a broad scale in South Africa. The South African Soul City Institute
created the Kwanda Reality TV Program. Five townships in different
parts of South Africa were chosen for this effort. People in each of these
townships received training in Asset Based Community Development
(ABCD).[37] Receiving a small working budget, the townships were challenged to use their own wisdom and local resources to make their communities great places to live. The TV program filmed it all — people
talking, people disagreeing and agreeing, people working together to
build new parts of the community and the physical improvements that
resulted.

In 2009, it became one of the most popular television shows in
South Africa. I know. I was there when week after week people inter-
rupted whatever they were doing to turn the television set on. All five
townships improved. One was a big winner and received additional
resources and support. People all over South Africa and other neighboring countries were both informed and inspired by the way these
communities used what they had to build the communities they wanted. The ideas demonstrated in the program reverberated across the
whole region. They shared a new way of organizing, of building from
what they had — a new story.

---

37 Something almost identical to ABCD is what's called JIMOTOGAKU in Japan.
Gaku is school and jimoto is the local area. So, literally, learning from the lo-
cal area. The first wide scale of jimotogaku in Japan started in Minamata,
the town made infamous for the mercury poisoning that occurred there.
Later in Chapter 8 it is the core of one of the Stepping Stones: "Use What We
Have"

Speaking about Kwanda to people in Japan helped to open their eyes and stimulate their thinking. They saw how it was similar to a popular daytime TV program in Japan that is built around a television personality who shows up in different cities and towns to interview people about their lives and their treasures.

There's something very powerful about being witnessed — by a TV series or by a television personality or even by a neighbor. This is a process of honoring and when work is honored, it becomes more visible to those doing the work. There are powerful lessons here: Seek out what's working and figure out how to amplify it. Concentrate less on solving problems and more on magnifying opportunities.

Warriors Without Weapons from Brazil

Much of my work in Japan has been with people in their 20s and 30s who had a strong itch to take action now. They were happy to be in dialogue with each other and older folks as well — but they were eager for action. I started introducing another way of making new stories called Warriors Without Weapons, developed by my Brazilian friends at the ELOS Institute. ELOS was formed by young architectural students who had the radical idea that what they were learning could be used to help people improve their own lives. They didn't want to just engage in endless talking; they had a deep hunger for immediate action.

They developed Warriors Without Weapons as a month-long program which literally builds community. Started in 1998, it continues today. Each year, about 60 people, mostly in their 20s, come together from all around the world. Originally, they spent a month in Brazil; now they gather in other parts of the world as well. But they typically work in three communities in the same region of Brazil — designed so they can all be together as well as working in three separate teams. They come into relationship with the people in each community and then they dream together about what would make a difference in the community. Immediately, they begin to build that dream together. Relationships create a fabric that holds dreams; dreams make a horizon towards which we can walk visible.

WE LEARN TO SEE ABUNDANCE
where others see scarcity

WE FOSTER KINDNESS
before fear and judgement

WE VALUE DREAMS
as the best impulse to create change

WE WALK TOGETHER simultaneously taking care
of ourselves, of each other and of a common dream

WE GUARANTEE AN EXTRAORDINARY RESULT
in the form of a gift for oneself and for others

WE RECOGNIZE AND CELEBRATE the individual
contribution to the collective achievement

And **WE EVOLVE ON THIS JOURNEY** propelling the
CONSTRUCTION OF NEW DREAMS!

This graphic is from the Warriors Without Weapons manual.

Warriors Without Weapons events are now organized all over the world and there is even a new virtual course. I hope they will come to Japan one day. This is one time when I think bringing in the form, whole, might work. Though, of course, it will be digested and reborn in a Japanese way.

It's clear to me is that youth in Japan and all over the world will be the ones who see and drive the changes needed. Those of us who are older need to come into respectful relationship with youth. We have much we can learn from each other. Together we are wiser and stronger. Warriors Without Weapons, and efforts like it, can help youth develop the confidence they need to step into this role of creators of a new future. To the benefit of all.

Each of these different frameworks presented in this chapter are ways of creating new stories. I could offer numerous other examples, but I think this is enough to give you the idea. The frameworks used are different; the stages are essentially the same. In each case, it is about people coming together and living their way into new stories. A small group of people begin to talk about an idea. They figure out who they should invite to join them — always with an alertness for diversity. They engage people and use dialogue in its many forms to help people build trust. They dream and imagine and yearn together — and then they begin to bring their imagination into physical form. They take action.

This is how we begin to create new stories. We create them through relationships because life everywhere is a relational ecosystem. We are part of what Duane Elgin has described as a living universe. No matter how brilliant we think our ideas are, we err and we create damage when we forcefully apply our own ideas and models on others. There is a balance between making things happen and pausing to watch for what is trying to emerge. I keep strengthening my capacities to listen and when appropriate offer some idea or insight from my listening. This is key to my evolving understanding of the dance of intention and surrender. And it is core to my own evolving understanding of leadership that is summed up in an expression from Lao Tzu:

Go to the people. Live with them.
Learn from them. Love them.

Start with what they know.

Build with what they have.

But with the best leaders, when the work is done,
the task accomplished, the people will say,

We have done this ourselves.

Discovering
Right
Action

CHAPTER

7

Discovering Right Action

As I worked around Japan in 2013 and into 2014, the situation had stabilized, but much remained unclear. Things continued to shift. There was so much to do. In my teaching and hosting I made regular reference to three particular ways of sensing what to do and figuring out how to act. These were Otto Scharmer's Theory "U", Joanna Macy's framework for Active Hope, and David Snowden's Cynefin Framework. I believe each is a powerful lens to look toward new possibilities. I won't try to fully describe any of these here, but I'll share the basic ideas as I've presented and worked with them, with references for your further exploration.

Discovering New Directions with Theory U

I'm an organizer and an activist. I like to get things done. Sometimes, in my haste to get things done, I do the wrong things. Truly embracing systemic change requires that we slow down, even stop, and step outside our habitual patterns of response. I've been working on cultivating patience and slowness for decades now. I turn to Theory U[38] because it reminds me to slow down!

---

38 Otto Scharmer's *Theory U* was published in 2000, and it has been a powerful guide for many large and small change initiatives around the world. The Presencing Institute, global home for this approach has many useful resources.

I introduced the basic elements of Theory U in many FutureSessions in Japan. Some people already had some knowledge of the concept because Otto Scharmer's *Theory U: Leading from the Future as It Emerges* was translated into Japanese in 2010. Perhaps more importantly, aspects of the approach resonated with Japanese culture.

In the early 2000s, Otto Scharmer and I exchanged e-mails from time to time. It felt to both of us that there was a deep connection to in our work. But it wasn't until I was reading some of his working papers and articles that I discovered some commonalities in our research. Otto found that business leaders he interviewed when developing his Theory U were guided by the same first three practices I found when working with younger activists to develop my theory of Enspirited Leadership. Our language is different (Mine: let your calling find you, stop and be still, stay connected. Otto's: opening our minds, our hearts and our will), but the essence is the same.

This illustration from the Presencing Institute shows the different dimensions of Theory U

THEORY U

FOUR LEVELS of
LEARNING and CHANGE

1: REACTING	DOWNLOADING PAST PATTERNS		PERFORMING by OPERATING from the WHOLE
2: REDESIGNING	SUSPENDING	OPEN MIND	EMBODYING
	SEEING with FRESH EYES		PROTOTYPING the NEW by LINKING HEAD, HEART, HAND
3: REFRAMING	REDIRECTING	OPEN HEART	ENACTING
	SENSING from the FIELD		CRYSTALLIZING VISION and INTENTION
4: PRESENCING	LETTING GO	OPEN WILL	LETTING COME
		PRESENCING CONNECTING to SOURCE	

Presencing Institute - Otto Scharmer - www.presencing.com/permissions

PRESENCING
INSTITUTE

But before offering a brief introduction to Theory U, let me explain why I find it so valuable. It helped me see that I can easily get trapped at Level 1 Change — just reacting. I download information as quickly as I can and act immediately. Everything I download is filtered through my existing biases and perceptions, which means I miss a lot. This capacity to act quickly is helpful when there's a life-threatening crisis or emergency or when we're dealing with something simple and ordinary — but it is not really helpful if we're trying to create something new.

Theory U is an invitation to pause, to be still and to open our mind, our heart and our will. It asks that we throw ourselves wide open and suspend the voices of suspicion and judgment that often preclude us from seeing what else might be possible.

- **Opening Our Minds** means engaging in an open-hearted inquiry about what else is possible in particular situations. We step away from the easy conclusion or course of action that is based on what we think we already know, and we step into inquiry. This inquiry can take many forms. It may simply be a dialogue in a FutureSession where we generate ideas and gather information and insights from those present. It might be compiling a list of diverse people to interview. Obviously, it can also include more conventional research in libraries and on the Internet. Perhaps it includes a learning journey where a group of people goes together to explore how others are addressing the issue under consideration.

- **Opening Our Hearts** means listening to what we encounter with all of our senses — listening more deeply than we ever have before. We listen to draw ourselves into a territory where the unseen becomes visible. In addition to looking at what we have gathered with our open minds, we listen just as deeply to the knowledge and wisdom within ourselves. We dwell in a place of openness rather than in a place of rushed conclusion. Often, we do this together, speaking to each other from a place of wonder and curiosity with an eagerness to unveil more and more possibilities.

- **Opening Our Will** means going deeper still. We take the insights from our minds and from our hearts and we go into even deeper silence. Often times this means going out and spending hours or days in nature and in the quiet, alone. It means accessing our creativity through journaling or writing poetry or painting or drawing. It means sitting with uncertainty and ambiguity with no need to come to a premature closure, but to stay in openness watching for what else will arise. We wait for the glimmer, for that which arises from a new place and attracts our attention.

This brings us to the bottom of the U, to the luscious place of letting go and letting come. I'd been working for years on letting go, long before I ever heard of Theory U. But letting come? What a delightful extension. It means, simply, from that place of letting go, being able and willing to stand in a place of complete porousness to see what arises, of its own accord. We find an access to a deeper intelligence. Some call it "soul's knowing"; others speak of it as "collective intelligence." I think of it as a field beyond all names where wisdom and insight live, ready to come to us when welcomed in. This for me is the realm of KAMI, the Japanese spirits — where insight, wisdom and help are available just beyond the boundaries of our rational minds.

> *Out beyond ideas of wrongdoing and rightdoing,*
> *there is a field. I'll meet you there.*
> *When the soul lies down in that grass,*
> *the world is too full to talk about.*
> *Ideas, language, even the phrase each other*
> *doesn't make any sense*
>
> — *Mewlana Jalaluddin Rumi*

In that place of letting go and letting come, we start to see possible ways forward. It is not time to rush. It is time to be slow and filled with care as we work to bring something with new form into the world. Scharmer describes this coming in three stages:

- **Crystalizing** is the work of taking an initial insight and giving it shape and form. The insight is the raw material. We work with it; look at it from different angles. We talk together about it. We ask questions about what might be served through this insight: *"What territory might it open?"* We stay in an open-minded inquiry with ourselves and others so that we begin to see more and more of the idea.

- **Prototyping.** As our insight begins to crystalize in our minds, we begin the work of giving it form in the material world. Perhaps we bring in some different media — clay, drawing, pipe cleaners, Legos — to see what shape we can give to the idea, to see what it would actually look like. Whether we're working on something that is intangible, like a new local currency system or a plan for a new co-working space, we use physical objects to map it out. We begin to make the possibility visible. Initial prototypes that we develop in a room give way to the actual working prototype we will construct and learn from in the larger world. For instance, before creating a new hydroponics factory to grow massive amounts of tomatoes, let's begin with a small version where we grow the first 500 and learn from our efforts.

- **Performing.** Eventually we learn enough through our prototypes and experiments that we're ready to go to the next stage. We've developed confidence and figured out how to tell the story in a way that we're able to raise the additional support we need — financing, labor, investments of all sorts. We begin. And, of course, even in beginning, we continue to learn.

The full description of Theory U is much more complex and filled with a wide variety of considerations. I invite you to explore it further.

For my part, I will add that I often experience the right-hand side of the U itself as a prototype, which is constrained by a linear orientation towards production and performance. I suspect that prototyping is most powerful when it is released into an ecosystem of energy and possibilities rather than being pursued in a more limited, controlled and owned fashion.

Many of the workshops I've hosted in Tohoku and other parts of Japan have followed the trajectory of Theory U. We come together. We pause. We go to a place of letting go and letting come. We see new possibilities and we act together to make them real.

Moving Grief: Finding Active Hope

The air was thick with grief when I first arrived in Japan after the disasters. One of the dynamics of a collective culture like Japan is that grief spreads quickly, everywhere. The entire country was in mourning. When we convened our first Youth Community Leadership Dialogue in May of 2011, we knew we would need to do something with the grief in the air.

I turned instinctively to the work of my longtime friend and colleague Joanna Macy[39]. Referred to originally as despair and empowerment work, Joanna has identified a journey of four stages that helps to transform the anger, sadness, fear and emptiness of despair into fuel for active hope:

- Discover Gratitude

- Honor the Pain

- See the World with New Eyes, Not as a Problem, Just as It Is

- Go Forth

In Japan, where there is always an eye to the aesthetic, we instinctively knew that beauty would need to be an integral component of this work as well. The presence of beauty would make the work of each of these four stages more accessible.

I often recall our first Youth Community Leaders Dialogue in May, 2011. Coming together as a community, we sat in circle and then sent everyone out into the surrounding beauty of nature. We asked them to go and return in silence, thinking about their experience of the two months since the disasters. We also asked them to bring back an object to place in the center of our circle. When we came back into the circle an hour later and began to build the center, someone jumped up immediately and placed a large pine bough in the middle. It was a

---

39   Joanna Macy's work stands at the intersection of Buddhism, Systems Theory and Deep Ecology. In the U.S., her work is usually referred to as The Work That Reconnects or The Great Turning. Eventually in Japan we started referring to it with the title of her 2012 book *Active Hope* — which translates easily and clearly.

little unusual for her to have moved in so quickly; usually there is more silence in Japan. Later, I understood why.

One by one people stepped forward in silence and placed their objects in the center. I was amazed. Collective beauty started to emerge: a center to hold us and the work we were doing. Later, I spoke with Toshiko Yokoyama[40] about why she had stepped forward with a pine bough as we began. She explained her background with Ikebana — flower arranging — and said she had consciously gone out to seek a foundation for the center that would be able to hold it all.

We used one of Joanna's exercises as part of this Youth Community Leaders Dialogue. We knew we needed something powerful to honor the pain in the room. I e-mailed Joanna; she happened to be home. She sat down and typed out the "Seven Generations" exercise, where people are in a circle within a circle, facing one another. In the inner circle, facing out to people on the outer circle, are "present beings" — people from these times. On the outer circle, facing in, are "future beings" — seven generations from now. What happens over an hour is a powerful dialogue across these generations. Hosting this process takes a lot of energy and, frankly, I wasn't sure I could do it — but I knew it was essential.

In the beginning, I asked a question on behalf of the future beings to their ancestors living today:

1. Ancestor, I have heard stories about the times in which you lived. Some of what I am told is very hard for me to believe. They tell us three disasters descended on Japan at the same time: earthquake, tsunami, nuclear radiation. They tell us that even before these disasters, chemicals were being released into water, soil and air when people actually knew that they would cause sickness. They tell us that billions of people around the world lived without clean water, food and shelter while others lived in great luxury. Is that really true? Tell me. And if it is true, what is that like for you?

---

40 Toshiko is co-founder of the Process Works Center of Japan and one of the facilitators for this first dialogue.

The ancestors are always quiet in the beginning, and then they begin to speak. After a short period of time — 5 or 6 minutes — I asked the pair to bow with thanks to each other and for the future being to move counter clockwise to the ancestor on their right. I then asked a second question, followed by a move, and then a third:

2. Ancestor, I have heard the songs and stories that tell of what you and your friends did back then to bring us back into right relationship with each other and this planet we love. What I want to know is how did you start? You must have felt lonely, facing great obstacles especially at the beginning. What were the first steps that you took?

3. Ancestor, I know you didn't stop with those first actions on behalf of Earth. It is clear to us that it is not so much what you are doing in this instant that is most important, but the fact that you don't stop — that you keep on going. Tell me, where do you find the strength to do what you are doing?

Then I asked the fourth question to the future beings, on behalf of their ancestors: You have listened to three ancestors speak, now speak to the one in front of you as if speaking to all three:

4. What is in your heart and mind to say to them, having listened to their stories? What is important to you in your own life, now?

Something incredible happened. As I began to host this circle, I felt the strong presence of Fran Macy, Joanna's husband who had died in early 2009. Fran was a good friend who had spent many years working with people near Chernobyl after the horrifying accidents there. Fran knew about the grief caused by nuclear disasters. I could sense that Fran's spirit was there, hosting me as I hosted this circle. This may sound "woo woo" to some, but these are the kinds of experiences so far beyond my imagination that I can't make them up. Japan is the land of non-material beings, the land of KAMI — the godlike essence present in every tree and animal and rock and ancestor. Fran's KAMI, beyond any doubt, was with us that day.

Since this small beginning in 2011, a number of us familiar with Joanna's work have been finding ways to introduce it in Japan. It took until May of 2014 to find the right opening to bring it into Fukushima. My good friend Hide Enomoto and I held a two-day workshop at Renshoan, a place of deep beauty near Koriyama City in Fukushima Prefecture.

We led people through the four stages:

- **Discover Gratitude.** We began by helping people reconnect with their gratitude for life, for their relationships and for this beautiful planet that nurtures us. It's a little like asking people in disasters what they have, rather than what they need. Gratitude turns our eyes and our hearts to what we have, to all that we have to be grateful for. Sometimes a little time and patience is required to help people redirect their gaze from their pain and grief to their gratitude, but when they do so, they begin to find a place to stand.

- **Honor the Pain**. Next, we worked together to honor the pain that was present. The intent was not to transform the pain or try to make it go away — both pretty impossible tasks — but rather to let it freely move through us. Expressing the pain, letting it out, no longer holding it in, doesn't transform the pain so much as it transforms the person. When we hold it in, it becomes poisonous and eats away at our hearts and spirit. When we let it out, it becomes fuel for active hope. Once it is out, we stay present to it, honoring it.

- **See the World With New Eyes, Not as A Problem, Just as It Is.** The next stage is using a variety of processes to open our eyes further. We seek to see the world for what it is. The intent is not to make things around us wrong or right, but just to look squarely at them and see them for what they are.

- **Go Forth.** Looking at the world as it is, we begin to find our own place. We look for greater clarity about the work we can do to transform ourselves and the world. We look for next elegant minimum step.

This May 2014 workshop helped me see the deep power of this framework. The grief was palpable. I remember the exquisite silence as one woman spoke of how she returned each week to clean her home in Itatemura, which she was forced to evacuate in the weeks after the nuclear explosions. She will likely never be permitted to live there again — but she returns each week to honor it. I recall a sense of gratitude and ease in the room when one middle-aged activist who had worked non-stop for more than three years declared she would begin to take one day a week for herself. There was a collective sigh of relief.

People connected with their pain, their grief, their hope and their resolve in those three days.

I've had a chance to introduce these four stages in a variety of settings since that first youth dialogue in 2011. The experience is always a powerful one. It is not about healing or changing anything. It is about simply creating a place of safety where people are able to look their anger, fear, sadness and emptiness in the eye. The effect is transformative.

A community has been forming in Japan around the framework of Active Hope. In 2015, my friend Hide Enomoto and I were offering workshops on Active Hope all across Japan, and in early 2016 the Japanese translation of *Active Hope* was published. The network of people who Hide called together to publish the Japanese translation have become a community of practice that is now becoming a system of influence as it offers workshops on Active Hope across Japan.

Locating the Starting Line: Cynefin Framework

Sometimes those of us working in Tohoku since 2011 got discouraged. It seemed like evertime we took three steps forward, we took two steps back. This seems true everywhere we are working to create transformative change.

Isn't there an easier way? Can't someone figure this out?

I have found myself turning to the Cynefin[41] Framework to help me make sense of all of this. It has helped me understand our current realities and how to move forward.

The Cynefin Framework suggests that when we're doing our work in the world, we find ourselves in four different kinds of situations:

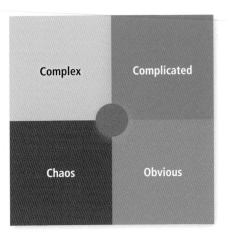

- **In obvious,** we know what to do. We just need to go ahead and do it.
- **In complicated,** it takes a little longer, but we can figure it out and get things done.
- **In complex,** we start to be confounded, not sure how to proceed
- **In chaos,** we're usually overwhelmed, uncertain and unsure.
- The space in the middle is **confusion**. Where it all starts.

---

41   A more complete overview of the Cynefin Framework is available on the NewStories website

These five domains are different sizes. My own default state is to picture them like this:

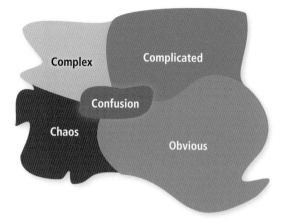

At first glance, a lot seems obvious and straightforward — let's get on with it. Some is complicated and will take a little more time. There's a little bit that's complex and then there are some things that are chaotic. Oh, and yes, there is still some confusion in the middle.

But when I pause, what I am able to see is that our world — especially our world in Tohoku — looks more like this:

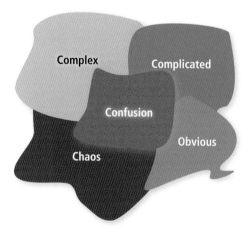

Right after the Triple Disasters, much of what we did was obvious. But I do not in any way mean to say it was easy. It was heartbreakingly hard. But it was obvious. Feed people. Shelter people. Find those missing. But then, in some ways, as we started to make progress on the mess, things actually became more confusing!

I have to admit I don't like confusion very much. Especially, I think, as an American, I tend to look at a situation through the lens of the skills and experience I have and I want to act immediately — remember Level 1 Change in Theory U from a few pages ago. I want to ignore any confusion. Many of us are much more comfortable with incorrect certainties than we are with correct uncertainty.

But after we've taken care of the obvious, the space in the middle is where we always must begin. We find our next steps by being in our confusion together.

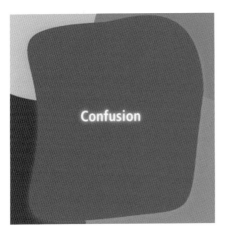

Confusion

As I look back on the spring and summer and fall of 2011, mostly I spent time being with others in our confusion. It was so important to stay there! The Triple Disasters were confusing and overwhelming; we all had to stop, connect with others, before we could begin to find pathways forward. It is in places like this that I'm so thankful for Theory U, because it reminds me to open myself to what is truly present in the whole system. Usually it's best to do this kind of presencing work together — which is where all my emphasis on dialogue comes from. We sit together, sense together, and begin to realize which of the four domains will help us understand how to approach the work ahead.

Obvious

We usually know what to do in obvious situations. We take a deep breath, look around, gather up our courage, think about where this problem fits, and get to work. It is possible to actually know what is going on.

This is the space where "Best Practices" usually work. People have been in similar situations and have figured out what to do. We can learn directly from past experience and apply it. We still need to take the time to step back and develop an overall sense of the situation, then organize or categorize that sensing, and finally respond. There's often hard work, but the way forward is pretty clear and we often have a good sense of the obstacles we are likely to encounter.

Complicated

Complicated is, well, a little more complicated.

The work required in Japan after rescue and emergency was more complicated. People had to stop and think. They needed to sense what they could about the situation and then begin to analyze what's needed and what's possible. Getting roads rebuilt and trains running, cleaning up and removing mega-tons of debris, rebuilding shops and services — these are all things with many moving parts, complicated but with a predictable relationship to each other. Things that are complicated are still knowable.

Sometimes we need to ask for help from outside experts. Systems thinking, different kinds of scenario planning, various means of categorizing and analyzing are all very helpful here. We may not know what to do in the beginning, but this is a domain of the knowable — we can figure it out. And while there usually isn't a single best practice for how to proceed, once we have analyzed the situation, there are often several different good practices, depending on the skills of those present in the system. We can get this done!

Complex

Now it gets more difficult. More daunting. We have moved to the complex and unpredictable. Indeed, this is the domain of much work in the coastal areas and Fukushima today — where we must create a new future.

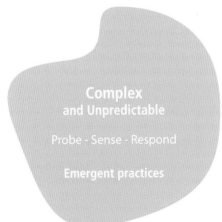

Complex
and Unpredictable

Probe - Sense - Respond

Emergent practices

In Japan, around the world and in our own minds, we keep asking — why can't we just get this done? Why does it feel, often, like we are almost frozen in place? It is because everything in this domain is unpredictable. We like to think we live in a universe where when we do "A," then "B" happens. We like predictability. But that predictability doesn't exist in a complex world. We are beyond the space of cause and effect.

Since we don't know what will happen, we have to reach out and probe – gently touch the system, try stuff and watch to see what happens. We begin with a number of different experiments and watch for the results. Going back to the last chapter, this is the space of early innovation in the Two Loops diagram, where we are trying new things out to see what will make a difference.

Remember, most of what we do doesn't work, at least not entirely. But we learn from our mistakes and we keep trying. We know that something is needed. We connect with each other formally and informally and learn together. We act, pause, examine, reflect, learn and then act again. We begin to build some new practices — emergent practices — that help us move, eventually to building new systems and processes.

Learning how to measure and evaluate the results of our work is essential. Reflective approaches like Theory U are helpful at this stage — just as they are helpful in cutting through the initial confusion. Developmental Evaluation, Outcome Harvesting and Most Significant Change are all useful here. Transformative Scenario Planning, mentioned in the last chapter, helps us place our work in a larger context so we can discover more about the new story we are building. Prototyping is essential here as well.

This is not an area of rapid response. Things are slow, sometimes painfully slow. It takes time to get anything done because we are in a complex, unpredictable stage. While we are learning as fast as we can, there are many unknowns and so much to learn. We have to learn how to hold urgency and patience at the same time. And it's hard. People all over the world are quick to criticize the Japanese government and TEPCO for not getting the many aspects of radiation under control more quickly. Many of the complaints are justified *and we have to remember that the situation is enormously complex.*

Chaos

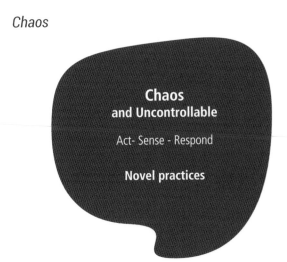

And, of course, there is the space of chaos. Right after the disasters there was so much chaos. Much of what is going on in terms of radiation in Fukushima is still in chaos. So how do we act in chaos? We act. The situation is unknowable and uncontrollable. We move into action, unsure of ourselves. In the best of worlds, we would have "Pause-Act-Sense-Respond-Reflect and Repeat." But in chaos, we often do the best we can with the three steps, Act-Sense-Respond, reflecting later on and hopefully sharing our learnings with others. Sometimes we refer to this as rapid prototyping: we do something and watch closely to see what happens. Some good things happen, some not so good. We increase our actions that cause good things to happen and decrease our actions that have led to unfortunate results.

In Act-Sense-Respond, we begin to develop new and novel practices for dealing with our current reality. As these novel practices become visible, we actually move out of chaos and in to one of the other spaces where we can get more done. But it is in this space of chaos that the new is born.

While this discussion just scratches the surface of the Cynefin, I wanted to introduce it because I have found it valuable to me in my work. It is so helpful for me just to pause, stay in my confusion and talk with others about which of these domains is home for a situation or issue we are confronting. It helps me know where to start.

There's another aspect of this framework I also want to mention. It is about where to draw the strength and leadership to get something done. Not surprisingly, it is different in each of these four domains:

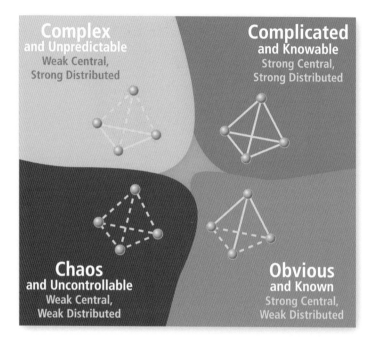

- Obvious: When dealing with the known and obvious, it works to have someone at the top in charge — giving orders.

- Complicated: When dealing with the knowable and complicated, depending on what's being done, sometimes it works to centralize authority, sometimes it works to decentralize it. It is situational.

- Complex: In complex situations, one of the worst things that can happen is that someone tries to be in charge and tell others what to do. It doesn't work. Small, agile teams deep in collective learning and action are needed.

- Chaos: Finally, in chaos it is just a mess. Frankly nothing works — but we still must act. We learn as fast as we can in order to situate actions in one of the other domains.

The Cynefin Framework helps me remember what I already know — that all situations are not the same. It helps me find a place to begin. The framework helps me remember that most community change work is some combination of the knowable and complex. Taking this last Cynefin illustration into account means that decentralized, distributed patterns of action and authority often lead to the best results — but not always.

Theory U, Active Hope, and Cynefin are frameworks I have introduced to help people find themselves, find their work, and find where to begin. They each remind us to look for and take in the largest possible picture of our work. They help us go deeper, to really seeing what is going on.

Creating
a Future
Together

CHAPTER

8

Creating a Future Together

IN THE YEARS FOLLOWING THE DISASTERS, I traveled to Japan many times. In the first three years alone, I took 14 trips there, each from two to six weeks. All told, from 2011-2016, I spent about 25 months in Japan. Even now, at the beginning of 2017, my work continues there, though I have also begun to turn my attention back to North America and other parts of the world.

My time in Japan itself sparked many questions. In Japan, people would ask me why I was giving so much to Japan. Outside of Japan people would ask me how it all worked — who asked me to come, who did I work for or with, where does the money come from. Like much of the rest of my story, the answers to these questions have many nuances. First, my heart invited me. I just had to go. Once there I began connecting with people who were also determined to be of service. We didn't have government grants. We were not members of large nonprofit organizations. We had each other, and a desire to be of service. I was able to raise some funds from U.S. friends to cover most of my expenses. There was no funding for my time for more than a year. It was delightful when, in mid 2012, Give2Asia gave us a grant supporting this work.

The people I started connecting with first were those I had met in 2010, when I was invited to offer workshops across Japan on dialogue, leadership and building resilient communities. Because of that work, I was invited in 2010 to be a TEDxTokyo Speaker with my daughter Annie, which gave me a little more exposure and credibility as well.

Gradually I transitioned from being just another foreigner coming for a visit to someone who increasing numbers of people knew and trusted.

The limitations I faced as a foreigner with modest fluency with Japanese language were humbling. That humility was perhaps one of my greatest strengths. I could only go where invited. All I could do was to make myself available to receive those invitations. I came not as an outside expert, but as an unpretentious friend, ready to listen and create spaces of listening. People invited me to join them in hosting safe spaces where people could come together to talk about their true feelings — their fears, their hopes, their grief.

People trusted me with their stories and I shared those stories with the world through my blogs.[42] I needed to write — it was my way of being connected to a wider community and my way of trying to make sense of my experience. Looking back over my writing, I began to discover patterns, and these patterns began to seem like stepping stones. Not stones laid down in some grand design, but stones that we have collectively and tentatively placed to mark our way and share with others. While putting the final touches on this English edition, there have been devastating earthquakes in both Japan and Ecuador, and more problems are regularly revealed at the Fukushima reactors. People in Japan tell me they return to my book and to these stepping stones to help them find their way forward.

This path into an invisible future needs to be rediscovered time and time again. And, we can learn from the journey of others. We still thrash about in the wilderness. It is not an orderly process. It is chaotic, messy, inconclusive. It takes time — so much time — no matter the urgency. It is long-term work. And, I believe, it takes us all, together.

We make the path by listening together. We make it through dialogue. We make it through finding just enough clarity to take the next step, and the next. I know that we can do more when we come together to share both dreams and grief, begin to develop ideas, gather more information, prototype possibilities and invite others to join with us in taking the next elegant minimum step. When I write those words, it makes it sound like a linear process, almost orderly.

----

42 These blogs are available on our NewStories website if you want a deeper look: www.resilientjapan.org

It isn't. And it doesn't start that way either.

It starts as people begin to find themselves and find each other and do what needs to be done, now. At first what's often created is a hodge-podge of interesting, but not necessarily significant, actions. This is how change happens. People try stuff. Some of it works, some doesn't. We amplify what works and let go of what doesn't. These experiments and prototypes begin to give us the learning and the relationships we need to create successful work at a broader scale.

These paths are made when people gingerly step forward, find their footing, take small steps, and move slowly forward, stepping their way into a new future. The path is not a straight path laid out in front of them. Their stories mark the path for others.

In gatherings large and small, I heard stories of people's lives and their losses and their finding a way forward. I heard their stories of salvaging what was left, reclaiming lost ground, and recovering their sense of a present, and finally stories of looking to the future.

There is not a visible destination. The challenge is to simply take the next step, to open to self and each other and mystery. Let me begin with two stories of this trailblazing as I begin to describe the markers I have seen.

The tsunami hit Otsuchi with unbelievable force. In minutes, so much was gone. In the harbor area, of the villager's 250 fishing boats, only one remained. The downtown was decimated — houses, shops, businesses, government buildings, gone. The rice fields near sea level were flooded with salt water and ruined for years. The picturesque beauty of the past was obliterated.

When the last wave had come and gone, Haga-san looked around. Town — gone. Friends — gone. Boats — gone. Crops — gone. Way of life — gone.

He turned away from the sea and looked behind him at the forest and surrounding hills. And he said to himself, "With the forest we can survive."

Ever since he was a child, he wanted to work in the forest. It called to him. But he could not make a good living working in the forest and he had a family to support. He spent most of his life as a car mechanic. Not long after the beginning of the new century, when he turned 52 and all his children had moved away, he asked his wife if he could now learn how to work in the forest. And he began.

Haga-san said, "After the tsunami came, everyone was the same. Rich people, poor people, people with college degrees, people without. We were all the same. Many of us didn't know each other, even though this was a small town. But we lay on our pillows next to each other in the emergency shelters with only candles for light. We lay next to strangers and we began to talk about our lives."

It was four days before the National Guard came to help. Because Haga-san was strong and because his family had all survived, he was able to join the townspeople in the search for other survivors. They kept finding bodies, he said, "Children, old people, people in the middle of their lives." The first night, Haga-san was unable to sleep – he kept seeing the faces of the dead. The second night, he was unable to sleep – he kept seeing their faces. The third night, he couldn't bear seeing the faces again, so he went outside to look at the many fires that were still burning. He was without hope. But somehow, looking into the fire, he knew he would dedicate the rest of his life to the memory of those who had died. He would build a new future for their descendants. He would build it with them.

It was the forest that gave him hope. During the Tokugawa Period, Japan's feudal age, Japan had perhaps the most advanced forestry management practices in the world. But when the modern age arrived, many of those practices were lost. People began to cut trees and plant trees as quickly as they could. The result has been extensive soil erosion into the ocean, depletion of the soil that remained, and ultimately a decrease in what could be harvested from the forest. Haga-san said that we can learn from our ancestors how to live with and from the forest. He created a nonprofit that would do exactly that.

"The forest teaches us how to live," he said. "It can bring us a livelihood until we can fish again. The forest can sustain us."

A second story takes place one hundred seventy-five miles to the south of Otsuchi. There Hakozaki-san worked in Minamisoma, a town of 70,000 about 15 miles from the Fukushima reactors. I met him a year after the disasters at the Minami Mirai Center — a small FutureCenter in Minamisoma. He wanted to tell me why he thought a FutureCenter was essential for hosting the important conversations his community needs.

Hakozaki-san came from Itatemura, a village near Minamisoma. Itatemura used to have a population of 6,000 and was known throughout Japan for its clean air, delicious water and fertile soil. Hakozaki-san's family had a lumber mill and had worked in the forest for many generations.

Today, Itatemura is still deserted. It is a ghost town. All the residents were required to leave because of the radiation.[43] Hakozaki-san's forest is toxic and can no longer be harvested, even if he had a lumber mill he could use. Right after the shock and emergency of the disasters passed, Hakozaki-san began to think about what he could do.

He moved to Minamisoma, where 50,000 of its people were being evacuated. His clarity was that *this is home*. He told me his thinking at the time: "It is risky to live here, but it is home and we must deal with radiation. We don't know the truth of the accident. We don't know when things can start again. We don't know what human rights we really have." Hakozaki-san remembers talking with others in Minamisoma. At first, they didn't know how to talk to each other about something they knew nothing about. But they had to learn. The government's hands were full — and they needed to start working now.

He noted that by the end of 2012 many people were coming back to Minamisoma, not just because this is the only place for them to live, but also because they wanted to live here. "They have come back for many reasons — but mostly because this is home and we need to start figuring out how to live at home in as safe a way as possible. It's time to learn about decontamination — removing accumulated radiation from ground and walls and roofs and leaves."

"We have to start now," Hakozaki-san said. "No city our size elsewhere in the world has reimagined and rebuilt itself after being exposed to nuclear radiation. We do this work because we must for our community and we do it because we know, unfortunately, a nuclear

---

43   In the next chapter, I'll share a bit more of Itatemura's current story.

accident will happen again, somewhere. Our work will help the people in that future community as well."

From the very beginning they kept meticulous records of their work — what they did, how they did it, what the radiation was before the explosions, immediately after, and in the coming weeks and months. They did this for themselves, and to support others when a nuclear disaster happens somewhere else.

Hakozaki-san founded the Institute for Decontamination in August, 2011, to treat fields, houses, and nature, to remove contamination, to measure the impact of the decontamination — to document it all. They started with decontaminating a school. First, they collected data on radiation from 500 places at the school. Next, they washed the roof and walls and removed the surface soil. They then measured all 500 places again.

"When we began, radiation levels were reduced by the cleaning, but were back up to the starting levels within weeks. We returned and cleaned again. By early 2012, the increase in contamination levels several weeks after the cleaning was much, much smaller than in August. Originally the radiation in the air was moving very quickly, and that was why the re-contamination was high. Now radiation is staying in fixed locations. There doesn't seem to be more air borne radiation coming from reactors. We need an effective plan to remove contamination. Need to do it safely. Need to measure it afterwards. Then design the plan again for the next site based on experience. And make a report to share our conclusions with others. Research is very important in all areas: worker safety, effectiveness of decontamination, planning, and evaluation."

Most of the decontamination work was done by volunteers. Many experts came to help, and each had different ideas they tried to give us. We had to organize the experts rather than having them direct us."

Hakozaki-san went on to say:

> The government of Japan has enough money to pay for decontamination. It would be best to contract with local companies in Minamisoma, but the government pays only after the work is done, and local companies don't have the financial capacity to cover up-front costs — so work goes to Tokyo companies. Money gets

taken out at the top and knowledge stays in Tokyo. Neither money nor knowledge finds its way to the local level. This is a really embarrassing system of public works in Japan.

Beyond the contamination, the disaster makes us think about our lives in new ways. Living standards were brought down by 3.11 and it will take more than 30 years to recover our old living standard.

Instead of trying to recover the old, we must find new ways, a new society: we have to shift the way we measure happiness. We had many problems before; we don't want to go back to that past. Even here, in the past, the gap between rich and poor was increasing. Is that what we want?

We need dialogue about what kind of society we are going to create and how. How are our children going to become adults in this situation? We must think of new good jobs for young people. This is the way we rebuild community. Our work is to overcome the disaster and realize a new way to be happy. The emergency phase is over, now we need to bring people together to build a new, good society. We have to become a dreaming town so our children can have hope for the future. It will take at least 30 years.

It is difficult to change our way of valuing happiness. It will take a long time. Some people will leave; others will be attracted here. We need to be in dialogue with each other to discover what is truly important now. Then we will make our future together.

For me, Haga-san and Hakozaki-san are heroes, ordinary heroes. They don't have positions of power. They do not have budgets from the government. They have no staff to hire or fire. They talked with their neighbors and figured out how to use their own resources to do the work needed now. And they kept listening and talking with their neighbors to foster a new, positive future. They created stepping stones — and invited and welcomed their neighbors to step with them.

Of course, they can't do it alone. There is work for the government to do. Other things can be done by businesses and universities and nonprofit organizations. I'm not even going to try to argue which is most important. It takes us all to create a new future. What I will say is that I am going to stand with Haga-san and Hakozaki-san and other people who are rallying themselves and inviting their neighbors to take the initiative to build the future they want.

Where did people in Japan leave their marks as they stepped forward? Each next day was the new time AfterNOW. Looking back through hundreds of pages of stories, there were seven stepping stones that stood out to me.

Stand Up!

"The nail that sticks up gets pounded down" is a common expression in Japan. When someone stands up, raising their head above the harmony of the collective, they risk being pulled back down and chastised for standing out. While collectives have many strengths, part of their shadow is they often place a stranglehold on individuation.

The Triple Disasters became an invitation for many to step outside of this expression and stand up for what they believe and want. It reminds me of what I wrote in my journal entries in Chapter 2 about the Bonanza story of a bunch of sticks being stronger than the single one. Stand together and you can't be broken.

In Japan these days, people have been standing up while standing together. This combination may be one of the most powerful forces in the world. I see this capacity all over the world, but I believe the collective culture of Japan gives it a greater potency. In collective culture, people turn to each other to get things done. Their prosperity depends on it. Turn back the clock 2000 years and people in Japan lived in villages separated by precipitous mountains and life was sustained by rice grown in paddies that took a village to cultivate. They became interdependent, relying on each other for life. There's a shadow to collective culture: it typically represses individual expression, and differences are shunned. But it also has many aspects that create harmony. What happened with the Triple Disasters is that while continuing to be part of the collective — standing together — people started to individuate and stand up for what was important to them.

How does a new normal get created? Are there special people with extraordinary insight who lead us to a new tomorrow? Does it take a five-year plan from the government? This may be our default mode — waiting for others to step forward or for the machinery in place to logically and cautiously move us forward. But I don't believe that either is up for the challenge. I believe we create it together. And usually, we create it while looking forward, but realize what we've done only when we look back. A new beginning gradually emerges through the combined seemingly small efforts of large numbers of ordinary people. The future is created when individual people stand up together.

There is no single right place to begin anew after a disaster. Start. Just start. Act on the possibility you see. Find the courage, the confidence and the clarity to step forward.

At the conclusion of a major community festival in Minamisoma, almost a year after the disasters, one woman who never had thought of herself as a community leader stood up and spoke in the NOMIKAI (the party after working). She said, "They used to say that people in Minamisoma were polite and waited for government to tell us what to do. We're not waiting anymore."

All across the land, people were discovering how to step forward, offering what they could to create a new Japan.

During the weeks and months after the disaster, people saw that they couldn't rely on government to do everything — everyone needed to pitch in. They stepped forward to do what was needed — coordinate an emergency center for volunteers, drive a truck with supplies, shovel the mud, clear the rubble. Each act was an act of leadership in community.

And, as hearts and minds turned to the question of how to build a new future, they also saw that many needed to stand up and step forward with their ideas and initiative. This book is filled with the words of many people who stood up and marked the trails of their journeys with their stories.

Stand Together

The saying from Africa, *It takes a village to raise a child*, became popular around the world a couple of decades ago. In the disaster area, a corollary idea became visible: It takes a community to build a community. And the building started within hours of the Triple Disasters.

Early on I heard from Laurel Kamada, who teaches at Tohoku University. She was in her office when the earthquake came. She and an assistant hid under a table as hundreds of her books fell to the floor, along with everything else in the room. "The quakes went on forever," she said.

Finally, they carefully made their way outside, where snow was falling. Dazed and confused. Alive. Later she was able to make her way back to her wrecked apartment. She and others from the apartment building gathered at a nearby shelter for the next three nights, packed closely together, not having known each other all that well before sleeping in each other's breath. Finally, they all went back to their apartment building and began cleaning. One man on the first floor invited the others, "Bring what food and supplies you have left; I have a gas stove." And so, they gathered and made two hot meals a day, sharing what they had as they began to make their spaces livable again.

People stayed together. They found places to start.

Chiba-san was a sea-going engineer born in Osawa, a small village in Iwate Prefecture, which he returned to permanently after retiring. His village of 188 households was near the ocean and was totally destroyed by the tsunami. Forty minutes before it struck, the warning came. Those who heeded the warning and retreated to higher ground were saved. One hundred and fifty people died.

When the temporary housing certificates were issued, Chiba-san and several others from Osawa were assigned to a temporary housing project about one kilometer from the old Osawa. Chiba-san immediately approached friends in the local government and asked if people could trade their housing assignments — they said yes. Trading their housing assignments with others, he and his old neighbors were able to gather most of those from Osawa into the same housing project. They created a space with shared relationships and a common history. The people of Osawa had their community again. Then, they started helping themselves. They started to self-organize to get things done – no waiting for government here.

Their temporary housing was like a series of small narrow trailers stuck end-to-end. Without the entryways and porches of their original homes. When someone stepped out of their front door, they stepped onto bare dirt. They got together and constructed small roofs, porches and sitting areas outside of everyone's door. Each person had a small entrance-way again where they could leave their shoes, put out a tomato plant and chat with a neighbor. Next, they said that they needed to take care of their own security, so they organized volunteer patrols to check on the community every night. Then they realized they could and should start growing their own food — so they started gardens. By the time their first summer together was drawing to a close, they said, "We're alive. Let's celebrate." And they organized a village festival.

By the end of 2011, just nine months after the tsunami, they told the nonprofit organization that had been working with them that they no longer needed their help: "Please go help someone else who really needs it".

Chiba-san is a very modest man, but it is clear that his determination played a key role here. He's a natural community organizer. As I listened to him, I heard several key principles:

- Do whatever is needed yourselves as soon as you possibly can. Don't wait for anyone.

- Don't ever wait for government. When you want something, go to them until you get it.

- Don't let problems grow. Bring people together immediately to talk.

- Make as many relationships beyond the community as possible. Stay connected.

The story of Osawa is quite different from that of most temporary housing settlements. In most cases, people were given temporary housing by lottery, in order to ensure fairness of distribution. People who had lived for months in emergency shelters were thrown into new housing with complete strangers. They didn't want to be where they were. For the most part, they were not interested in being in community. Osawa was different. Their relationships gave them a place to begin.

In the late summer of 2012, I hosted a learning journey for young people from around the world in Jusanhama, a small fishing village near Ogatsu. Sitting around a table, we heard stories as we learned how to work with the WAKAME (seaweed) harvested that morning and prepare it for market. One grandmother, offering a huge welcoming smile, said she had been sitting at tables like this one for 40 years. Later we had a feast from the sea — crab, shrimp, seaweeds, scallops. A bounty. We sat in a small fish factory, newly built since the tsunami. We asked, "What was the story of this village, Jusanhama? How did you stay together?"

One woman said, "It was the hope we could start again that held us together." Another man said: "We had the boats. We could still fish." And another said, "We still had the sea." We heard that the first 100 days were very hard; it was a struggle each day to find food and water and clothes and warmth. "We had no idea what the new day would bring. Then, young volunteers started to arrive and they had so much enthusiasm," the first woman said. "They had come to help us and we couldn't give up hope."

How had they managed to make their way forward? "We had each other," they said. There were 40 families here before. Now there are 15. "We found a place where temporary housing for our community could be built and we cleared the land. We went to the government and said we have to stay together to rebuild our lives — we have prepared the ground. Please build our temporary housing here."

Such lovely people. Kind, proud, laughing, somber. Since then, some have died. Others have left. Those who remain are making a life together. There is always more to do. They need permanent homes. They need more ways to sell their products. They need a bigger community. But they have begun!

A different story of staying together comes from a small non-profit organization in Fukushima called Peach Heart. One evening in the fall of 2012, their leadership asked me to help them have a difficult conversation with each other. One Peach Heart founder, Chika, was a television personality who lived in Sapporo to the north. Chika was raised in Fukushima, and would not live there now. She visited frequently. A second woman, Chiki, was also born and raised in Fukushima and felt called to work to support the people who could not leave, even if they wanted to. A third woman, Maki, was evacuated to the province to the south. She found a way to move back because she wanted to organize a way for the voices of young women from Fukushima to be heard in Japan and the world. The three were very close friends.

Chika had just recently returned from a visit to Chernobyl to report for her television station. Even before her trip she had been urging the others to leave. Her visit to Chernobyl was painful and shocking and she was even more convinced that they should leave. But the other two didn't plan on leaving. They didn't want to hear her stories from Chernobyl. Their response was painful for Chika; it also left her unsure about what information she should share in what ways on television.

As with many aspects of life in Fukushima, it was messy! Part of the complication, of course, was that knowledge and wisdom was needed more than the information. The information they were given about what was actually going on with radiation and cleanup tended to be very incomplete and did not answer their questions: How were Chernobyl and Fukushima similar and how were they not? What were the similarities and differences in Japanese and Ukrainian cultures? What more did we know now than was known 25 years ago when Chernobyl exploded? Undoubtedly there are things for people in Fukushima to learn from Chernobyl, but what are they?

Chika, Maki and Chiki kept talking. Would Chika be accused of withholding information if she didn't tell everything she knew? When is it better to remain silent? Is telling the truth the same as telling everything you know? We talked about how trying to convince someone that they're wrong just makes them dig in their heels and refuse to budge. Is it sufficient, and ultimately more helpful, just to speak our own truth — and our own hopes and fears and aspirations — to each other, without the intent to change the mind of the other?

These three wonderful young women knew that they wanted and needed to stay together. They knew they had different ideas. But they also knew that they didn't need to resolve their differences and would not let their differences separate them. In fact, they realized it was because they had different ideas that they especially needed to stand together — in order to find their own ways forward.

Staying together when we have differences — sometimes strong emotional differences — requires curiosity, respect and generosity. When we have those qualities in the BA, we can hold the tension of our differences, and a new clarity begins to emerge that helps us find our way forward. This has been the work of Peach Heart

— creating the BA where young women in Fukushima can stand together to find their own ways forward. It is not about convincing each other or all going in the same direction. It is about standing together to discover the next steps.

We continued to talk about these same themes the next day in Minamisoma. Just before we arrived for an evening FutureCenter session, the biggest quake since 3.11 struck nearby! Minamisoma is about 3 miles inland from the coast and 15 miles from the Fukushima reactors. The quake's epicenter was 150 miles off the coast and 7.3 in magnitude. There were tsunami warnings.

We joined 20 other people who were sharing quiet and intense conversation as well as laughter. Had the earthquake damaged the Fukushima reactors? Was more radiation coming their way? Would a tsunami come? I was in the middle of the reality the people of Minamisoma live with each day. There is no certainty. What should we do?

A decision was made, quickly, to begin the FutureSession. We knew that we wanted each other's wisdom and insights. If we received an alert to evacuate, we would take immediate action. Perhaps that was one of the core lessons from 3.11 — whatever the problem; we're likely to find our way forward if we begin by turning to one another.

We formed a circle and began to check-in with each other. My own anxiety, which had been rising, settled down. I knew that I was not alone and that we would make wiser decisions together than if we all rushed out the door going our separate directions.

The alert passed. There was no major tsunami this time. We had a powerful evening, talking about how to live with uncertainty.

Many people are talking about resilience these days. It has become a favorite "buzz word" — right up there with innovation, design thinking and social impact. But what does it mean? What promotes resilience? Some bring it down to another overused term: social capital.

Resilient communities make good use of their social capital. What does that mean? It means people stand in relationship with each other. They know their strengths and resources and capabilities. They may or may not be friends — but they are in conscious relationship with each other, doing together what they cannot do alone.

Go Alone

Another lesson from the disasters was that while staying together is essential, sometimes it is also necessary to go alone.

Far too many school children and teachers died on 3.11. Sometimes it was because they stayed together. Teachers led the students as quickly as they could to what they thought would be safe shelter — on top of the roof of the school or of a nearby building — and sometimes they died.

It was both heartbreaking and inspiring to talk with a Junior High Principal from the village of Ogatsu. His school was totally destroyed. The building stands, but rubble, not students, populate the corridors. When the earthquake came, he sent the children outside. "The waters are coming," the principal told them. "Run up the surrounding hills as fast as you can." His instructions saved their lives. If they had gone to the third floor of the school — a fair distance inland from the ocean — most would have died. The waters covered the three-story school.

It took the Principal eight days to find every child from his school. That night was freezing cold, as were the next several days and nights. Some of the children spent up to three days in the hills, finding others and waiting for the waters to recede. Others made it to rescue spots and emergency shelters. He found them all. They survived. Miracles do happen.

In Kamaishi to the north, there was a similar story. In that city, fewer children died than any other place along the coast. The teachers in Kamaishi decided that the government's teachings about disaster preparedness were not good enough. They came up with their own approach — which in itself was a bit unusual! They drilled students with three principles and one teaching from ancient wisdom. Simple. Direct. Easily remembered.

The principles were:

- Go as quickly as you can.

- Don't wait for anyone.

- Do it now.

The ancient wisdom was:

- Don't look for your family.

The last piece of wisdom is, of course, the hardest. But the ancients knew that people died because they went to look for others. If everyone went as quickly as they could, more would be saved.

One particular story made this step of going alone most vivid for me. It's from the same fishing village I wrote about that stayed together, Jusanhama. You may have noticed that I wrote they still had their boats. How?

Sasaki-san's family had worked with the ocean for many generations. On March 11, 2011, he had traveled to Sendai for a graduation ceremony for his son, arriving back in Jusanhama in the early afternoon. Just after he reached home, the earth began to shake, more than ever before. All his life, his father and his father's father had said: "If the tsunami comes, take your boat and go to sea."

He rushed to the harbor, quickly loosening his boat. Nine other fishermen came for their boats as well. Together they started towards the open sea. Their ancestors had told them, you have to make it to a depth of 150 feet before the tsunami comes, or you will die. Signaling each other by hand, they traveled together. They listened to their radios, hoping for news about what was happening to their families.

Their world was unraveling. Would they see their families again? Would their families make it to high ground? Would they and their boats survive the storm? They could only follow the ancient wisdom and hope they would make it out to water 150 feet deep.

Everything was quiet and then their boats began to roll; the tidal wave passed underneath. Then the ocean was unhappy: rough, wild. The snow started to fall — so thick that they could no longer see each other. It was cold, so cold. Their radios spoke of unimaginable destruction. They could see fires. They turned on their lights so their families could see them, if their families were still alive.

They returned the next day, found their families, and began. They had gone alone into an unimaginable present so that they might create a new future.

You've probably noticed that in each of these stories of "going alone," people actually also went together — together with someone else. These ideas aren't exclusive. But how is that so?

Maybe I should call this stepping stone: "Follow your heart" or "Don't ask for permission." Included in each is the core experience of going alone — separating from what might appear to be the easy or convenient or the conventional path. One quickly figures out what's right to do, looks around for mates who will join in the journey, and moves — without asking anyone for permission. It seems to me that resilience flows from deepening this capacity to know what's mine to do and doing it. Now. Guided both by ancient wisdom and present circumstances. Now. Go as quickly as you can. Don't wait for anyone. Do it now.

Hold Hands Across the Generations

Across the world, the energy and commitment and vision and questions of youth are one of our most important — yet most unused — resources.

We need people who will think outside of the box, who are willing to discard what doesn't work in the present for what will work in the future. It's not the experts or the people with big budgets. It's the youth with their energy, commitment, questions and insights that are essential to our search for a future that can work for all. They can't do it alone; we need to stand together.

In 2010, when I convened dialogues across Japan, I became very aware that many young people felt lost and disillusioned. They weren't particularly interested in the old economy — they could see it wasn't working very well. But many of them were unclear about what they could do, how to get on with their lives. Then 3.11 happened and brought with it even more uncertainty, and more questions. But it also brought a huge need and opening for youth to step forward to help.

By May 2011, some of us had started organizing gatherings for youth from across Japan to gather in dialogue with each other about what 3.11 meant for them. Yuya Nishimura, who had brought me to Japan for "Art of Hosting Conversations that Matter" in 2010, was the primary convener. Later in 2011 Yuya, who had just turned 30, would create Miratuku,[44] a new nonprofit organization focused on using dialogue for social innovation.

On the first evening of our first post-disaster, three-day dialogue, a woman from Fukushima said, "The disaster made us all the same age." She made it immediately obvious that we were all in this together and that the disasters offered an opportunity to construct new partnerships involving the gifts and strengths of people of all ages.

Over the next six months we gathered five groups of 50 or so youth in their teens and twenties and thirties at the KEEP at Kiyosato, which I mentioned in Chapter 2. Using methodologies from Art of Hosting and FutureSessions, we became a community exploring questions of how we each might serve.

Each time we met, a few older people showed up as well. I especially recall one man in his fifties from Fukushima who came to our first session filled with grief and anger and hopelessness. He said: "When I saw the flyer for this gathering, I knew I was too old, but I had to come. Perhaps I could find something here that I could not find at home." I could tell that before the disasters, he was the kind of person who was the life of the party, openhearted, gregarious, and ready. He spoke of himself as being broken-hearted, frozen in place, unable to muster clarity or energy to do anything at all. The land he loved was destroyed. He had shut down and grown more inward and despondent as the weeks turned. At our closing circle, our broken-hearted friend ran around the circle shouting, "I have hope again; I can move again." I don't know how long this feeling lasted. As he left, I trusted that he would be able to remember the smell of hope and that it would help him go on.

This was happening across Japan both through organized gatherings and by individuals stepping forward to answer the call. In Tohoku, the heart of the Triple Disasters, there has been a remarkable intergenerational dynamic. Young people have been going to the region. They're known as U-turns and I-turns. U-turns were those who had grown up in the region and moved elsewhere. They thought they

---

44 Miratuku is a nonprofit organization that uses dialogue and other participatory processes to invite people into learning and action. It focuses mostly on youth in their teens and twenties and thirties.

would never return, but they did. Their hearts had called them. Or their grandmothers. The I-turns were people who had no direct connection with Tohoku. The disasters happened and they were called to come. They just had to be there.

I was privileged to meet a number of these younger leaders, sometimes over coffee, sometimes in workshops, often working side-by-side. Let me tell you about a few of them.

Yuji Suzuki was in his late thirties when we first met. He came to Sendai, a city in the Tohoku region, from Tokyo in early April, just weeks after the disaster. He had to help. He did whatever was needed and he learned his way forward. Today he is the founder and leader of the Sanaburi Foundation. Sanaburi is the name of an ancient festival of giving thanks to the ancestors after the seeds have been planted. The Foundation's work is to support the planting of a variety of "seeds," the many projects needed to bring health and vitality to this region. He and others established Sanaburi as an intermediary to match the funds of those who want to invest in Tohoku and the needs of those who have work they want to undertake here.

Oyashiki-san put his undergraduate degree at University of Tokyo on hold. He came to the small community of Takajo just two months after the disasters. By November, the 340 families in emergency shelters in Takajo were relocated to temporary housing. They were made up of the elderly, the people hardest to employ, and those with the least resilience. In the temporary housing, they were isolated in separate housing units, disconnected and unemployed. Soon there was an alarming number of suicides as well as people getting sick and sicker as they tried to live without the surrounding relationships so core in a collective culture. Oyashiki-san supported them, creating community for them by doing things such as visiting all of the shopkeepers in the neighborhood and making a directory of the shops and what they offered. He also made sure everyone was visited on a regular basis. His calling was to build a bridge from the old community to the new.

Yuko Endo came from Toyama, in central Japan. She didn't know how she could help, but she knew she had to try. For the last two and a half years, she has worked with a number of nonprofit organizations doing reconstruction work. Part of her work has been reading

English language newspapers published in Japan and researching what's covered in those papers as compared to the Japanese press. Her NPO wanted to see what might be learned by a view from the outside. She has also served as my interpreter, especially in Fukushima and elsewhere in Tohoku. Deeply spiritual, she helps other people improve their lives.

KEITA OGASAWARA was finishing off a graduate degree in education in Yokohama when the disasters hit. He came to Sendai in March. He started off driving trucks of supplies needed in the region. He kept working and working and looking for where he might be of the most service. Two cooperatives in different parts of Japan have since provided the initial funding for his project, the "Foundation of Cooperative Community Creation." Like Yuji, his purpose is to collect funds needed for work in Tohoku and to distribute them to those who can use them well in a way that satisfies the donors' desires for accountability.

Before the Triple Disasters, these young men and women and hundreds like them had no idea they would soon be living and working across Tohoku. They came because they felt a deep calling. While typically strangers are regarded with a bit of suspicion, usually treated politely but not particularly welcomed, in part because of their youth, they have been able to walk through the isolating boundaries common in the region. They have been able to enter into relationship with other young people as well as older folks. They've stepped forward with commitment, passion and willingness into work that needed to be done.

Shortly after the disasters, ETIC (Entrepreneurial Training for Innovation Communities), a Tokyo-based nonprofit organization, saw that there was a need for volunteers who could come for three to nine months to give long-term help in communities. By the end of 2013, nearly 200 people had served through ETIC. I've had the chance to meet and work with many of them. These ETIC volunteers and hundreds like them entered into communities across the region, and in many places, magic has happened.

In many cases, they came thinking that they, as bright young women and men from Tokyo, would come and show the people in Tohoku how to do things right. They smile when they mention that to me — and say that it didn't take them long to realize that they were really there to listen and learn from the wisdom and kindness of the local people.

I've heard many of these young people talk about how they were searching for meaning in their lives before the disasters. They found that meaning in Tohoku. The rhythms of rural life combined with its unpretentious wisdom were immediate attractors. They found work to do that has meaning — work that seems to make a difference. They entered into contexts where their ideas and perspectives were welcomed. When they joined groups of older people, their enthusiasm sparked new conversations and new relationships among both older and younger generations.

This sense of value and worth goes both ways. Older people have told me that many times after the disasters they just wanted to give up — but they couldn't disappoint the young people who had come to help them. I had one man tell me: "You know, the youth left Tohoku because we older people told them to leave. We told them to go to Tokyo and make something of themselves. We just never realized how much we needed each other."

Sometimes the voices of different generations are raised in anger. Young women, high-school students in Soma, a community 25 miles away from the reactors, made DVDs in the summer of 2012 so that their voices would be heard: "A year ago, before 3.11," they said, "we were living ordinary lives, but now we don't know what is safe. Government says we can plant crops now, but we worry about it. We doubt the safety of the vegetables. We don't know what we should trust and what we shouldn't. We can't get away because this is the place we live and we have many good memories. But we can't get the truth.

"This year our voices have more anger: our freedom has been stolen. We cannot drink water or breathe the air. If we get pregnant in the future, what if our babies have diseases? We want to have babies, but maybe it is not something we can realize. This mess is not our responsibility, but we have to be responsible for our children if they have diseases or problems. Being healthy depends on what we think health is. We are in good health right now physically, but not mentally. We have no idea about our future health. Our law covers basic rights like the right to live in health, but will we be healthy?" Spoken forcefully and with the passion of the young, many of these questions transcend all generations.

Just to complete the picture of hands across the generations, the ancestors are present as well. Ancestral wisdom has helped guide many during the disasters and after. One example is the way in which ancient wisdom guided school children to run from the tsunami in the section above on Going Alone. Another is the old stone markers in the hills throughout the coastal areas which all say the same thing, "Do not build below this point. The tsunamis will come again." The communities that honored these markers were safe; those that didn't were destroyed. Ancestors are part of daily life in Japan - cemeteries were among the first places restored in most communities. Throughout the coastal area many Shinto shrines that honor ancestors and the KAMI mysteriously escaped the damage that ravaged neighboring properties.

Ancestors are present in daily life. There is more present here than we know. We live in a wide web of life that holds both the seen and the invisible. Children, youth, older adults, seniors, ancestors — we all need to be together, those here before, those yet to come, and all of us in the middle. When we are aware of all our relations and approach each other with respect, curiosity and generosity, magic happens.

Use What We Have

All around the world, people are remembering how to build community with the resources and knowledge they already have. It's really nothing new. It's the way we have always built community. But over the last stretch of time, we've sometimes forgotten. In the United States this approach started to attract attention in the 1990s and was known as Asset Based Community Development (ABCD). But ABCD wasn't invented in the US — it happens everywhere.

In Japan, it goes by the name JIMOTOGAKU[45] (Learning from the Local Community) — JIMOTO means "local area" and GAKU means

---

45   See AfterNow.Today Additional Resources bibliography section for more information about JIMOTOGAKU. I've seen this spirit of working with what we have in other cultures as well. It is part of our legacy as human beings.

"school," so JIMOTOGAKU means learning from the local area or community. It was first popularized in the 1990s in Minamata, a small city on the island of Kyushu. Minamata had become almost a pariah after mercury pollution poisoned the population in the 1950s. Jimotogaku was a core process used to help the community recover pride and rebuild itself.

JIMOTOGAKU focuses on existing local resources and facilitates people's initiative to utilize those resources. "Stop asking for what we do not have: let us start from finding out what we have," is a principle of Jimotogaku. It also emphasizes collaboration among "Soil and Wind" (community people and outsiders), working together to make things better right now.

The Shimizu family in Kesennuma — one of the fishing towns north of Sendai hit hardest by the tsunami — had never heard the term Jimotogaku. But after their fishing factory was completely destroyed; they instinctively operated from its principles. They looked around to discover what was left after the tsunami destroyed the fishing boats, ice plants, fish processing plants and more. One thing they saw they had in abundance was ship's canvas — rolls and rolls and rolls of it — that wouldn't be used again soon. "What can we do with it?" they wondered. They talked and brainstormed and they came up with an idea. "What if we dyed it bright colors, screened on the names of the devastated towns, and started making handbags?" Within a few weeks, the eldest son of the family, a young entrepreneur named Kenyuu, took some of the first bags produced on a trip to Seattle where they were an immediate hit. Twenty of the 200 people employed in the fishing plant had jobs by mid-May, just two months after the disasters. Soon they were making everything from iPad covers to baseball caps from the ship's cloth.

One of the things Jimotogaku produces is a changed attitude — a new look at what one has — and a clear sense that you start with what you have and follow it wherever it leads.

More than a year after the tsunami, in the Iwate town of Otsuchi, a series of four FutureSessions were held to help people reimagine their future. The tsunami was devastating in the town Otsuchi. Many survivors were leaving town both out of grief and because they didn't think they could make it here. But the ones who chose to meet to reimagine their future were different. They looked at what they had. They still had the clear water once used to grow wasabi that could be grown again. They saw that their pure water might also be an attractor in creating a tourist destination. They realized that their long-time local knowledge of flowers could lead to a new dried and pressed flower business that could be competitive with flowers from Europe now popular in Tokyo. These were not complicated ideas. They were a set of first steps to bring the community back into relationship again.

They found a place to start. Perhaps their initial ideas wouldn't work out. That's often the case. Often when we try something new it doesn't work like we had hoped or imagined. But we act and learn, act and learn. Build relationships and build community. Find first steps and begin.

In Fukushima people were learning how to coexist, and more, with one of the things they have — radiation.

I heard about a town that wanted to have a festival with an outside play day for their children. But playing on the ground was prohibited. They spent days and days cleaning one park so that it was radiation free and for one morning their children could play outside. They knew that the radiation would be unsafe the next day — but they could begin.

Jimotogaku is the story of beginning with what you have, right now, without waiting for permission from anyone. As you step into Jimotogaku, it can begin to change the entire way in which you see your life.

I remember ten years ago, I was sitting in the courtyard of a home in Udaipur, India, talking with Vishal. He was working with small tools to turn old rubber car tires into beautiful handbags. At some point, Vishal got a look in his eyes, sort of a "you don't get it, do you?" look. Then he said: "You know, Bob, this is not about making bags." I asked him to tell me more. "Working like this," he said, "changes the way I see my world. I slow down, begin to see what I have, and begin to see new possibilities."

In our modern society, we have given so much of ourselves away. Our children think milk comes from stores, not cows. We act as if only teachers are responsible for our children's learning. We consume art as if it was just another product. We have moved further from the essence of life itself. Jimotogaku calls us back to our communities and to a fresh view of what we already have. It directs our gaze to what is right in front of us. It makes us remember the abundance with which we live rather than waiting for someone else to make our lives better.

Start Anywhere — Start Now

Jimotogaku ties directly to the idea of just starting. Start now. Start anywhere. Make a new path into the future, step-by-step.

Rikuzentakada is a small town on a beautiful curved bay that was totally destroyed by the tsunami. Fukuda-san, a former government official of the town, talked about how government can't create anything new. "People need to do that. Government goes in circles, ending up in the same place. Upward spirals are what are needed now. We need to unleash the creativity of people to make a new future that combines old traditions with new technologies. We need to plan and build differently for a future we want, not the past. We need to talk about new building styles and zero-emissions. Crazy ideas like, perhaps the young people who can run from a tsunami should live on lower ground than old people — but in 30 or 40 years they'll be old people so that won't work!"

Creating a new future means being willing to be a little unusual. To stand out. To try things that will, perhaps, not be successful. This is most obviously true in the places where the past is gone — in Fukushima and in the coastal areas. There is not a past to return to. This opens up the question: What is the future we will build?

A farmer in Fukushima offered, "We have to open our minds and hearts and become aware of what we are feeling. We have to open up and accept other people. We must change our ideas. I've come to realize that we need to tell our children that college probably isn't all that important for them - we have to learn how to live in and open up to nature and we have to learn how to relate differently to our natural world. Colleges don't teach important things like this."

Another Fukushima farmer added, "Let's focus more on what we can control. We know we can't control the radiation, but we can learn to live with it. The government says it will spot check crops for radiation. That's not enough. We must check all crops for radiation and have very high standards. We must not sell crops with any radiation. If we have high standards, people in other parts of Japan will begin to trust our food again. They will remember that they used to think rice from Fukushima was the most delicious in all Japan. We must discover what we can grow on our land that's needed here and in all of Japan."

Working with what you have, you just start. Early in 2012, local friends got together in Minamisoma and decided to hold a future festival. More than 1,000 people from the community participated. There were music performances, presentations, dialogues — many different activities to engage people and invite them to think about their future together. At the end of the day, Mikako Takehashi, one of the organizers, who also runs a local laundry, offered a toast, "Before *3.11* we had a reputation for being quiet and just waiting for the government to do what they wanted. Now we know we must do it ourselves. We cannot wait for government. We must join hands and create a future together." And that's what they were doing.

In June 2012, they opened a Minami Mirai FutureCenter on a street corner in downtown Minamisoma. "Minami" means "south" — this town is a little south of the town named, simply, "Soma." "Mirai" means "future" — so it translates as the "South Soma FutureCenter." People started to use it immediately. Those who organized it said: "We don't actually know what a FutureCenter is, but we know we need a place to create a future together — so we started."

The Minami Mirai Center's leadership circle is a delight — a truck driver, a laundress, a dairy farmer, a nurse's aide, a bartender — ordinary people who have come together because something had to be done. One had been evacuated from Minamisoma to a town several hours to the north. It took her more than a year to be able to make her way home. Another spoke of how his family had been torn apart - he and his wife wanted to stay here, in their home with their children. Fukushima was home for them; they had no anxiety about staying and safely raising their family. But his parents moved north to Miyagi Prefecture and accused him of killing his children by exposing them to radiation in Fukushima. He thought that perhaps they would never speak again.

These people have stepped forward because they must. This is home. There are dangers - but there are dangers everywhere and this is home.

This region, the beautiful Tohoku, is home, and many are doing whatever is necessary to stay in their beloved home.

Monitors in public places throughout Fukushima carefully measure radiation levels. Safecast,[46] the world's most extensive open source radiation monitoring initiative, has hundreds of people with monitoring devices transmitting data as they travel throughout the province. But this isn't just about data. Even now, 70 years after the atomic bombs were dropped on Hiroshima and Nagasaki, our knowledge about why some people are affected by low dose radiation and others are not is pretty sketchy. Arguments and disagreements are often based on fear.

People in Minamisoma know this is long-term work. One person spoke of how "we hold individual FutureSessions and that is good. Things happen in them, but what we are really doing is working to gradually change the mindset of the community. We are helping ourselves realize that we can and will create a future together."

They are ordinary people who are working together to create a life. They don't have positions of authority in the community or in businesses or other institutions; they are just people who want to make things better. With each other. Now.

It leads me to ask the question, *"Where does change come from?"*

I think it comes from people everywhere who reach out — often with a little trembling — and do what they can. Sometimes, like Nobel Peace Prize winner Wangari Maathai, they look back 20 years later and see that they've led a movement that planted millions of trees. They also remember that most of the first trees they planted died. But they learned how to do it right.

Other times it is two government officials who look each other in the eye and say, "We can make this idea work." It's the farmer who decides to grow vegetables hydroponically, with water, no soil. It is the business owner who commits his company to a bold new experiment.

Change happens when people see a place to start and find enought clarity, courage and confidence to begin. Usually they don't know what will happen — even if they think they do. Progress is most often seen when we look backwards, when the path we've walked is revealed. It happens when we huddle with friends and come up with the

---

46   See Safecast for an astonishing array of data on radiation levels throughout Fukushima.

best idea we can and find a place we can begin. And then we watch what happens. We talk. We chew our experience and learn. We talk some more and we decide what to do next. And next. When we do this for long enough, we discover what to amplify and what to let go of. We begin to discover what works and we discover how to do more of it.

Gradually we begin to see what works and start to amplify and expand it. It's no longer change. It's doing the same thing again and again because we like the results. It's the next important stage.

It's actually one of the stages we need to see more and more of in Tohoku. It took three years to just get things stabilized. Many were exhausted. Most were tired of dialogue and of networking. They were ready to do something that works and would make life better. Continual experiments are needed that help people see what's possible — they have to keep starting somewhere and following it everywhere. Then they need to take what's been learned and use it at broader scale — not "scaling up" or "replicating", which rarely works, but finding the ways in which knowledge and experience can be used by others.

The five years since the disasters have been about finding confidence. The next period is about getting focused, discovering what we need to learn with each other, and walking the long road of building a future together.

Grieve What's Gone

The afternoon of March 11, 2011, a young woman in Ishinomaki was rushing to the hills and came across a grandmother moving slowly. "Let's go together," the young woman said. They hurried along for a while, but slowly, so slowly. Minutes passed. The grandmother sighed, "Please go ahead, save yourself; you have your whole life ahead of you; please go." With regret and a heavy heart, the young woman ran up to the mountains. Hearing the tsunami surging behind her, she turned and watched as the grandmother was caught, tossed and surrounded by the waves.

The magnitude of the disaster was unimaginable. In my first visit to Ishinomaki four weeks after the disasters, I traveled through kilometer after kilometer of devastation. Ishinomaki's past was completely swept away. With a pre-disaster population of just over 160,000,[47] Ishinomaki had 22,000 people homeless living in 152 shelters, and many of those whose homes survived had no jobs because so many businesses were destroyed. Huge numbers of cars were destroyed in the tsunami and the roads were turned to rubble. Add the destruction of train lines and Ishinomaki and its citizens were isolated and alone. The losses and the destruction in Ishinomaki and elsewhere were staggering and opened up a huge rift in the collective emotional field that stretched across all of Japan.

In Japan's collective culture, everyone and everything Japanese is held in an empathic field. Sometimes it is stifling and other times it offers safety and a deep, deep sense of connection that breaks out in a variety of ways - some quite raw.

People in Tokyo felt guilty for feeling grief and other emotions — after all, most didn't lose friends, family and property. In Fukushima, where many had lost so much and had no income, some people felt anger towards the workers being paid by TEPCO[48] while risking their lives in the nuclear power plants, and then guilt because of the anger. Silently, people who had lost everything took their own lives. Some people were finding ways to "turn the switch off" or go back to sleep. They tried to act as if everything was normal - even while they knew it was not.

This emotional response stretched across the whole country. A month after the disasters I was hosting a FutureSession at a regional television station in Shikoku, 600 miles southwest of the disasters. At the end of the first day, one of the senior executives started to share his story with me. "I couldn't escape from the news. It kept grabbing me. I thought Japan had died. I thought our lives were over."

A month later I was at another FutureSession with a business leader from a large manufacturing company in Nagoya. We had met several times in the previous year. When we first greeted each other

---

47 Ishinomaki's population in 2015 was just under 146,000 people, about a 10% decrease.
48 TEPCO, the Tokyo Electric Power Company, is the owner of the nuclear power plants that exploded in Fukushima.

and I asked how he was, his response was casual, "Oh, you know, just working along." That changed as the afternoon progressed. Later his response was more powerful, "I don't watch the news anymore. I can't. I pretend everything is normal with my family and then I go to my office and pretend even more." Tapping on his heart he says: "It is all different in here and I am sad and confused."

More than a year and a half later, I was back in Ishinomaki hosting a small learning journey of people in their twenties from Japan and around the world. In learning journeys, we come together to learn with each other and from local people doing extraordinary work. We were with the president of a local fish processing plant when he wondered out loud, while telling the story of a close friend who had died. "Why did I live while my best friend died? Why was it he who was trapped in the car, unable to open the doors or windows, as the waters rose? Why was he allowed only that last gasp of air before the waters closed around him?"

We learned that all 76 of his employees, including his wife and son, managed to successfully evacuate to higher ground. By the end of 2011, he had managed to build his business back to about a third of its former size. They had a year-end party to celebrate their survival, with lots of good food, but for the first time, no alcohol — a staple at many parties that numbs memory. Of course, each one has stories of family and friends who were killed or physically and emotionally scarred. After eating they had a circle to talk about the meaning of their lives. "We are here to remember. 6,000 of our 120,000 died. We are alive. Why?"

The room was filled with silence as he spoke. Hard words. Grief. "What about all those families in Japan that have found success? You know, they have a nice house with new appliances and a shiny car. Their children have gotten into good schools. But are they happy? Is this all there is to life? I'm okay today, but sometimes it is so hard to go on. A good friend of mine thinks about suicide almost every day. But each time I would begin to give up, miraculously one of my 800 or so business partners across Japan would show up, here in Ishinomaki, just to be with me and help in whatever way they could. They helped me shovel the ten tons of mud out of my factory. When they would leave at the end of the day and say ITTEKIMASU (see you later) only then did I believe there would be a tomorrow. Some days I was all alone. Just me, the mud and my grief."

Many times since the disasters, I've sat with circles of people in all parts of Japan. We came together to be in dialogue with each other about what the future might hold. Part of what the future holds is our grief. It will always be part of us. If we try to hide the grief, we become sore and sick. So many have found it too much and have died in temporary housing, sometimes by their own hands, others with deep suffering.

But our capacity to let grief work through us can also give us strength. We discover our ability to come back into right relationship with each other by not making our feelings out to be good or bad, simply accepting them as feelings. When we willingly embrace the ambiguity and the uncertainty that always accompanies grief, we are ready to find the next step forward.

I put this stepping stone of grief last. It is the most powerful. As I share stories since the disasters, I never know when the tears will come, unbidden, ready to work me through to another level. Grief is fuel. I remember those who have dedicated their lives to the descendants of those who died. I remember those who have wondered why they were chosen to live while others passed. I remember the tears I've seen as people mourned the past, gone forever.

When we can speak our grief, and let it speak through us, it is the fuel for a future waiting to be born. We are not alone as we look for what comes AfterNow, today. This journey of finding the future in our present, or discovering new stories, or making a new normal — it is a human journey. We can mark the path as we make it. We can lay down stepping stones.

what Now

WhatNow

PEOPLE KEEP ASKING ME to comment about the current situation in Japan. Beyond the occasional report of the latest incident in the endless catastrophe of radiation in Fukushima, precious little is being shared about what's happening in the disaster area. Even in Japan, not to mention the rest of the world, it can be difficult to get a sense of where things stand today. And, depending on what you look for, there are many answers. Everything has changed and nothing has changed. In some ways, it appears that Japan is back on its feet, having successfully put 3.11 behind it; or that they have fallen back to old ways, belying progress made in response to the disasters; or that there is an ongoing revolution, quiet perhaps, taking place in Japan today, leading to a new future.

The story is far from over. Richard Samuel's book, *3.11: Disaster and Change in Japan,* offers one of the best overviews I've come across. The good, the bad and the ugly are all happening at the same time.

On the plus side, infrastructure has been reconstructed throughout the region. Businesses and factories have been rebuilt. Inland, where the only damage was from the earthquake, not the tsunami and nuclear explosions that decimated the coastal areas, things look much the same as they did before the disasters. Shiny black markers in cemeteries replace those destroyed. New and old buildings stand side-by-side.

On the other hand, the construction of permanent replacement housing has been delayed and delayed again because materials and workmen are building for the 2020 Summer Olympics, not for the people of Japan. Now, the small emergency housing trailer-like units built for close to 300,000 people within six months of the disasters stand mostly empty, with people who have the fewest options feeling trapped there. Many have moved on: some into other parts of Japan; some into permanent housing that has been constructed; others living with friends or relatives and waiting, waiting.

Even worse, nuclear radiation continues to be a challenge on many levels. Nationally the country is divided on whether or not they should restart the nuclear power plants turned off after the Triple Disasters. The current government insists that their restart is necessary for the Japanese economy. About half the population agrees. The other half says not so fast.

What of the progress towards a new way of being, towards a new future? On this front, it sometimes seems that little has changed from the time before the Triple Disasters. The same problems Hakozaki-san talked about in the beginning of Chapter 8 persist: a vibrant new economy is needed — indicators of success for Tohoku that are different from Tokyo's are still needed.

That cracking open I described back in Chapter 2? The relentless pressure to return to the old normal has closed most of those cracks. The current administration of Prime Minister Abe continues to promise a return to the 1990s, when Japan's economy was strong, combined with an increasingly powerful military to stand against real and imagined threats from China and North Korea.

The relationships that were forged in the early stages of rescue and emergency, where people who never talked to each other were reaching out? Some of those relationships persist and grow. Many have returned to the comfort of their old relationships and ways of being.

In Fukushima itself, the tragedy will last many lifetimes. Thousands and thousands of gallons of radiated water pour into the ocean daily, with no end in sight. Of course, the ramifications of this goes far beyond the residents of Fukushima, affecting the health of the planet and all its people. The spent fuel rods in Dai-ichi Four, with its compromised structure, is one of the most dangerous places on earth. Efforts to decontaminate and dismantle the reactors meet overwhelming obstacles and new dilemmas on a regular basis. Tons of low-level nuclear waste gathered as part of the decontamination process are stored in big bags that have a five-year life, piled on temporary sites, waiting to be moved to temporary storage with a promise of a long-term solution that no one sees. *And* the proud and resolute people of Fukushima are making their way forward, one step at a time.

The people of Fukushima reveal that, at the same time, everything has changed. In Chapter 4, I shared the stories of activists who were deeply involved in the Triple Disaster relief and community building. Their stories give a hint of the critical, subtle changes that are taking place. I come into contact with a lot of people in Japan. To be sure, they are not a representative lot. The people who talk with me and come to FutureSessions and other workshops I am hosting are the ones who are stretching towards an invisible future rather than dwelling in a predictable past. With each other, they are discovering their resolve and their confidence to step into a different AfterNow. My old friend Willis Harmon,[49] used to talk about how the world changes when large numbers of people change the way they think a little bit. This is the change we are seeing in Japan. Large numbers of people looking for a new polar star, making and blazing a trail into a new future. I want to share stories from three places I've been recently to give more of a sense of this continuing story.

Fukushima

Where to start with this impossible tale?

It breaks my heart and stirs my hope like nothing else. The people of Fukushima are very real to me. The ones I've known for five years now and the new ones I meet each time I enter the region. Their lineage is ancient; their connection to their land eternal. Towns in the coastal area nearest the reactors, which were completely evacuated, now have some areas open for those who want to return.

Many former residents have moved on to other parts of Japan; now it's becoming clearer who are choosing to return. In 2016, I was talking with Takaai Kanno who had dedicated the last four years of his

---

49 Founding President of the Institute of Noetic Sciences (IONS), Willis was a prolific author who started life as an engineer, then systems scientist and then futurist.

life to the people of Namie, a town of 20,000 a little more than a mile from the reactors, which was 100% evacuated.

Thanks to Safecast, radiation in Fukushima is the most monitored in the world. Everyone has their own opinions about radiation and there's no need for me to add mine. For those who are returning, and for those who never left, there's a fierce determination to make a good life knowing the danger of radiation lurks nearby.

For four years Kan-chan, as he is called, had been reaching out to all of the 20,000 former residents who had been scattered from one end of Japan to the other to help them decide what to do. He was excited to tell me that they had passed a critical milestone. A thousand of them — mostly older — were clear that they wanted to come home to Namie and were committed to building a new community together.

Now, Kanno finally has a group to work with on the future of Namie. To the south, in the 10,000-person town of Okuma, about 2,000 have said they will return. Older men came back first. "We can risk our lives more easily," they said, and have been making plans for their new town.

The story of Itatemura, just over the mountains from Namie and the reactors, is one that breaks my heart and that I want to share here. Itatemura, a small village about 30 miles inland, had a population of about 6,000 at the beginning of 2011. It had a growing reputation all over Japan for its clean water, delicious air and fertile soil.

On March 11, 2011, when the earthquake struck and the tsunami washed in, Itatemura had no damage. But when the reactors exploded on March 12th, Itatemura received one of the largest dumps of radiation in the region. There was so much confusion about what had and was happening and there were so many communication breakdowns that it took almost a week to realize what had happened. When the news came out, the entire village was evacuated. The beautiful village became a ghost town. I was shocked when I visited for the first time in: the silence, the weeds growing in rice fields, house after house shuttered and closed.

I've been there many times. Watching the changes. I was unprepared for what I saw when I visited in November of 2015, and then again one year later.

Some of you may remember the infamous headline during the Vietnam War: "We destroyed the village to save it." That's what is happening in Itatemura. In Tokyo, the decision was made – way over the heads of people in Itatemura – to decontaminate the village by removing all the radiated earth — the top 6 inches — which, of course, is the top soil carefully built up over hundreds of years. It also requires washing the trees and brush by hand, and then removing the soil newly contaminated by this process. The waste is stuffed in black storage bags that will fall apart in five years; the bags are placed in big piles in temporary-temporary-temporary locations for resettling in temporary-temporary locations before being moved to temporary locations before arriving at the non-existent destination of permanent storage.

The waste is being removed at a huge industrial scale and the field and hillsides of the village are being completely ravaged. It is not being done in a way the people who have lived in and loved the village would have proceeded. The "clean-up" proceeds at the direction of Tokyo. Profits are being made, by companies based in Tokyo. It is the

second disaster — and it feels almost more tragic and greater in magnitude than the first! Different choices about how to clean up the radiation are available. For example, remediation by growing mushrooms is definitely experimental and has never been done at this scale, but it works. The chosen path of cleanup was comparatively fast and could be measured (how many new bags of waste), but it leaves behind barren land, bags of waste, and radiation leaking in from the many adjacent lands not cleaned. The human choice to build a nuclear power plant at ocean's edge in a area where earthquakes are common precipitated the first disaster. The human choice to sacrifice the village to clean it was the second.

Such travesties

Some say it is necessary — but, really? By anyone's account, the village will remain uninhabitable for 30-40 years. What else was possible? What would have become visible if absolutely nothing was done for 2-3 years except local people really listening to each other and listening to the land? It is not for me, another outsider, to decide this question — but it is a question intimately important to the people who live in and love Itatemura.

But the "cleanup" is being done with the same mentality that created the nuclear power plants and the ensuing disaster. This is the mentality that says humans dominate and control and the earth is our dominion. We can do whatever we want and we will fix any problem we stir up. Progress is necessary, so come along or step aside.

This beautiful village is being turned into a terra-farmed mega waste site with no regard for anything except to clean it up as soon as possible and then forget about it. Of course, *cleanup* is a relative term. The Tokyo firms have contracts to clear the forests within a particular boundary, but on the other side of the boundary, no action is taken. Guess what happens when it rains? Or when the winds blow? Immediately the certified decontaminated lands are re-contaminated. But the contract work has been carried out and the certificate issued, so the job is done.

It is a heartbreaking mess. And it is an exquisite example of the exercise of "power over" rather than "power with." The central government listened patiently to local people for a while – and then the government made those "hard decisions" that local people "can't make for themselves." What's missing in this picture?

I will stand with the people of Fukushima whenever I can. I will tell their stories. I will help make sure the world does not forget.

Ishinomaki

Further along the coast to the north is the sprawling town of Ishinomaki. About 145,000 people live there now, 12,000 fewer than before the disasters. Homes, shops, businesses, fishing boats and fish processing plants were all destroyed. Most of the first-floor shops in the downtown area were shuttered until 2013, and the train service was only restored in 2014.

My good friend Hideki Iwai has been working in Ishinomaki since shortly after the disasters. I want to share a bit of his special story.

I met Hideki in 2010. He was a Senior Vice President for Tokio Marine & Nichido Systems Co., Ltd.; he knew that the company needed to make many changes to enable it to provide the best possible service.

He also knew that the people in the company needed to find ways to solve existing problems and create new opportunities. But they did not have a process for bringing together their knowledge to create innovation. Hideki had heard about work being done in Europe to create a space — a FutureCenter — to give birth to dialogue and innovation. He was part of the first group to travel to Europe to explore  this new possibility. In 2010, he created one of the very first business FutureCenters in Japan and started to see that when employees had a place for deep, action-oriented dialogue, changes could ensue.

Then, like so many others, Hideki watched helplessly as the countless images of destruction came through on television broadcasts. "I felt overwhelmed," he said, "by the horrible conditions in the disaster area. By looking at the images, I felt I wanted to do something for Tohoku, but I was working with Tokio Marine at the time. The company's employees, including myself, were doing their best to pay out insurance claims as quickly as possible to support the disaster victims. We were taking turns, even during the weekends and holidays, to answer phone calls from the disaster area. There were also people who were not insured and it was so hard to tell people we could not pay them. I was feeling regretful because in my mind, I had this desire to do something, but there was also the work of the company I had to do. Day after day I kept holding this sense of guilt."

By the summer of 2011, Hideki found a way to spend more and more time as a volunteer supporter of JEN, a nonprofit organization working in Ishinomaki. By 2012, he had left his job at Tokio Marine to concentrate completely on Tohoku. This region was different from his hometown in Kyushu, but he was familiar with some of the patterns of rural life. "In the beginning," he said, "people just worked together to do whatever was needed. Jealousies and old fights and fears were put away. But as things got more stabilized, people started look at those they didn't know well with less trust and openness. People started to isolate in the silos of the particular issues they cared about most, or they started paying more attention to the needs of the funders than the needs of the community." Hideki knew something more was needed.

He found places and ways to show up to help. He listened a lot. He started explaining FutureCenters to people. He told them, "It's nothing fancy, but there are ways we can work better together." He interviewed people about their ideas and concerns and then held meetings to ask them help him find meaning and make sense from the interviews. He introduced people to different ways of having dialogue — World Café, Open Space Technology, Circle, Appreciative Inquiry, Transformative Scenario Planning and others.

Mostly what he did was he persevered. He kept coming back, time and time again. Knowing that it takes time to build resilient communities, he stayed at it. He built trust by showing up and acting with integrity. By 2013, he created a new nonprofit organization — Kohaku — to serve as his base of operation. Of course, money was scarce. Hideki had to do consulting work to pay his family's bills, raise money to support Kohaku, and do the FutureCenter work.

What Hideki knew was that people had to find their way back into enough relationship with each other so that they could get stuff done. They don't even have to like each other — but they do need to respect each other and their differences. And then make a path forward, one step at a time.

A year after Kohaku was created, Hideki and I had a conversation about what was changing and what was possible now. He said,

> By 2013, reconstruction of the hardware side started to become visible: fishing ports and factories to process fishery products, plans for road construction and other things on the physical side. The phrase "creative rebuilding," which was often said right after the disaster, has been taken over by just simple reconstruction. Some of the local fishermen and farmers were trying new ways of adding values to their business, literally practicing "creative rebuilding," but when I came to have an overview of what local people and industries were doing, it seemed to me that the momentum to jointly re-create the community to better places than before the disaster had started to fade away. Or maybe I should say that many people had not had such an image from the beginning. I came to see, more and more, how long this work would take.

Most of the local people had enough on their hands to just re-build their own lives. It was natural for them not to be able to imagine new ways of living which were even better than before the disasters. In order to have such imagination, serious deep discussions and information sharing was needed across the sectors, including the governments, residents, agriculture, fishery, service industry, etc. But that did not happen.

All the rebuilding efforts after the disaster can be an opportunity to realize new ways of living and new styles of communities, proposed as the "Vitalization of Regions" initiatives by the government, in advance of the other parts of Japan. But, so far, it seems that we need a lot more efforts and time to make it happen.

What is most important is for people in the communities to love and take pride in their communities. That pride is the source of creative ideas. I know many people have the pride in their community from the beginning. But efforts and time are needed to make people become aware of the pride within, take actions for the community, and cooperate with one another. It has been almost four years since the disaster, and the rebuilding of hardware has been making progress. But, on the other hand, negative aspects of time passing have been emerging. For example, the weak members of society, who are having difficulty in recovering economically and/or mentally, are facing increasing challenges.

The key to create new ways of living and community, based on the strengths of Ishinomaki, is for all the Ishinomaki people to remember their love and pride in this community and to share that feeling.

The work to build community continues. Kohaku is helping people make a new future now. Frankly, the work is frustrating and rewarding, energizing and exhausting. But Iwai-san keeps connecting people back to what they love. He keeps asking what brings them happiness. He reminds them to find joy.

Here are some current examples of Kohaku's work in Ishinomaki.

Kohaku supports **Civic Pride Ishinomaki,** which is connecting local people to their love and pride in Ishinomaki and asking them to visualize that love and pride as a souvenir. The souvenirs catalyze

a sense of oneness among the residents and invite more interest from outside. Kohaku creates meeting spaces — BA — where people can share their honest feelings with each other. They meet, they talk, they drink tea. They talk with each other, remembering the past and seeing the future.

The **Minamihama Memorial Park** is scheduled to be open in the spring of 2021. The establishment of the park has not been easy;

it has been a hard, emotional time. The long-time residents have mixed feelings about the park plan because 400 people were lost in the area, and another 150 people have yet to be found. Something special was needed to help residents, together with the city, prefecture, and central governments, plan the best possible park. Kohaku worked with local leaders and supported different governmental jurisdictions by designing and facilitating workshops for engaging the citizens in constructive dialogue.

In the **Kawanokami** area, just a few miles inland from the Ishinomaki port, permanent housing is being built for two very different towns — Okawa and Ogatsu — both decimated by the tsunami. Ogatsu was home to fishers. Okawa was home to farmers. Their ways of looking at the world and being with each other are very different — and it is not easy to communicate across those differences. A wise community leader said, "We need a BA where we can get to know each other and start working together." And then he said, "I know the right place." He arranged for the use of an empty rice storage building and together people from both Okawa and Ogatsu raised money to turn it into a new center for their blended community. Kohaku supported the local dialogues where people designed the center. Now Kohaku is now hosting necessary conversations in the center, among the residents in the Kawanokami area — both new and old — for them to build a better life together.

Of course, Hideki has also discovered that he needs to take care of himself if he's going to do this work for the rest of his life. He must see to his own happiness. He's woven his love of motorcycles into a way to connect people with the deep beauty of Tohoku through "Go for Ride in Tohoku!" which aims to keep the memory of 3.11 alive and to showcase this incredible region. Motorbike riders from across the country come to tour along the Sanriku Coast in Aomori, Iwate,

Miyagi, and Fukushima. A successful pre-event was held in 2015, and in 2016 motorcyclists from across Japan toured along the Sanriku Coast from May to October.

These are small steps. But they add up to something, they have begun to build community and create a new future for the area. They may be small, but they reveal a new view of how change happens. I'm sure there are times and places for master plans — including a lot in Tohoku right now. But plans only build what we know and see. They mostly re-create the past.

We need to be co-creating a future, *now*. We do that when we figure out what's really important to us — what it is that brings us joy — and come together with others who care to figure out how to make it happen! When people come together in this way, there is a delicious taste in the air. More laughter. People looking carefully and kindly at each other. Passion. The confidence that we have vision, relationships and a place to start.

In Ishinomaki, Kohaku offers the design and facilitation skills for people to co-create a future. They provide a means to explore what is possible now. Across the region others are doing similar work. I offer

Kohaku's story because of my respect for Hideki and the possibilities to which he has dedicated his life.

Onagawa

Onagawa, a town of 10,000 on Japan's northeast coast, is part of the larger Ishinomaki area. It was hit by a tsunami wave towering 60 feet and rushing forward at 60 miles an hour. The devastation and destruction were beyond imagination. 85% of the town was destroyed. As I wrote in Chapter 2, I visited Onagawa in April, 2011. In January of 2016, I returned for the first time in almost five years and was amazed by the stories I heard.

I took this picture of the harbor five weeks after the tsunami came. We had traveled through mile after mile of rubble and debris to reach the harbor. The destruction was overwhelming.

In January 2016, I hosted a three-day leadership learning journey for executives of a Japanese company. The view is different now. Rebuilding continues.

Local government, citizens, business, and national government have all been working together to create a new future. Aoyama-san, from the Chamber of Commerce, took us back to the day of the disasters:

Onagawa Harbour, January 2016.

> We had breakfast that morning, my wife and kids and I. I was in my office when the tsunami came and I climbed the water tower on top of our building. As the water came as high as my chest as I clung to the tower that night, I wondered, why didn't I pick up my kids and kiss them goodbye as we left for our jobs and day care? It was so cold and so hard as wave after wave came in. I wanted to give up, but I wanted to see my children more. It's not so much

that I was afraid of dying — but I wanted to do more things for my kids.

The tsunami helped me see that none of us have to be excellent alone. We just need to stand up together. I'm a high school graduate and I don't speak any English. But I can help. With passion, we can overcome anything.

Our beautiful town of 10,000 was 85% destroyed. Unimaginable. 827 people died and another 257 are missing, their bodies never recovered. Our school gymnasium was converted into an emergency shelter where my family and I lived with 2,000 other people. Some were there for nine months. Within a week of the disasters we were starting to talk about where to begin. We couldn't tell who was in government and who was in business or how people used to spend their days. We knew we had to get together and do something.

Fifty of us came together to form FRK, a rebuilding association at the Chamber of Commerce. Most of us were in our 30s and 40s. Our community elders said to us, "Rebuilding will take 20-30 years. We will support you as you provide the leadership and vision this community needs now." We all knew that local government can help — but can't do everything. Citizens are needed. What's most important is unity of the people and most especially the energy of young people.

There used to be divisions and blocks between local business, big business, government and ordinary people — but we had to get together. Everyone began to think about "the town we can leave for our children. We started out drawing pictures in our FutureCenter and we began to see that we wanted a town that:

- Is eco-friendly
- Has clean water
- Has food security
- Is kind to children, elderly and disabled

It continues to be a very challenging time. 37% of the people living in Onagaea before the disasters are gone. And even today, nearly five years later, 2003 people live in temporary housing and 654 live in various shared spaces.

Sato-san, a public health worker in the Onagawa Town Office talked about how so much care was and still is needed — not just for those who have critical life-threatening needs, but for everyone. "We were all traumatized by the disasters. In some ways, it has been especially hard for many men who lost whatever status they had from their jobs or their volunteer associations and who, in the shelters, started to drink more and more with no purpose in their lives.

"There are many limits to what government can do," she said, "so we began to focus our attention on creating the conditions for citizens to take action themselves. One good example of this was that we realized that more than anything people just needed someone to listen to their stories. We created a program of "volunteer listeners" who organized themselves to go out and listen to people's stories. As health care workers, we tend to focus only on health care, but our real focus needs to be on quality of life. Relationships with others is the basis for quality of life. Specialists and supporters won't be here forever — we must do what's needed ourselves. How do we continue this community building spirit when things look more normal?"

Downtown Onagawa

As the community worked together, beauty has started to grow from the rubble. The main shopping street opposite the train station is one example. Shopping streets in most small communities are pretty drab affairs. Even on the shopping streets where cars have been eliminated, utilitarian storefronts, shuttered at night, give little sense of beauty and vitality. The people of Onagawa wanted something different.

And what they've created is just lovely! The Train Station across the highway from this shopping street complements its beauty and even has an ONSEN — a Japanese hot bath — on the upper floor. Come to town, have a relaxing bath, stroll to the shops and restaurants while watching the sunset!

I first met Onagawa's Mayor in early 2012, not long after he had been elected. I was at a planning forum in Tokyo with seven mayors from the disaster area. Six were near 70 and talked about what they needed. In contrast, Suda-san, Onagawa's Mayor and 43 years old, talked about what they had and how they had an opportunity that comes along only once in 1,000 years, to build a new community from zero. And that's just what they have done.

Suda-san was elected in November of 2011 after having spent three terms on the Miyagi Prefectural Council. The former mayor was a friend who encouraged him to run for office, saying that his vision and insight was needed now. Suda-san is quite a guy.

"We have a very small city staff," he said, "and I knew right away that we had to collaborate with everyone to make anything happen. From the very beginning, we said that whatever we do in Onagawa it needs to be sustainable, efficient and useable:

> I have spent much of my time as mayor building consensus and communicating. Government is not above people; we are all equal partners. Each citizen must be involved. Four days after becoming mayor, I looked closely at the plan for redeveloping Onagawa and I felt something was not quite right. I talked to the former mayor, and he mentioned that he had some anxiety as well. I called together a group of nine people and discovered that we each had misgivings about the plan.
>
> I knew something more was needed and that it had to come from all of us. To make it easier for people to be involved, I participated in 80 information groups, which led to creating citizen working groups for specifics. Government's job is to decide the broad picture with specifics decided by the working groups — it became everyone's plan, not just mine. People worked hard and once a month we published all information on the plan as it was developing. By January of 2012 we had a completely new plan developed

with citizens. We changed some things thought to be permanent — like the topography of our town.

Soon after becoming mayor I realized I had three roles. First, I was just another citizen with my own hopes and dreams. Second, I was a politician and my work was to convene people, listen to them and help them listen to each other. Third, I was mayor with the job of directing local government to build and run what citizens want in our community.

These three stories offer a glimpse of what is happening now. Everything is the same and everything is different. People are living into a future which is both new and yet the same. They will continue to find each other. New lives and new communities will emerge. It just takes time.

These are also proxy for similar stories of what is happening in communities across Tohoku, throughout Japan and in communities everywhere on this lovely planet. They are the stories of people who have stepped forward to make the difference they can. I know in my bones that this work makes a difference.

I also know it is time now to elevate it, make it visible, connect the people doing the work, and start to get much clearer about the difference we want to make. New terminology is flying around — *combining emergence with rigor* and *co-creating collective impact* are a couple phrases I am working with. In a time when old systems and old ways of making meaning are collapsing and new ones are still often tentative and weak, we must be persistent and patient, persevering in our efforts to live in ways that make sense again.

I know the stories of the courageous, ordinary people in Japan who have faced disaster and come out of the other side will have opened up questions and possibilities for you. I hope my own story of my journey in Japan will help you in taking your next steps. And I hope the ideas I have shared here will be of use to you in your life and work.

These are remarkable times. May we continue to find our way forward, one step at a time!

Living in the messy middle

CHAPTER

10

Living in the
Messy Middle

Tao Te Ching #15

The ancient Masters were profound and subtle.
Their wisdom was unfathomable.
There is no way to describe it;
all we can describe is their appearance.

They were careful
as someone crossing an iced-over stream.
Alert as a warrior in enemy territory.
Courteous as a guest.
Fluid as melting ice.
Shapable as a block of wood.
Receptive as a valley.
Clear as a glass of water.

Do you have the patience to wait
till your mud settles and the water is clear?
Can you remain unmoving
till the right action arises by itself?

The Master doesn't seek fulfillment.
Not seeking, not expecting,
she is present, and can welcome all things

— translated by Stephen Mitchell (2006)

I KEEP COMING back to the third stanza of this chapter of the Tao Te
Ching. Do *I* have the patience to wait till *my* mud settles and the water is clear? I've been on an incredible journey. Like the people whose
stories I have shared throughout this book, I have been shaped by the

Triple Disasters. I have seen what happens when the present collapses and the future disappears. I have also come to understand that disasters bring great pain and they also open the way for new possibilities. Even while the future is very muddy, I am clearer now, more sure about what can happen when people come together in community.

We are in the messy middle these days. At a societal level, old structures and forms and ways of seeing our world that no longer serve us still dominate, while the new, barely born, is often weak, isolated, disconnected and fragile. The same is true in institutions in which we work and play and pray and learn and heal. The same is true in our own personal lives. Going back to the Two Loops, the old loop is much easier to see than the new. I have learned how important it is to be able to stand, together, in this messy middle of our times and discover the hope and energy in that space.

This book is my story; this is just the way I see and understand the times we are living in. I am not alone in seeing this story; hear this story expressed by many voices in Chapter 11. Each idea and method in this book is one I know intimately and have worked with in many settings. That Two Loops diagram back in Chapter 6? It lives in me. The Cynefin structure I introduced in Chapter 7? Same thing. I return to it time and time again because it helps me not get lost in our sometimes overwhelming, confusing times.

I know in my bones that we are in the midst of major transformations. We all have a long road to walk. The greatest challenge, I think, is to learn how to stand tall rather than collapse small in the messy middle of our times. Twenty years ago, Charlene Spretnak wrote that in our hypermodern world there are still three things that were negotiable: body, place and nature. But many of us have fallen out of healthy relationship with our bodies, been distanced from any sense of place and separated from nature. We must reclaim these three aspects of our lives. And we can learn to prosper in this messy middle. I suspect most of us will be there for the rest of our lives.

One key, I think, is learning to live in an alchemy of opposites, holding the tension of ways of being that pull us in separate directions.

We're in a time when we must have clear intentions — but we must surrender and let them go, time and time again, as we find our way forward. Clarity is helpful, but it is often in our confusion that we find the right way forward. Sometimes it is still possible to plan and organize while other times we must work with the emergent. We have to know when to push for change and when to accept what is — at least for now.

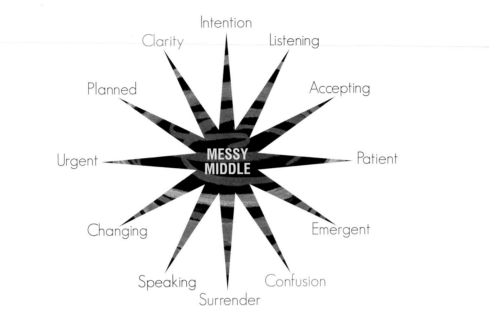

This list of seeming opposites goes on and on. They surround the messy middle. The stepping stones I described earlier in this book help us walk in the mess of our times. But where do these stones lead? I don't know. The future is invisible. We proceed, together, step-by-step. This is what it is like to live in an epoch of transformation.

Even when the future is invisible we need a sense of direction, a polar star that we can see at times, a horizon that beckons us. Our values, principles and beliefs help to provide that direction. The stories, companionship and insights of those who are also searching sustain us on the journey. We also need images and metaphors to help us understand what the hell transformation actually is.

For me transformation is like what happens in a garden. It can be beautiful and bountiful, but there's a lot of work to do. The soil has to be prepared. Research is needed about what plants play well with each other and in what temperature zones. Seeds have to be planted. The ground has to be tended and watered and the seedlings need to be nourished. Weeds need to be removed. Seedlings need to be thinned. Gradually things of beauty and things that are edible begin to emerge. They are harvested and arranged, or cooked and eaten, in one way or another. And then they become compost, returned to the garden.

This is a different image from that of the butterfly that is typically used as the metaphor for transformation. In the butterfly story, the caterpillar dissolves into primordial ooze, imaginal cells triumph and the beauty of the butterfly simply emerges whole and complete. That may be the way it is for butterflies, but for us humans the story of transformation is punctuated by intention, hard work, abundance, and cycles.

It is a long road. And we have the tools and processes, heart and spirit, creativity and innovation to find our way — together.

My delightful editor tells me I am putting too many new images and frameworks here at the end of this book. She's right, of course. But this ending is a beginning as well and I have a chance right now to share some of what is clear and confused for me right now. I do the work I do because I continue to learn. I am changed, challenged, informed and inspired by each group of people I meet.

As I moved towards the completion of this book in May, 2017, I noticed myself becoming more and more unsettled, almost anxious. Zaid Hassan, a dear friend from the UK as me an obvious question: "So what are you going to do with the book when it is published?" I went wide-eyed like a deer caught in the headlights: I had no idea! As my unsettleness grew, I assumed I was that I was in the land of author doubts, questioning the value of this book and the amount of time, energy and money it has taken to complete the English edition. A very recent conversation with my good friend Laurie Adams from River's Bend in Northern California on her birthday helped me see a very different view. Laurie asked, "When did you start writing this book?" I was shocked when I realized I started to write what would be the Japanese edition more than 4 years ago, in early 2013. That book was published in Tokyo in June of 2015, and I started working on the English edition in the fall of 2015. Altogether, it been more than four years! As we talked further, I realized that this book represents the culmination of more than 17 years of learning and work, which started in 2000 when NewStories joined with The Berkana Institute and PeerSpirit to launched From the Four Directions. *Seventeen years.*

My unsettleness, almost anxiety, is not about the chapters of this book, it is about what feels like the culmination of a chapter of my life!

Guess what? I am here in my own messy middle with little clarity about what comes AfterNow and uncertain about how I find my way into my invisible future!

I'm so grateful for this insight. It makes me feel so much better about this book. It lets me take in the kind things said as endorsements by voices from my larger community in the next chapter. A sigh of relief has welled up inside of me. I know a little bit about being in the messy middle. I know something about finding my way with an invisible future!

While I don't know many specifics about what comes AfterNow for Bob, I will find my stepping stones. I know that whenever and however possible, I will support the wonderful people in Fukushima in all ways that I can. I have special relationships there that have touched my heart. My work has taken me to many other parts of Japan as well: Tokyo, the Kansai region of my Kyoto home, and Hokkaido, Shikoku, and Kyushu. I will continue to help people build the confidence they need to step forward into the stories they want to create.

I will also support the work of Kohaku FutureCenter, described in Chapter 9, however I can. I believe that Hideki and his team will continue to expand the use of FutureCenters in Tohoku. Likewise, I will support the work of FutureSessions and Taka Nomura throughout Japan. We need special BA to create a new future.

I'll support my good friend Hide Enomoto to bring Active Hope into Japan. Mentioned briefly in Chapter 7, Active Hope is one of the best ways of working with the energy of grief that I have encountered. As I end this book I realized that I haven't talked at all about the incredible work of the Co-Cre Community (Co-Creation Community) that I helped to start in 2014 with my dear friend Ai Sanda from Recruit. I'll continue to support, and to study, co-creation in Japan.

Nor have I mentioned the action learning cohort of leading facilitators of social innovation in Japan that I've created with Hide Enomoto and Taka Nomura that started at the end of 2015 after a week at River's Bend, when I asked Hide, *How might I best serve in Japan, now?*

There's renewed and growing interest in my enspirited leadership framework described in Chapter 1. In just the last six months it has shifted into enspirited being and leadership — I keep learning and learning.

In Japan, I will support ETIC and anyone else I can in their efforts to develop the new structures for learning that we need. I will do this everywhere I can — in North America and around the world.

For me, it is also time to focus more of my attention back in the country and culture of my birth. Others can do a better job than I can in designing and hosting FutureSessions and other opportunities for collaboration in Japan. In this life, my facility with the Japanese language is just not going to get that much better!

And there's a new story emerging in North America. People are coming together and creating healthy, thriving, resilient community again. The work and voices of those engaged in these efforts are frequently drowned out by the shrill and acrimonious voices of a contentious and fearful culture. But these new stories are present. And they will grow.

I'm learning to take better care of myself, placing a priority on my own health and wellbeing. Time for more space for my own enspirited being. I am in training to be a sacred outsider, arriving with listening and presence and offering what I can as a dialogue host and a teacher.

Right now, in the U.S., my work in 2016 with the Robert Wood Johnson Foundation on creating a culture of health is leading me into more work that is focused on health. My work with a Foundations for Education project in Washington State is inviting me to engage more around our systems and institutions for learning. I'm also focused now on developing and practicing better ways to evaluate and communicate the results of the work many of us are doing to use emergence to co-create collective impact.

Writing these last paragraphs makes it sound like I know what I am doing. Truthfully, I don't. I need to listen. I need to quiet myself. I want to pay attention to all these possibilities and I want to show up for what is invisible. I want to stay in the messiness. Wish me well, and join me!

Voices
from my
Larger
Community

CHAPTER

11

Voices From My Larger Community

In early May, 2017, when this book was far enough along that I could label it as "Review Copy," I started sending it off to friends for review, comment and hopefully endorsement. As time went on, I reached out to other authors, friends and colleagues in Japan, and to my wider community of innovators and creators. Every day or two, I would think of someone else and send off another e-mail.

I was bowled over by the response. And I quickly turned it into a problem! How do I choose which to include in the book? It took me weeks to realize that these were not simply endorsements; they were the voices from the community in which I've been cooked and baked, eaten and born over the last 17 years. While I have been the one to write this book; its ingredients are the insights, wisdom and experience of hundreds of people with whom I've traveled for almost two decades. Their comments offer valuable and important windows into and from *AfterNow*. I decided to include them all to share their perspectives on the insights in this book, which are not mine alone, and to honor this beautiful community with whom I've made this journey.

They offer many windows into *AfterNow* from the personal experience from many who have been on this long road, together.

Words from Other Authors

I have deep respect for the wisdom of my author friends, who, like me, have taken the time to distill their experience into books. For us it's our best way to share our insights and experience. It is our art form. Meg Wheatley and Mary Catherine Bateson, who wrote the Foreword and Afterword, are also, of course, master artists among this company of friends.

"Bob Stilger has written a brilliant, personal account of how to apply a learning orientation to complex issues of community renewal. His engagement with events in Japan after the Triple Disasters represents a real-world application of working with volatility and uncertainty in groups, social networks, and organizations. *AfterNow* is alive with theory, models, practices, and processes that can enliven any group."

Alan Briskin, USA, author, The Stirring of Soul in the Workplace

"For well over two decades, we have been both witness to Bob Stilger's work and the beneficiaries of his deep learning. *AfterNow*'s wisdom, stories, principles and practical applications come from Bob's life-long work all over the world, working with people on the ground and learning together on behalf of the common good. Not only is this a fascinating read for anyone interested in how real change happens, it's an essential teaching for anyone who aspires to be of service to those seeking to transform their organizations, communities and the larger world."

Carole and David Schwinn, USA, co-authors, The Transformative
Workplace: Growing People, Purpose, Prosperity and Peace

"Following the Triple Disasters of 2011 many things floated across the Pacific Ocean to North America. But until now, we have yet to have the impressions and insights of a faithful witness who accompanied, learned from and interpreted the experience of his Japanese friends and colleagues as they lived with the disasters and the subsequent changes in their lives and society. Bob Stilger is a passionate observer of resilience and he has dedicated his life to weaving together the disparate experiences of peoples around the world so that all may benefit from the collective learning of human communities. *AfterNow* is powerful artifact of his own learning in Japan and offers grounded maps and practices for our times. It is a gift from a troubled present to a hopeful future."

Chris Corrigan, Canada, author, The Tao of Holding Space

"In *AfterNow*, Bob Stilger brings the unique perspective of the Sacred Outsider, someone who offers profound listening and presence. In this book, he offers that listening most directly to the tragedy of Japan's Triple Disasters, but the thread of his compassionate presence brings the reader into an understanding of the patterns of crisis and resilience that permeate our global culture today. He invites us to consider what else might be possible if, rather than waiting for disaster to strike to remember what matters, we in this moment, now, reclaim our commitment to community and connection."

Deborah Frieze, USA, author, Walk Out Walk On: A Learning
Journey into Communities Daring to Live the Future Now

"In this brilliant book, Bob Stilger offers a welcome guide to strengthen our personal and community capacities for resilience and prepare for the inevitable upcoming changes, challenges, and crisis. Bob draws deep insight from his work helping communities around the globe discover the power of their collective wisdom. Offering inspiring examples of the courage, clarity and community that can emerge when people gather to discover and create new potentials when old certainties and assumptions of the past have been shattered and washed away."

Joel and Michelle Levey, USA, co-authors: Living in Balance:
A Mindful Guide for Thriving in a Complex World

"Bob and I have been colleagues for decades and I've followed the evolution of his thinking and professional practice over many years. His work in supporting community resilience under devastating conditions is a lesson for all of us as we seek to navigate the uncharted territory that awaits so many communities facing unprecedented challenges. We live in a time of tsunamis, tornadoes, financial crisises, wars, oil spills, political/institutional breakdowns, and climate change. Many of us around the globe are or will be facing situations that Bob has so ably helped communities to navigate after the tragedies in Japan. The lessons and principles in *AfterNow* have already been useful with many facing the Japanese disasters. I have confidence that his message and the practical frameworks he offers will find resonance with all of us facing uncertain futures under unknowable conditions."

Juanita Brown, USA, author, The World Café: Shaping
Our Futures Through Conversations That Matter

"If I could only have one book about leading social innovation on my shelf, AfterNow would be my choice. To read Bob Stilger's stories is to sit next to a master practitioner — one who is both humble and generous with his teaching. AfterNow provides much more than a set of principles and methods for community-based change. It invites us into a way of being that unleashes hope, imagination and resolve in the face of confusion and despair."

Larry Dressler, USA, author, Standing in the Fire: Leading
High Heat Meetings with Clarity, Calm and Courage.

"I was very fortunate to be part of the team that worked with Bob on *AfterNow*. I have greatly appreciated his openness, wisdom, humility, and good humor. Through our work together, I have gained both a friend and valuable insights into how we, by working together in community, can find ways forward even in times of chaos. It gives me hope for our future."

Megan Scribner, USA, editor, co-author, Teaching with Heart.

"In Bob Stilger's beautifully crafted and life-affirming book, *AfterNow*, we hear the echo of the poet John Keat's line: 'There is nothing stable in the world; uproar's your only music.' We hear this music every time we are surprised by those many aspects of life that are not controlled by us. *AfterNow* guides us towards finding faith that even in the presence of harm; life knows what it is doing. Our encounter with the unknown is not only something to accept, but to be sought after. By following the path through anxiety, grief, and sudden loss of place, life can be transmuted into something of beauty within which a deeper truth can be found."

Michael Jones, Canada, pianist and author The Soul of Place: Re-imagining Leadership Through Nature, Art and Community.

"Complexity, self-organization, emergence, resilience — Bob Stilger grounds these abstractions in real experiences of upheaval and change, movingly captured in stories of his work following Japan's Triple Disasters of earthquake, tsunami and nuclear explosions. If you seek the means to navigate through uncertainty with a spirit of community, *AfterNow* offers insights, wisdom, and practices to help you on your path. I recommend the journey."

Peggy Holman, USA, author, Engaging Emergence: Turning Upheaval into Opportunity and co-author, The Change Handbook.

"Each now
AfterNow
Asks: "Are we 'We' yet?""

AfterNow is triune gift for unleashing powerful we-ness. Bob offers readers:

- a culminating artifact that gathers together social innovation practices he has collaboratively honed over the past 20 years in communities addressing dire circumstances and daring opportunities;
- an invitation to plumb the depths of transferable wisdom for these times made visible by his masterful storytelling about Japanese resilience in meeting their 2011 Triple Disasters of earthquake, tsunami, and nuclear explosions; and
- evidence that collaborative attentiveness to restorative beauty works. Bob offers his many gifts wrapped in a bow of courageous compassion."

Rachel Bagby, USA, author, Divine Daughter: Liberating the Power and Passion of Women's Voices, and Daughterhood.

"Bob Stilger has given us all a tremendous gift of insight, guidance and wisdom. This book is about a way forward that we can each help to build. And at its heart, it is a book about the triumph of the innate human spirit and capacities for placing us on a path of possibility and hope in a troubled time. Read this book and you will cheer."

Rich Harwood, USA, author, The Work of Hope: How
Individuals & Organizations Can Authentically Do Good.

"Bob Stilger has written a heartfelt guidebook for our tumultuous times. It's not easy to think and behave in new ways when facing an unknown future. Working with Fukushima communities following Japan's Triple Disasters, Bob demonstrates the power of new stories rooted in an ecological worldview, where the healing power of community allows us not only to survive but to thrive. Full of models and tools, *AfterNow* is an artful manual for creating a positive future in this chaotic historical moment."

Rick Ingrasci USA., co-author, Chop Wood, Carry Water: A
Guide to Finding Spiritual Fulfillment in Everyday Life.

"Reading *AfterNow*, I immediately thought of my journey across North America when I wrote *The Revolution Where You Live*. We've both been looking at what happens when people stand up and stand together to do what's needed to make life better. Bob shares the stories of his own journey into Japan's disasters of earthquake, tsunami and nuclear explosions. He writes about what he heard from people as they found how to step forward. He describes the tools, views and approaches he used and taught to help people create a new normal. It's a remarkable book, based on years of direct experience witnessing and supporting people who knew they had to make the world they wanted."

Sarah van Gelder, USA, author, The Revolution Where
You Live, co-founder of YES! Magazine

"Among the many patterns I see to make participatory culture wiser are the determined use of uncertainty, possibility thinking, spaces for dialogue, the power of listening, feeling heard and collaboration. We can make creative use of diversity and disturbance, partnership culture, life-enhancing enoughness, the commons, powerful questions, story sharing, working through feelings, generative interactions, and integrity with authenticity. Having worked with Bob Stilger, the compassionately insightful author of *AfterNow*, I am not surprised to see every one of these patterns manifest in the book. Bob highlights them in relationship to our encounters with disaster, and thus in our encounters with each other, to whom we must turn in times of need. In so turning we can begin to discover the wisdom that can come alive among us as we co-create what is next, *AfterNow*, today. Japan is exemplar in *AfterNow*, but we all can recognize our common ground and learn from Bob's important insights and stories."

Tom Atlee, USA, author, The Tao of Democracy.

"For me, *AfterNow* is one of the most eagerly anticipated pieces of writing in a decade. The practice that Bob embodies and describes has elegance and grace coupled with steel. I am reminded of why the work matters. Thank you."

Zaid Hassan, UK, author, The Social Labs Revolution: A New
Approach to Solving our Most Complex Challenges

View from Friends and Colleagues in Japan

While I wrote this edition of *AfterNow* for people outside of Japan, I reached back to my friends and colleagues in Japan to share their impressions of my work over the last seven years. I knew none of them before 2010. Now, we've seen the tears in each other's eyes and we've listened to the laughter of our souls. We have experienced disaster together. We have created hope and possibility together.

"Bob Stilger is a genius who weaves the future from the here and now, when we don't know what is right and are in chaos and confusion. I've worked with Bob for many years in Japan and have been with him when

he senses into the invisible atmosphere — the BA — and then poses the questions the BA needs. He loves Japan deeply and wholeheartedly and is able to be in the BA with a perspective, position, insights, and professionalism. This love and determination is only possible for a person who believes in people and BA. I believe that is what happened in Bob's work in Japan in our time of chaos. AfterNow is a hint to shed a light on what's next in the world. I hope the love and wisdom of this book will reach many."

Ai Sanda, Japan, founder, Co-Creation! Project, researcher, Jalan Research Center - Recruit Lifestyle Company, LTD.

"*AfterNow* made me feel as if I was experiencing the events and leaning since the Triple Disasters first-hand. It shows how Bob has helped people stay "enspirited" while taking action amid waves of confusion and changes. I'm just so glad that this sad but significant event which took place in Japan can be witnessed through these stories from Bob and everyone around him. Many people around the world, and in Japan, are already forgetting what happened six years ago. We need to learn, not forget. I've known Bob and worked closely with him since 2010 when Bob was introducing Art of Hosting in Japan. First I was just his shadow as an interpreter, but over years Bob has become my teacher, friend, and brother after working together in so many dialogue sessions in Japan, and some in US. *AfterNow* is relevant to everyone who lives in the messy middle — which might just be literally everyone on the planet. We all do live in the time of great turmoil."

Chie Aikawa, Japan, social-focused interpreter / diversity facilitator at GiFT

"As the coastal region of northeast Japan was shaken by the earthquakes and was wiped out by the tsunami so was our belief that tomorrow will be just an extension of today. Although what happened that day was extreme in its scope and scale, I think "3.11" is now happening every day in our lives. Unexpected events can happen anytime and things usually don't move according to our plan. In spite of this obvious fact, we still spend so much time and energy in setting goals and laying out plans as if we can control the future. *AfterNow* offers a different perspective: we need to shift our paradigm in terms of how we create our future. Bob clearly shows that the way we used to create our future no longer works. His point is that we always have to start from the present and also from the people turning to one another. We must let the future emerge rather than manufacturing it. He makes the case through sharing stories of people who worked and are still working tirelessly to create a different future made possible by this historical disaster. The message and the methods contained in this book apply to people everywhere who are trying to create a different future by creating it differently!"

Hide Enomoto, Japan, co-founder of Transition
Japan and Seven Generations

"We still remember when we first visited Tohoku with our friend Bob Stilger a month after the unimaginable tsunami hit. It was the beginning of his journey to create the space for many people — including us — to embrace our pain and focus not on what we lost but what we have within. *AfterNow* has had a significant impact for people in Japan. Bob offers beautiful and precise articulation of what happened in our mind at those moments. These stories remind us of the new possibilities which become present and visible after tragedy. We sincerely hope the English edition will connect our experiences and learnings with further new stories of people around the globe!"

Hideyuki and Yuki Inoue, Japan, co-founders, Inno-lab International Inc.

"In a world of exponential change the importance and power of collective intelligence is like never before in history. Bob shares key insights on how to build communities, react to rapid unexpected change and how to be in your heart when finding your true purpose in life. Seeing Japan's resilience from an outsider's perspective also provides useful insights into being civil in a crisis."

Patrick Newell, Japan, co-founder TEDxTokyo

"*AfterNow* is a great resource of knowledge for those who want to create a better future through personal, organizational and social change processes. Disruptions that make us vulnerable come suddenly. The vulnerability causes our life and work to derail in troublesome ways, but it also offers a tremendous opportunity to create a future we want. It requires a balance of patience and swiftness, preservation and agile learning. Bob not only offers useful tools and frameworks such as the Two Loops and Arts of Hosting, but more importantly portrays how human beings can bring themselves to the present moments with people in great distress, tensions and needs so that we can co-create futures. His humbleness and compassion, among his other characteristics, provides a role model for facilitators and designers for organizational and social changes. I highly recommend *AfterNow* for navigating our time in all the continents of the globe."

Riichiro Oda, Japan, general manager, Japan for Sustainability;
chairperson, Society for Organizational Learning Japan Community

"Bob is always illuminating ahead for me. When we had the Triple Disasters in 2011, he told me that the indicators of success in Japan would change soon. Since then, he has been sitting beside us for more than five years, and weaving "new stories" of how we cultivate viable cross-sector communities, re-creating our social systems by ourselves. The Japanese edition of *AfterNow* was truly a valuable reminder and a resource of knowledge for the people of Japan. This edition will help social innovators around the world who develop resilient communities."

Takahiko Nomura, Japan, Innovation Facilitator,
Founder of Future Sessions Inc.

"Bob Stilger shows us that crisis and confusion are opportunities from which we can make a new future. Grassroots conversations make it so. *AfterNow* invites us to listen to our inner voice — the answers are always within. Dialogue with others helps people find their way forward when they cannot see a future. Bob's story made a deep impact on readers in Japan. May this edition serve the world."

Tatsunari Takano, Japan, senior editor, Eiji Press,
publisher of the Japanese edition

Comments from Innovators and Co-Creators Around the World

Since NewStories joined with PeerSpirit and The Berkana Institute to launch a global leadership initiative — *From the Four Directions* — in 2000, I've had the opportunity to be with people all over this lovely planet of ours. We've met around campfires and in ballrooms as we've listened to each other to develop insights and perspective to help guide our work. Together, we've created and worked with the many ideas I used in Japan and that I've shared in *AfterNow*. This is the lived experience of collective intelligence!

"What I love about *AfterNow* is its provocative invitation to stay in the confusion and "messiness in the middle" long enough that right action may emerge. This book is both extremely timely on a practical level, given the many global crises we face at this time, as well as a great resource for any of us facing difficulties or disruption on a personal level. I found Bob's wisdom deeply insightful as I struggle on my own journey, beginning with the very first page: "We need to let go of the pretense that we can know what will result from our actions. We need to embrace radical uncertainty, showing up as fully as we can each moment, each breath." YES! Thank you, Bob Stilger, for your courage, your perseverance and your dedication to sharing the stories of the Triple Disasters in Japan and all of the amazing learning that has come forth from Japan and all around the world since that day the earth trembled back in 2011."

Aerin Dunford, USA and Mexico, former program coordinator, The Berkana Institute

"Every once in a while, a book appears at the exact moment that humanity needs it. *AfterNow* is such a book. It shines light on the ways that we, as a civilization, are living in a trance, and how disaster can be our wake-up call. Yet, as Bob notes "Disaster changes everything. And it changes nothing." How do we take our sacred moments of despair and use them to find our way back to a deeper, more authentic life — as individuals and as communities? Bob's premise is that everything we need to face disaster is in our present moment. Filled with depth, beauty and the soaring of the human spirit, his stories call us to face forward into the great unknowable future together."

Alicia Korten, USA, CEO, The Culture Company

"The messages in *AfterNow* have relevance far beyond the amazing stories Bob tells of the devastation of the 2011 Triple Disasters in Japan and the responses they sparked in the people affected by them. They are a timely support for all of us who are learning how to navigate the anxious uncertainties of today's world. *AfterNow* reveals a way to move forward together with grace, cultivating curiosity and a profound trust in ourselves and each other."

Amy Lenzo, USA, steward, The World Café Community Foundation

"I have grown up hearing tales of the vibrant, defiant, quixotic individuals and communities that my father has worked with around the world. I have grown up in Japan. I have grown up with the chance to meet and work with those whose stories wend through these pages. This book brings to life the richness and wisdom that I have always found in those voices, that show me that another world is possible, one in which 'moving beyond business as usual' is not just an empty catch phrase. They give me hope. My father is a father figure to many; he has an innate ability to listen and to sit with the things that are most difficult without trying to change them or lighten them prematurely. He can echo back what he has heard in a way that opens new truths and possibilities, in a way that creates grounding where there was none. Early in the book, he says: "We arrive quietly, working from our listening. We hear their stories. In the process, they begin to see themselves in a different light. They are able, literally and figuratively, to re-member themselves, to discover more of who they are." This book comes from deep listening. It sheds light on how people and communities in Japan and around the world are living in and rising from disasters. The words in these pages are a powerful reminder of how to embrace disaster and uncertainty — whether ecological, sociopolitical, or personal — as we live our lives in uncertain times. They are also authentic, a reflection of my father and how he lives his life in all of its messiness and ridiculousness and grief and joy."

Annie Stilger Virnig, USA, Knowledge Management, Learning, and Capacity Building Specialist, UNDP Global Programme on Nature for Development

"I'm a teacher who wonders, what are we educating ourselves for? Is it to continue on a path many of us do not really want? If we know that we want a different future, where do we begin? To answer these questions, Bob weaves stories and deep wisdom with practical advice. Building on his vast experience and knowledge of change, he brings together many approaches showing that they all have much in common: they begin with being present to what is emerging and then moving collectively to create positive shared stories. I've known Bob since my days as a founder of social enterprises in post-war Croatia, where our work was guided by his wisdom and advice."

Ante Glavas, USA and Croatia, School of Business, University of Vermont

"In *AfterNow*, Bob Stilger accomplishes something truly remarkable — simultaneously capturing both the unique experiences of Japanese survivors of the 2011 earthquake, tsunami, and nuclear meltdown while sharing lessons and practical advice that have direct value in our own communities. It is all too easy to dismiss "3/11" as a tragic anomaly, but, as Bob reminds us, acute and chronic disasters are everywhere and growing more likely as we face economic, energy, and environmental crises. Drawing on his humility and practical experience, he provides a roadmap for all of us to begin working towards the after now, today."

Asher Miller, USA, executive director, Post Carbon Institute

"As a member of the team in the creation of this book I had a close-in view. What I noticed through the process was the quality of open exchange in the collaboration, the spirit of encouragement, kindness and leaning in, the willingness to make requests and then hear what was possible and the inclusion of everyone's opinion in how to proceed. The making of this book was a reflection of its contents - creative, appreciative and loving."

Barbara Bash, US, artist and author

"Sooner or later we arrive at a stage in our lives where we wonder what happens next. In his book *AfterNow*, Bob Stilger shows us how we can occupy that space with poise, presence and purpose."

Brian K. Bacon, UK, executive chairman, Oxford Leadership Group

"*AfterNow* is a work of brilliance that captures both the unique essence of the Japanese rebuilding efforts and the power of working within community in uncertain times. Part memoir and part manual, Bob's story of love and commitment grows out of the tragedy of March 11, 2011. I work in and with Japanese contexts, and *AfterNow* speaks to the heart of the rebuilding efforts and the transformational power that rose from the destruction. Read this book and you will not only be filled with hope, but will also take away some practical tools as a contributor to the greater good in the world."

Britt Yamamoto, USA, executive director & founder | iLEAP

"Bob openly shares his story of resilience based on deep relationships. These stories remind us of how important it is to build relationships and open our hearts and minds to one another. This is where we get our strength to be present to what the world brings to us every day. I have seen this kind of resilience over and over again in my work in communities that have faced disasters. Even now, as coastal Louisiana residents face challenges from climate change, communities find strength and creativity in working together."

Bobbie Hill, USA, partner — Planning & Engagement, Concordia, New Orleans

"Bob Stilger has given his life to learning and serving individuals, groups and communities to discover the power of community and connection. *AfterNow* chronicles his journey. Whether read from cover to cover or opened at any page, you will discover gems of wisdom and practical tools to help transform groups, communities and yourself! Bob shows us what it means to shift from problem to possibility and provides tools to open our hearts and minds to seeing strengths within each of us. He reminds us of the importance of seeing whole systems and what is possible when we come together to co-create a future distinct from the past."

Charles Holmes, Canada, facilitator, co-founder
Academy for Systems Change

"This book was very difficult for me to read, yet healing. When Cedar Rapids was hit with a surprise raging flood in 2008, destroying 10 square miles in the center of our city, we went through the stupefaction, grieving and conflict common in large disasters. The approaches outlined in *AfterNow* are very helpful for getting a community back to making progress following such a disaster, and have wider application as communities work to develop positive and constructive narratives in our rapidly changing world."

Chuck Peters, USA, chair of the board, Folience

"*AfterNow* awakens my heart with a vision of how communities of care and collaboration can be created in response to disaster, suffering and grief. It shows how hearts opened in grief and suffering can be healed and how we need and thus can create life-giving relationships that enable us to rebuild individual lives and vital communities in the wake of tragedy. In a polarized era when the leader of our country, the United States of America, frames the world as a competitive jungle, we need hope, we need a vision rooted in reality of how we human beings can find ways to collaborate, celebrate human dignity, and embrace our fundamental interdependence on planet earth. We need a different story: *AfterNow* provides such a story."

Dean Elias, USA, leadership professor, St. Mary's College of California

"This book is a testament of the true resiliency of the human spirit. I have been working with Bob since the early 2000's as I've learned to untangle many complex issues. *AfterNow* captures the spirit with which we worked to find ways for community to discover the solutions to their complex challenges. Bob is a great listener and harvester of learnings and this comes across very clear in *AfterNow*. It focuses not only on what has been happening in Japan but also what is being noticed in other parts of the world. The book provides a cocktail of ways and methodologies, as well as approaches, that we could use to solve complex challenges and even emerge from disastrous situations."

Dorah Marema, South Africa, director, SEED Community

"Bob Stilger combines many years of experience as a leader and teacher with his deep learning and love of community to write *AfterNow*. His work in Japan to facilitate healing, visioning and transformation after the incredible devastation, is an inspiration for so many of us working in these times of tremendous change. Full of insight and practices, *AfterNow* invites us to step into the unknown, knowing we are not alone."

Gretchen M. Krampf, USA, consultant, Process Experts LLC

"Bob has walked a path many of us find ourselves on: no longer being able to navigate by familiar maps because the territory has changed so radically. Amidst pain, noise, loss, grief, upheaval, disillusionment, how do we find our way, together? With *AfterNow* I feel myself understanding how we might collectively navigate a path forward that is grounded in such deep regard for life, that life itself shows the way. I have underlined half of all of the words written, they resonate so deeply. Appreciating the persistence and patience, deep listening and courage that makes visible this new way to navigate these times."

Heather Johnson, USA, executive director, Whidbey Institute

"*AfterNow* provides great insights on how we as humans move forward when we face catastrophes, deep tragedy and pain. It is in these times that we must dig deep, ask new questions, realize the true gifts within ourselves, truly connect and build relationships with others, and imagine and create the lives we want. This inspiring book resonates with me as it reflects what I have experienced on a personal level at the worst times in my life. It is often following dark times, that I have been able to truly focus on what is important, grow tremendously, be present and intentional, and springboard into a new light."

Jessica Eva Jensen, USA, Trail Runner & New
Mexico Health Equity Partnership Strategist

"I believe that we can create the world we want together and that the opportunity to create is always in front of us. It becomes more visible and of course more necessary in crisis. I love the way Bob invites the possibility in. When my hometown of High River, Alberta, Canada was flooded and I found myself struggling to rebuild, a dear friend introduced me to Bob. I knew we needed him. He helped us see a version of a new future. *AfterNow* describes the practices that helped us to imagine a new way forward together. We all need Bob's lessons - I am still practicing with them today."

Jodi Dawson, Canada, economic development director, High River, Alberta

"'What does it take to live with the messiness of a new normal, keeping focused on personal calling, co-creating positive, sustainable shared futures with others?' That was the question I took into reading *AfterNow*. Many concepts in the book are helping me *live with the messiness of my present reality*. One that really stands out is what Bob calls *Enspirited Leadership*. It helps me stop being anxious about "what is the correct thing I must do," I now find myself looking for time to s*top and be still* and *chew on my experiences*, while I let my calling find me! *AfterNow* is definitely a must read for anyone who dares to host meaningful conversations among those who will create, not predict, our future."

Juan A. Kanapi, Jr., Philippines, chairman, Future By Design Pilipinas

"In this noisy world, truth has become hard to hear. And yet, we know. Deep down within us, somewhere, we know. *AfterNow* is an invitation to seek our truths, and a pathway to find them and hear them in others. In a time where we are embattled in noise, *AfterNow* reminds us that listening is power, and in order to truly listen, we must quiet ourselves enough to hear the subtle, small, quiet truths, the truths that offer an escape from this noisy distraction that surrounds us today. Bob illuminates a different way forward, a path that he has been living for many years now. This is our invitation into the years of experience and wisdom that Bob has cultivated with a warm, open, and humble heart. It offers a roadmap of practices, mindsets, and values, that can help us find our way forward in these challenging and beautiful times."

Kate Seely, USA, board member, NewStories

"How do we create a life in this time when there is no certain future? Whether we face imminent disaster on the scale of a tsunami or the growing uncertainty shared by many of us on this planet, what we have is each other, right now. *AfterNow* is an immensely rich collection of stories, practices, reflections and resources that is informed by decades of experience around the globe. It responds to this question of what we do now with humility and wisdom. The loud voice of spirit Bob heard as he gathered with people in Tokyo weeks after the disasters — *we have been released from a future we did not want* — offers this release as a real possibility for all of us, now. *AfterNow* invites us to gather around the village hearth to listen together, and then to write a different future."

Laurie Adams, USA, director and steward of River's Bend Retreat Center

"Whether personal or collective, a sudden disaster rends not just the physicality of place but also the soul fabric of community. Bob's genius is that he is able to illuminate and activate the invisible warp of a healthy community's structure — the psychic rules of engagement that foster health and well-being. And at the same time, he names and guides the processes that help a community become the weft that weaves those tattered threads across difference and fear into a new, living, soul-connected tapestry that has its own wholeness. He gives us, through both his own participatory journey and the tools he has honed along the way, a guide on how to be with disruptive times. *AfterNow* helps us see how we can heal through dialogue with each other, and how we can bring who and what we are together to co-create a path forward. The future we want to live in will not be imagined by one person, or one idea, or one story, but by a respect for the whole and the gifts of everyone. How we dance with what's emerging in any of our worlds will make the difference about where we go next as a species."

Lynnaea Lumbard, USA, co-president, NewStories

"A Gift. Bob Stilger has given us a rare gift offered with such tender love and compassion. Called by his heart and friendship, he travelled into chaos and disaster to become a companion to the people of Japan. With his heartfelt listening and companionship he supported an organically unfolding response to the Triple Disasters. From the intensity of the Japanese cauldron comes a tapestry of rich lessons. In *AfterNow*, Bob brings us several simple but profound maps for how to find our way through monumental rivers of chaos and confusion together. He offers carefully harvested principles for how to co-create and build communities that bring people and connections alive. He shares guidelines gathered from countless stories for how to work with the natural arising flow of emergence in an ever changing and often tumultuous world; working with what we have here and now. His discerning reflections and insights carry important lessons for us all. What he offers here are skills for the future and capacities for Now. As Bob himself says: It's messy. It takes time. And it takes us all, together." I am grateful for the contribution of this book is to our collective journey."

Maaianne Knuth, Zimbabwe, founder, Kufunda Learning Village

"*AfterNow* is a fantastic book for those who are looking to roll up their sleeves and step into the 'messy middle' of doing real work on the ground. It comes from someone who has dedicated his life to working with communities around the world. I have known Bob Stilger for over 17 years, as a brother, colleague, co-inquirer, fellow troublemaker, warrior of the heart. We share a strong belief in the power of communities and their collective intelligence as the primary vehicle for driving deep social and systemic change. *AfterNow* opens a new channel for intercultural dialogue between the East and West and will resonate deeply with leaders in the Global South. Bob's deep love for Japan, honoring and reconnecting to the wisdom of Japanese culture deeply touches me. I am particularly inspired to see how his work with Enspirited Leadership has evolved and taken shape in Japan. New models of leadership which transcend the dominant logic of cost-benefit rationality, the Market, and techno-utopian fantasies are urgently needed. Bob not only names the challenge leaders face, standing in the messy middle and embracing uncertainty, but also offers many processes and frameworks on how to work from there. True leadership requires that we develop a deeper understanding on how to hold sensitive space for grief, generosity, re-imagination and practical action after a crisis. I walk away from reading *AfterNow* with more practical insights and tools on how to engage a crisis while the short window of opportunity is open. This book is an important contribution to the global and local conversations on systemic change."

Manish Jain, India, co-founder, Shikshantar

"The words and meaning of *AfterNow* come from the deep love that Bob Stilger has for the land and people of Japan. It has guided him in writing this book. He not only pays homage to the resilience and strength of the Japanese people who survived the Triple Disasters, he also surfaces from the depths of the despair and the universal lessons we all need to pay attention to. Bob offers us practical wisdom on how to turn disaster into conscious choice to meet new futures. *AfterNow* witnesses, translates and transforms the tragic events in Japan into a worldwide message to wake up before disaster hits and begin to participate in news ways in life. This book is a manual for stepping more fully into life, so that we can make daily choices to live consciously with the earth, our fellow human beings, and all life forms."

Maria Scordialos, Greece, co-founder of both
Axladitsa-Avatakia and the Living Wholeness Institute

"I first met Bob Stilger in 2008. It was his first time to return to his people, the Cherokee. He had not been raised in our Nation or been instructed in the Cherokee core values. But those values are woven into Bob's DNA. *AfterNow* is a book that gives hope to our uncertain future. It outlines how to organize, move forward and not leave anyone behind. Bob uses the experience of the Triple Disasters in Japan and his work in other communities to illustrate this process. Our Cherokee elders called this GaDuGi, people coming together as one and working to help one another. This is something many of us have forgotten. In *AfterNow*, Bob reminds us how we are to live in this uncertain world."

Mark Parman, USA, evaluation & outcomes measurement
specialist, Cherokee Nation Cultural and Community Outreach

"*AfterNow: When We Cannot See the Future.* Where Do We Begin — the full title is like a "Koan," a phase or questions that a Zen master uses to unravel greater truths. Questions quickly arise: What is

"AfterNow?" Where do we begin? What do we see? What is the future? What is Now? The disaster recovery process is messy — there is a sense of not knowing what to do next and a sense of not doing enough. Bob shows how to hold the space in which something appropriate will often happen, as well as how to just accept things as they are. Disaster creates a discontinuity with the past which can allow a new future to emerge. Particularly in this VUCA (Vunerable, Uncertain, Chaotic and Ambiguous) world, this book provides stories to inspire with multiple structures to guide the efforts to create a new future."

Mark Pixley, China, general manager, LEADERSHIP INC, Shenzhen

"I was at my desk at the U.S. Army post at Camp Zama, Japan at 2:46 PM on March 11, 2011 when life as we knew it changed for Japan. 250 miles from the epicenter, we experienced the forceful crescendo of rolling and swaying motion unlike anything we had experienced before, lasting an incredible 5 ½ minutes. With horror and helplessness, we began to see the images of the tsunami on Japanese television as it rolled relentlessly over homes, farms, cities. Days later, we began to appreciate the devastation at the Fukushima Daiichi nuclear power plant and the true extent of the tragedy. Bob Stilger's beautiful and insightful book, *AfterNow*, examines the Triple Disasters and other seismic shifts that happen after all types of tragedies and disasters. Leaning into hardship is anathema to many people, but it is in welcoming whatever change is at our door and opening up to community that we make sense of our new lives, no matter how painful. Bob shines a beacon through the darkness to help lead us to new growth and resilience. It is a deeply personal and enlightening book that embraces change in all its forms."

Michael Brumage, USA, executive director/health officer - Kanawha-Charleston Health Department. Colonel, U.S. Army (Retired)

"This is a time that I often feel like my feet are firmly planted in midair! I go from confusion to fear to uncertainty often in minutes on many days. How do we survive and even thrive in this time? *AfterNow* offers Bob Stilger's lived experience, interwoven with many other stories of ordinary and extraordinary people of courage and heart. AfterNow gives a glimpse of emerging truth. I have spent my life in community organizing and Asset Based Community Development (ABCD). I often feel that many books are not practical to the hard, daily work that must be done on the ground. I appreciate that AfterNow is very practical, offering ordinary people like myself a path to action amid all the confusion and uncertainty. It will build a growing community of courageous leadership."

Mike Green, USA, faculty, ABCD Institute

"In this time of seemingly overwhelming social, political and environmental challenges, Bob Stilger is a wise and compassionate guide to the possible and practical. *AfterNow* uses very personal stories and inspired examples from Bob's many years of work around the globe in helping communities facing challenges to envision and develop new futures. It is especially enriched by his recent deep and thoughtful involvement with Japanese communities in the wake of the disasters coming from the Fukushima nuclear reactor meltdown. This book, full of practical steps and ideas, will be a good friend to anyone committed to realizing our best possible futures together.

Michael Chender, Canada, co-founder, Shambhala
Authentic Leadership in Action Institute

"*AfterNow* affirms the truth that all we really have to do is be present to one another. There are no agents of change but meaningful presence to one another, true accompaniment, allows for change to emerge and develop. Listening with our heart, our mind, our will is key. No judgment, no cynicism, no fear. We must stay together, because transforming out of the complexities of today can no longer be addressed alone, especially how we move forward as the future disappears. This disappearance is real every day to Filipinos — indigenous peoples, urban poor, rural farming households — most of those in the periphery have lost their ability to dream of a future. It is in this time of chaos, all over the world, that hope and dreams are most important. Indeed, we must remember that we come alive in community."

Miren C. Sanchez, The Philippines, co-founder,
president & CEO, Future By Design Pilipinas

"*AfterNow* offers compelling road maps to find ways to counter the side effects that arise after the disaster. Keep the focus on people and allow them the space to find their way through dialogue and emergence. Action must remain grounded in the local which, when connected, leads to transformation. These lessons from Japan apply to India as well. *AfterNow*'s question 'what do we have' instead of 'what have we lost' is profound, it connects to hope and generates the energy needed to take the necessary steps forward. Bob's spotlight on his own learning, allowing his own anxieties and insecurities to discover new directions is fascinating. His is a quest to become a sacred outsider with listening and openness as the basic element to know the unknown."

Nitin Paranjape, India, co-founder, Abhivyakti Media for Development

"*AfterNow* resonates with me, lifts my spirits, and provides me a knowing that there is hope. I am sometimes not a fan of hope because it seems so often to me to be unwarranted and a distraction away from clarity, truth, stepping up and stepping in. Hope is warranted because of the work we do. It's no wonder that it is Bob Stilger who has blended teaching with story. His story is a long journey in place and over time, with all the whispering insights arising from small moments. It draws the deep movements and unseen power of community out enough that we can see them, if we pay attention. I am as thankful for the journal entries as I am for the clear teaching. They each make visible the invisible journey of an attentive wanderer, offering true insight. *AfterNow* is truly a pathfinder's guide toward the future. Best read, before disaster."

Peter Pula, Canada, founder and CEO, Axiom News

"Lynnaea and I joined others on a the 2014 New Stories Japan Learning Journey. I frankly did not know much about Japan or the devastation they had endured. Three years after the disasters, we were welcomed by group after group of community members whose lives had been torn apart in seconds, many of whom had been forced to relocate, unable to return to their homes. I was most impressed by the welcome we received. Bob was honored as a person who had come and listened and held these communities in their grief. I was touched by his gentleness as he approached these communities with an attitude of listening, respect, and caring which clearly had a profound impact of healing. I felt healed, being present with these new friends. It is beautiful to see these stories come alive in *AfterNow*."

Rick Paine, USA, board chair, NewStories

"Bob Stilger is a researcher on how we are going to reach the best future we can dream. One thing he knows for sure, the way to get there is by consciously building it together. AfterNow shares his experiences in Japan after the Triple Disasters of 2011, during six years of witnessing the present, researching what is possible now and sowing seeds for the future. Bob shares the best tools, processes and experiences he has harvested throughout his life of interaction with innovative and creative projects and people around the globe. Here you will find moving stories, highly relevant knowledge, and deep wisdom that flows from a professional and a person full of generosity and love for the people and for the planet. Welcome to AfterNow!"

Rodrigo Rubido Alonso, Brazil, co-founder and
executive director of Instituto Elos

"Bob has been my mentor since we met in Zimbabwe in late 2011, just after the triple disasters had happened. He's a unique combination of deep wisdom and youthful curiosity, that's a joy to be around. Since we met there have been many moments in my life where his questions and insights helped me move through my own personal disasters. *Afternow* is the condensed wisdom from a true servant of life. Deep bob of gratitude for to you Bob for giving birth to this incredible gift."

Simone Poutnik, USA and Germany, board member, NewStories

"Bob and I first met as 21-year-olds, traveling to Japan to spend our senior year in college at Waseda University in Tokyo. While I had a long-standing interest in Japan, Bob told me that he knew nothing about Japan, only that "it was over there someplace near China." What surprised and impressed me was that Bob soon became a serious and sincere student of Japanese language and culture. A second characteristic that drew me to Bob was his very unusual ability to listen deeply, without interrupting, without judging. Over the years, as we co-founded a nonprofit, got married, had our daughter Annie, and grew older, Bob developed a capacity to sit calmly, or at least relatively calmly, with uncertainty and murkiness. These three gifts — a great love of Japan, the skill to listen deeply, and the ability to live with and learn from uncertainty — anchored Bob's work in Japan and shine through the pages of this book. Having been involved in part of the work in Japan, as well as in both the Japanese and English versions of this book, I can attest to Bob's determination to tell these stories and share these tools, and to invite all of us into the stories of our own lives and the life of our communities. *AfterNow* is both a good read, full of intriguing and inspiring stories, and a toolbox for work in our world. It is a story of Bob's journey and at the same time a universal story of walking into the unknown. *AfterNow* offers us a compendium of tools plus the context in which these tools were effectively used. Page through it, dip into it, or read it cover to cover — you will be enriched by what you find."

Susan Virnig, USA, partner in life and work, spouse, best friend

"Bob's words transport us on a journey of exploration of what is meaningful action in times of transition. With Japan setting the context both literally and culturally, this book honors the human endeavour to save itself in times of upheaval - a lesson we need to learn the world over if we are to be ready for more turbulence and be able to face it with dignity and compassion. This is essential reading for social innovators ready to accelerate their learning trans-locally, with an understanding of how challenge can give rise to communities of action."

Tatiana Glad, The Netherlands, social entrepreneur,
Impact Hub Amsterdam

"Bob Stilger saw something in me when I was young man that I could not see in myself. His ability to see clearly into the heart of people and situations is reflected in this profound and practical book. Bob has harvested years of experience in leading change and the incredible relationships he has built along the way. Read *AfterNow*. You'll be better for meeting Bob; I know I am."

Tim Merry, Canada, change leader

"I've known Bob for 20 years. He's has a big heart, deep thoughtfulness, and knows how to get things done. Bob inspires me with his insightfulness in naming key principles, and then having the wisdom to ask and discover the right questions. In *AfterNow* you will find principles and questions that awaken you to Japan's resilience story. Perhaps also, you will find your own beginnings of where, how, and after now."

Tenneson Woolf, USA and Canada, board chair, The
Circle Way, steward, The Art of Hosting

"Bob Stilger has been instrumental in growing a global community of practice dedicated to learning how to create the future we want to live, together. His soulful work in Japan has helped us all look at disaster and change differently — learning how to lean in together regardless of the difficulty or complexity. In AfterNow we meet people and communities right where they are at, in the space between the honest, and often different, realities and in the dreams and wisdom of the community. The path forward emerges at our feet. Thank you Bob, for faithfully walking this path everyday and sharing the stories and powerful insights from life after the Triple Disasters. I hope we can all take to heart what it means to navigate radical change TOGETHER with grace."

Teresa Posakony, USA, Art of Hosting Steward

"*AfterNow* is a beautiful, heartbreaking, inspiring and important. This is a book with many people's stories including Bob Stilger's own - of how he asks burning questions, how he sees, how he shows up, how he serves the Japan he loves and has learned with and from most of his life. Seeing the past and the future from the Now is a wise perspective. *AfterNow* is a most helpful offering — a statement that there is not just one official way, one solution to complex disasters. There are many perspectives, practices, methods, wiser ways forward. This book is a profound, honest and heartfelt harvest of one unwanted disaster. There are many in our world today and I am so very grateful there are humans like Bob, who takes the time to harvest as he walks his own learning path and then shares it in service of the rest of us citizens of Earth now. This book is not just a book - this is a gift from the heart."

"Bob Stilger has been at the forefront of cutting-edge work in communities for several decades. He has worked creatively and courageously with very diverse groups around the world, hosting spaces in which people discover and embrace their power to create new ways of being. He has also helped launch and guide several practitioner networks that support our collective learning about collaborative leadership. In this context, I've always valued Bob's gift for reflecting on his work and highlighting the lessons it might offer for others. That's the promise of this book — to serve as inspiration and resource for the countless people in every field, and every society, grappling daily to co-create healthy, sustainable futures."

"As always, Bob tells the stories that bring life to the values and principles so many of us aspire to in our practice. *AfterNow* is a generous and beautiful book that elegantly guides the practitioner through the chaos and overwhelm of disaster, offering sage advice and practical tools for being of service."

"On the day before the final layout is due, sitting here reading all the other endorsements, I get yet another email from Bob asking me to write one myself. He says since my name begins with Z it will be the very last, and since I know the person doing the layout, he's sure it can be fit in. That's Bob. I have been part of the team who worked to make it possible for you to hold *AfterNow* in your hands today, I helped doing graphics, illustrations and coordinating the layout of the book. I was invited to be part of bringing visual beauty and clarity through design with the intention of supporting the meticulous weaving of stories. And this is how I get to read these voices from the larger community, before many other people. A mix of feelings engulf me. I have met some of these people, and read the books of the authors. I have quoted them in conversations, I follow with admiration many of their endeavors and recognize in them the authority to "have something to say." What have I got to say?

And then I understand what Bob is doing. Once again, he is bringing us into circle and hosting us, listening to us, meeting us with respect, curiosity and generosity, making visible our collective hopes and aspirations for a future we want to be part of creating. I can't help but smile and let the feeling of anxiety go. The anxiety of writing this comment and also for the huge uncertainties about the future: the future of Colombia, the country where I was born which is currently going through a long waited for peace process; the future of my parents going through very tough health and relationship challenges; the future of our pacha mama with the environmental and social challenges we are all facing. I hold my daughters' hands in mine and I accept wholeheartedly Bob's invitation to continue nurturing life-affirming relationships with myself, my family, my community and nature. Gracias Bob."

Zulma Sofia Patarroyo, Colombia, listener and graphic facilitator

AFTERWORD: Toward a Common Future
by Mary Catherine Bateson

IN THE EARLY PAGES OF THIS BOOK, Bob Stilger refers to Japan as "a deeply collective culture." In saying this he is not suggesting that Japan has been forced into a collectivized mold, as has been attempted in some societies; such forced collectivization has proven very brittle when the iron fist is lifted, unlike in Japan, where many individuals are engaged in shared choreographies of commonality. In the West we sometimes encounter flocks of Japanese tourists, each with a camera, dutifully following a guide around some monument and on and off a bus, but this is collectivity sustained by unfamiliarity and dependency on the guide, a caricature of shared participation. It is this cultural elaboration of collectivity, surely, that first drew Bob to Japan, for he has spent his adult life learning how to help groups work toward shared creativity. This is an aesthetic goal, as is hinted in his work of many years, "The Art of Hosting" — specifically of hosting discussions. How do we weave different goals and perceptions together into a pattern that is resilient, practical, and beautiful? As the American reader comes to the end of this work, she or he must wonder whether, with all our emphasis on individualism, we have the sense of collectivity needed to respond to the kind of disasters that lie ahead. Can we develop a spirituality of care for the earth that will include all peoples and strengthen us to work together?

In the colonial period, a strong sense of community was seen as necessary for survival. Alexis de Tocqueville wrote about it as a distinctive characteristic of the American colonies. But since the mid-twentieth century, the sense of community has been declining, as evidenced by book titles from David Riesman's *The Lonely Crowd* (1950) to Robert Putnam's *Bowling Alone* (2000). The Triple Disasters of Fukushima of March 11, 2011, had both natural and human causes — an underwater earthquake causing the tsunami and a nuclear reactor exploding — this provides a preview of the kinds of chaos that lie ahead, parallel to the mass extinctions that have occurred in the history of the earth. The Japanese reaction suggests the cultural variability of human responses, which will depend on alternative reactions to the challenge of cooperation in meeting local pressures and crises.

On a larger scale, however, I believe that our immediate challenge is to recover a sense of human unity *beyond all differences of race, religion and culture,* welcoming refugees, offering resettlement, adjusting our patterns of consumption and energy use, and resisting the temptation to make war for resources. We often say that the world has become smaller; this remark refers not to size but to intimacy, not to convenience but to the necessity for closer integration. The central theme of expanding human knowledge for many centuries was analysis: taking things apart and understanding distinctions. The development of systems theory as a central theme in the cybernetic revolution meant that the time had come to look at connectivity rather than distinction, interdependence rather than competition. We now understand more than ever before how the climatic cycles of temperature and precipitation and the composition of the atmosphere and of ocean water are global phenomena, moving in swirling patterns so that pollution is eventually spread globally and we can only preserve our local environments by protecting the planetary environment. We human beings must act as a global community. We are only likely to do so, as pressures develop, if we reclaim our capacity to act as local communities and to project this out to an inclusive and global human community. For a while this seemed to be happening, but it seems clear that increased regional conflict in many parts of the world that is often attributed to "populism" is a symptom of resource pressure and climatic stress of various kinds. We need to act locally *and* globally. Unfortunately, the need to recover community structures in the United States is complicated by defensive patterns that have been fostered by government in recent years, and slow progress toward human unity has been reversed in many places.

The series of civil conflicts referred to as the "Middle Eastern Spring" was caused by drought and bad harvests; the partial break-up of the European Union (i.e. Brexit) was partly caused by administrative pressure to share of various kinds. The 2016 victory of Donald Trump was in part a reaction to policies to create greater equality in the United States, even as inequality was increasing. At a deeper level, these stresses have been more about attitudes than about policy. Since 9/11, Americans have been urged by government to be suspicious of strangers, and this has undermined the possibility of working together in trust. Marketing not only encourages the desire to own and consume without limits, it insidiously suggests that everyone has a *right* to this luxury car, this diamond necklace, this latest computer, and that the lack of it is due to unfairness in the "system." Xenophobia is cropping up everywhere and racial violence is increasing. We are turning back the clock and transferring our concerns about lost global equilibrium to distrust for other human beings. With equilibrium weakened, the punctuation when it comes will be severe. Citizenship involves interdependence and cooperation. We can only be "citizens of the world" if we are citizens at home.

Bob Stilger's account of his work in Japan is a model for the gradual, patient creation of a new social climate, but one with roots in tradition. It is worth rereading at the end of the book the principles he set forth at the beginning:

- Start from a realistic understanding of the present situation.
- Seek unity as we move forward rather than demanding it as a precondition.
- Listen rather than tell. (There are many useful kinds of expertise, but no one approach is adequate, so expertise becomes a contribution rather than a solution.)
- Harvest useful knowledge from first-hand experience.
- Demand diversity; it brings rich perspectives.
- And, perhaps most eloquent of all, remember, "Intention must be braided with surrender."

He does not quote the familiar "Think globally, act locally," perhaps because implicit in his work is the assumption that we will only learn to think globally by building cooperative and non-competitive models locally. Children, for instance, need to experience cooperation that is not embedded in competition. The cooperation needed among members of a basketball team is after all directed toward defeating the rival team, and the same is true for cooperation learned in the military. Evolutionary theory today, rather than being focused on "the survival of the fittest," pays increasing attention to the fitness achieved by *not competing*, often by symbiosis.

I am reminded of one of Gregory Bateson's favorite quotes from Blake's Jerusalem: "He who would do good to another must do it in Minute Particulars: General Good is the plea of the scoundrel, hypocrite, and flatterer, for Art and Science cannot exist but in minutely organized Particulars..."

This work to build the new world that awaits us after now is granular, paying close attention to all that exists in the present moment while at the same time holding in sight and in heart the broadest view. Both are essential. Global and local are not only related. Indeed, they are each simply different views of the same pathway into our future.

There will be disappointment and failure as we step into this consciousness; it is new territory in which we learn to stand with the paradox of particulars rather than collapsing into old generalities and platitudes. There will be excitement and heart opening success as well.

In Japan, the ability to rebuild and move forward, without repeating past mistakes, is hindered by the deep sense of trauma, which can lead to paralysis and despair or to the temptation simply to replicate what has been lost without correcting its weaknesses. But the cost of replication is too high. Nearly 20,000 people died in the Triple Disasters and half a million lost homes or livelihoods, the structures of their lives. Outsiders working on site in the disaster area can only be humbled by the extent of loss and the effects still to come of radioactivity. But whatever succeeds or does not succeed, the world has much to learn from Japan, both about resilience and about vulnerability. Here, from the beginning of the book, are Bob's guidelines for those who would learn from these three horrific disasters:

> We need to surrender our fears. We need to embrace ambiguity. We need to radically accept that we are not in charge. We must demand diversity. We are invited to find our true calling and true

work. We can't do this work without the close company of others. Likewise, we can't do it without a spiritual practice. And we must always be in the space of learning.

I have come to think of willingness to learn as itself an ongoing spiritual practice that entails respect across difference of all kinds. Beyond respect, I have also discovered that when we learn from and with others, the result is often love. We can be thankful that Japan's Triple Disasters, hard as these lessons have been, did not come about as acts of war or deliberate violence, so the vulnerability to these disasters can be studied without guilt, and help accepted without blame. Life in the coastal areas ravaged by the tsunami is returning to a new and less vulnerable normal. For those nearest the radiation that spewed from the nuclear reactors in Fukushima, no new normal is in sight.

The world, and Japan, can reap a huge harvest of learning from this catastrophe for our human future.

Additional Resources

Please visit www.AfterNow.Today for additional resources including:

- Experimenting with Powerful Questions
- Methodologies for Dialogue and Conversation
- Finding My Way, One Story at a Time

Bibliography

Note to Readers

Websites

My home base is the nonprofit I founded in 2000. NewStories —
www.NewStories.org
For this book, NewStories has developed a companion website —
www.AfterNow.Today

Introduction

Books and Articles

Gersick, C. J. G. (1991). Revolutionary change theories: A multilevel exploration of the punctuated equilibrium paradigm. Academy of Management Review.

Stilger, B. (2015). 未来が見えなくなったとき、僕たちは何を語ればいいのだろう 一震災後日本の「コミュニティ再生」への挑戦 — When We Cannot See the Future, Where Do We Begin? (Japanese). Tokyo: Eiji Press.

Tainter, J. A. (1988). The Collapse of Complex Societies. New York: Cambridge.

Wheatley, M. (2017). Who Do We Choose to Be? Facing Reality, Claiming Leadership, Restoring Sanity. Oakland: Berrett-Koehler: Oakland.

Chapter 1

Books and Articles

Arrien, A. The Four-Fold Way: Walking the Paths of the Warrior, Teacher, Healer, and Visionary (1992). New York: HarperCollins.

McAdam, D., McCarthy, J. D., & Zald, M. N. (Eds.). (1996). Comparative Perspectives on Social Movements: Political Opportunities, Mobilizing Structures, and Cultural Framings. Cambridge, England: Cambridge University Press.

Nonaka, I., & Nishiguchi, T. (2001). Knowledge emergence: social, technical, and evolutionary dimensions of knowledge creation. Oxford; New York: Oxford University Press.

Scharmer, C. O. (2009). Theory U: Leading from the Future as It Emerges. Oakland, CA: Berrett-Koehler Publishers.

Stilger, R. (2007). Enspirited Leadership: Landmarks for Uncertain Times. Available at www.enspirited.newstories.org

Stilger, R., & Dunford, A. (2009). Alive in Community. Available at www.alive.newstories.org

Websites

For from 2000 — 2011, much of my work was in partnership with The Berkana Institute where I served for five years as Co-President. Berkana was founded in 1992 by Margaret Wheatley and Myron Kellner Rogers after Meg wrote *Leadership in the New Sciences* — www.berkana.org

In 2000, Berkana, along with NewStories and PeerSpirit launched a global leadership initiative called From the Four Directions, which brought together a number of people using different approaches to support dialogue and conversation. Many of these people, with a great deal of leadership from Toke Moeller of Denmark, went on to launch a community and framework called Art of Hosting — www.artofhosting.org

Future Center work in Japan started at the Knowledge Dynamics Institute at Fuji Xerox in 2009 and after the Triple Disasters moved to a new corporation, FutureSessions Inc. — www.futuresessions.com

In creating Future Centers in Japan, KDI received substantial guidance and support from the Future Center Alliance and KDI hosted the global gathering of the Alliance in 2010 — www.futurecenteralliance.com

Early on with FutureCenter work in Japan, Fujitsu started to ask an amazing question: *Whay can Fujitsu Do for People With Dimentia? See* www.runtomorrow.jp/en/?lang=en.

Bob and his daughter, Annie Stilger Virnig, were invited to do the first ever father/daughter talk at TEDxTokyo in 2010 — bit.ly/TEDxTokyo2010-BobAnnie

Early this century, Maaianne Knuth felt called to start a learning center in Zimbabwe as a place for new possibilities as the country entered a period of great instability. Kufunda is amazing — www.kufunda.org

The Popular Center for Culture and Development started in Brazil almost 30 years ago when people said there must be a better way for our children to learn. For more than a quarter century it has practiced emergence with rigor — www.cpcd.org.br/

Chapter 2

Websites

In Japan, as well as all over the world, people have become intrigued with the idea that happiness might be a measure of progress — www.grossnationalhappiness.com

The KEEP at Kiyosato in Yamanashi Prefecture was the location for my early work in Japan in 2010 and 2011. More than a venue, it is a space of possibility that has given birth to many dreams — http://www.seisenryo.jp/en/index.html

Chapter 3

Books and Articles

Agerbeck, B., Bird, K., Bradd, S., Shepherd, J., & Stilger, B. (2016). Drawn Together through Visual Practice (1 ed.). Kelvy Bird.

Alexander, C. (1979). The Timeless Way of Building. New York: Oxford University Press.

Atleo, E. R. (2004). Tsawalk: a Nuu-chah-nulth worldview. Vancouver: UBC Press.

Websites

Many useful resources, including The Art of Powerful Questions, are available in the World Café Store: www.theworldcafe.com/store.html

BALLE is a thriving movement to support growth of locally based, independent businesses. https://bealocalist.org

There are now many efforts around the world which recognize waste as our most underutilized resource — http://www.upcyclethat.com

ETIC has been doing extraordinary work in Tohoku since immediately after the disasters — www.etic.or.jp

Appreciative Inquiry, developed by David Cooperrider from Case Western Reserve University in the 90s, is a powerful process used around the world to focus and amplify what we appreciate as a starting point for deep change — https://appreciativeinquiry.case.edu

Chapter 4

Websites

The idea of "transition" was advanced and popularized by the Transition Network — www.transitionnetwork.org

Chapter 5

Books and Articles

Lebow, V. (1955). Price competition in 1955. Journal of retailing. Available at www.newstories.org/food-for-thought/making-consumption-our-way-of-life

Stilger, B., Poutnik, S., Seely, K., & Patarroya, Z. (2017). Communities Report: Culture of Health Listening Tour. NewStories. Available at www.newstories.org/food-for-thought/communities-report-on-culture-of-health

Websites

The Thriving Resilient Communities Collaboratory is a unique venture which brings a number of initiatives across the US into relationship with each other — www.thrivingresilience.org

Chapter 6

Books and Articles

Kahane, A. (2012). Transformative Scenario Planning: Working Together to Change the Future. Berrett-Koehler Publishers.

Websites

A brief history of the Tilth movement is available at www.seattletilth.org/about/abriefhistoryoftilth. The YouTube Video of Wendell Berry and Bob Stilger from 1974 is available at bit.ly/wendell_bob_1974

Ten years ago, the Dinokeng Scenarios helped to make new possibilities in South Africa visible — www.dinokengscenarios.co.za

Nossa Sao Paulo is a brilliant example of how ideas and aspirations can be made visible — www.nossasaopaulo.org.br/portal/node/9639

The Institute for Alternative Futures has been a foundation for many futures initiatives for nearly 40 years — www.altfutures.org

This reality television show on how to build community with vision, energy and available resources had a galvanizing impact on South Africa — www.soulcity.org.za/projects/kwanda

The ABCD Institute was an early pioneer in the US in help people begin to look and build from their assets rather than simply being preoccupied by their deficits — www.abcdinstitute.org

In Japan, it was Jimotogaku — learning from the local area — that was the equivalent of ABCD. Working with what we have is a naturally occurring form — www.japanfs.org/en/news/archives/news_id027966.html

Started by young architects more than 20 years ago, Institute ELOS was how ABCD naturally occurred in Brazil — www.institutoelos.org

Chapter 7

Books and Articles

Macy, J., & Johnstone, C. (2012). Active Hope: How to Face the Mess We Are In Without Going Crazy. Novato, Calif.: New World Library.

Patton, M. Q. (2010). Developmental Evaluation: Applying Complexity Concepts to Enhance Innovation and Use. NYC: The Guilford Press.

Scharmer, C. O. (2007). Theory U: Leading from the Emerging Future (1st ed.). Cambridge, MA: Society for Organizational Learning.

Snowden, D., & Kurtz, C. F. (2003). The new dynamics of strategy: Sensemaking in a complex and complicated world (Volume 42, No. 3). Available at www.cynefin.newstories.org/

Websites

The Presencing Institute is a powerful resource for those learning to be fully present to themselves and the world around us — www.presencing.com

The Process Works Center of Japan is a gathering point for people learning new ways to engage people around questions and possibilities that matter — www.jpwc.or.jp/english

Chapter 8

Websites

Miratuku is an important platform for social innovation in Japan — www.emerging-future.org

My blogs from Japan after the disasters, as well as other resources are featured at www.resilientjapan.org

For more information about jimotogaku — www.i-i-net.blogspot.jp/2009/02/jimotogaku-based-on-what-we-have-here-1.html

Safecast is the world's most extensive open source radiation monitoring initiative — www.safecast.org

Chapter 9

Books and Articles

Harman, W. (1988). Global Mind Change: The Promise of the Last Years of the 20th Century. Indianapolis: Knowledge Systems.

Samuels, R. J. (2013). 3.11: Disaster and Change in Japan (1 ed.). Cornell University Press.

Chapter 10

Books and Articles

Spretnak, C. (1997). The Resurgence of the Real: Body, Nature and Place in a Hypermodern World. Reading, MA: Addison-Wesley

Afterword

Books and Articles

Putnam, R. D. (2001). Bowling Alone: The Collapse and Revival of American Community (1st ed.). Touchstone Books by Simon & Schuster.

Riesman, D. (1950). The Lonely Crowd. New Haven: Yale University Press.

After Now

When we
cannot see
the future
where do we
begin?